D1064278

THE BLACK
CIVIL WAR SOLDIERS
OF ILLINOIS

THE BLACK CIVIL WAR SOLDIERS OF ILLINOIS

The Story of the
Twenty-ninth U.S. Colored Infantry

Edward A. Miller, Jr.

The University of South Carolina Press

© 1998 University of South Carolina

Published in Columbia, South Carolina, by the
University of South Carolina Press

Manufactured in the United States of America

02 01 00 99 98 5 4 3 2 1

Library of Congress Cataloging-in-Publication Data

Miller, Edward A., 1927–
    The black civil war soldiers of Illinois: The story of the twenty-
ninth U.S. colored infantry /   Edward A. Miller, Jr.
        p. cm.
    Includes bibliographical references and index.
    ISBN 1–57003–199–1
    1. United States. Army. Colored Infantry Regiment, 29th
(1864–1865) 2. United States—History—Civil War, 1861–1865—
Participation, Afro-American. 3. United States—History—Civil
War, 1861–1865—Regimental histories. 4. Illinois—History—Civil
War, 1861–1865—Participation, Afro-American. 5. Afro-American
soldiers—Illinois—History—19th century. I. Title.
E492.94 29th .M55 1998
973.7'415—dc21   97–4742

CONTENTS

Contents

ILLUSTRATIONS

Illustrations

PREFACE

This is the story of a black regiment in the Civil War. My choice of the Twenty-ninth U.S. Colored Infantry, the single black regiment raised in Illinois, was more or less arbitrary. Apart from the well-known Fifty-fourth Massachusetts Volunteer Infantry (Colored) and its sister regiment, the Massachusetts Fifty-fifth, few Americans have heard the story of any of the 149 infantry, cavalry, and artillery organizations manned by black troops. Many of their members fought as hard, if not as long, as did the Fifty-fourth, and each of them has an important history, about how mostly uneducated black men, the overwhelming majority of whom were just freed from slavery, adapted themselves to useful service in the armies of the Union.

Most black units had been in uniform for a year when the war ended, although some were kept on for another six or seven months, so their histories are short. Since few of the noncommissioned officers and other enlisted men could read or write, army paperwork was left to the often shorthanded white company officers, most of them former enlisted men commissioned without special training. Consequently, army inspectors faulted the Twenty-ninth for poor paperwork, a condition never corrected because the officers had the more pressing responsibilities of training and disciplining troops.

The stories of many white regiments are enhanced by the large number of letters written by officers and men during the war which have been preserved and by journals and recollections, published and unpublished. Bell Irvin Wiley found no more than twenty examples of letters by black men to add to his memorable work *The Life of Billy Yank: The Common Soldier of the Union*.[1] Forty years of scholarship since the publication of Wiley's book have turned up more. Those that survive, however, are often heavily edited versions published in newspapers and periodicals during the war.[2] This study adds a few useful letters culled from the military and pension records of soldiers of the Twenty-ninth Regiment as well as descriptions of events, most recalled many years after the conflict, in affidavits and depositions accompanying requests for pensions. My primary sources for information about the lives of black men in uniform were not the skimpy company and government files in the National Archives but, rather, the military and pension files of the individual soldiers at the same location. Being advocacy documents, the latter records are not always reliable; comrades often supplied supporting letters that were identical word for word because pension agents assembled the files for unlettered veterans. Consequently, some of what soldiers—and their officers—might say must be used with caution, since there is little other information to check alleged incidents and facts.

More than a century since Luis F. Emilio's memorable 1894 *History of the Fifty-Fourth Regiment of Massachusetts Volunteer Infantry, 1863–1865* (now in print as *A Brave Black Regiment*), scholars have still given little attention to any single black regiment. One would have assumed that more popular accounts of black regiments would have followed the motion picture *Glory,* based on Emilio's book, but there have been none. Perhaps this study will inspire others to undertake the tedious task of reviewing the sparse organizational papers and the thousands of individual files that hold the story of a single regiment.

Selecting the Twenty-ninth U.S. Colored Infantry came as the result of a request by Wanda S. Dowell and Susan G. Cumby, dedicated archivists at the Fort Ward Museum and Historical Site in Alexandria, Virginia. They asked me to assist in learning about two black regiments thought to have served in Alexandria during the war. We learned that both had passed through the city, but their short visits did not add much to local history. This preliminary look at black military history revealed the scarcity of published data, so I continued the project with the Illinois regiment. Ironically, my research revealed that the Twenty-ninth Regiment had enlisted many men in Virginia and Maryland, so there was a local connection, after all.

The history of the black soldier is in many ways a tragedy because the bright hope of freedom which brought many to the recruiting tables was not met in postwar America. The black veteran was not recognized as having earned his right to full citizenship. These poorly educated men gained little preparation for life after the army, and few of them had more than day-to-day employment in menial labor for the rest of their lives. Their contribution to the military victory of the Union was small, but a soldier's work is not measured this way. What can be said of the men of the Twenty-ninth U.S. Colored Infantry is that they did their duty. This is the best compliment one can pay to a soldier.

THE BLACK
CIVIL WAR SOLDIERS
OF ILLINOIS

Chapter 1

FINDING A PLACE

Black soldiers served in the American armed forces from the Revolution onward, but not until the Civil War were their numbers significant. No provision for black enlistments existed at the war's beginning. Still, groups of Northern blacks requested acceptance in defense of the Union, and antislavery and egalitarian-leaning whites supported their cause. Initial war enthusiasm was not sufficient, however, to overcome the common Northern prejudice about the ability of blacks and the limits that law and custom placed on their acceptance for military service in state militias and in the volunteer and regular armies. But more important than prejudice was the belief that the war would be over quickly and thus blacks were not needed. This changed when the Battle of Bull Run and other early engagements showed that the rebels would not be defeated easily, and preparations for a long conflict began. The initial surge of enlistments which followed the surrender of Fort Sumter slackened, and many militia regiments, signed up for only ninety days, went home, aggravating a persistent manpower shortage. Now, however, slaves were in federally occupied rebel areas, and more of them were entering Union lines. They could provide labor to help with building roads and intrenchments and working as porters and teamsters in the army's support system.

The problem with the use of blacks, and especially the escaped slaves who were among them and considered to be contraband of war, was the administration's concern for the loyalty of border slave states. President Lincoln's position was that these states must not be lost, so contraband slaves were initially subject to eventual—and sometimes immediate—return to their owners. Government policy held that the war could not be seen as a crusade against slavery, although for many it clearly was. The declared reason for opposing the Confederacy was to preserve the Union. Under these circumstances it was understandable that blacks could have no significant role in the war effort. Congress was not insensitive to the plight of contrabands, and in the Confiscation Act approved on 13 March 1862 it prohibited army and navy officers from using their forces to return fugitive slaves to their owners. The act further provided that any officer found guilty by court-martial of violating this provision would be dismissed from the service. Within a few months another bill, the Militia Act of 17 July, authorized the president "to receive into the service of the United States, for the purpose of constructing intrenchments, or performing camp duty, or any other labor, or any military or naval service for which they were found competent, persons of African descent." The act further provided that "when any man or boy of African descent, who by the laws of any State shall owe service or labor to any person who during the present rebellion has levied war, or has borne arms against the United States, or has adhered to their enemies by giving them aid and comfort, shall provide service under this act, he, his mother, and his wife, and children, shall forever therefore be free, any law usage, or custom whatsoever to the contrary notwithstanding." Based on a 20 April 1863 opinion of the solicitor of the War Department, pay was fixed at the same ten dollars monthly provided to black laborers, of which three dollars "may be in clothing," and blacks providing military or naval service were not to receive the federal bounty (then one hundred dollars) to which white enlistees were entitled. White private soldiers at the time were paid thirteen dollars plus a clothing allowance of three dollars and fifty cents a month. This and another law, the Second Confiscation Act, approved simultaneously, provided that all rebel-owned slaves within or who might enter Union lines or found in any rebel area occupied by Union forces would be considered prisoners of war and "shall be forever free of their servitude, and not again be held as slaves." As for slaves of citizens loyal to the Union, the act did not give them freedom but, rather, allowed persons who first made an oath that they had not served in the Confederate forces or aided those forces to have their fugitive slaves returned. The slaves of loyal citizens were somewhat protected because the law prohibited any person in the army or navy from deciding the validity of ownership claims and called for the dismissal from the service of anyone giving up such claimed slaves. In addition to other provisions, the Second Confiscation Act gave the president discretion to employ "as many persons of African descent as he may deem necessary and proper for the suppression of the rebellion."[1]

Lincoln implemented the acts by his 22 July 1862 executive order, directing military commanders in the states of Virginia, South Carolina, Georgia, Florida, Alabama, Mississippi, Louisiana, Texas, and Arkansas to seize and use all property needed for military purposes and "to employ as laborers, within and from said States, so many persons of African descent as can be advantageously used for military and naval purposes." The order said: "As to both property and persons of African descent, accounts shall be kept sufficiently accurate and in detail to show quantities and amounts, and from whom both property and such persons shall have come, as a basis on which compensation can be made in proper cases." This authority did not mean blacks would be accepted as soldiers to be armed and organized in military units but, rather, allowed them to serve in labor organizations.[2]

Some successful and unsuccessful attempts had been made earlier to enlist and arm blacks, the first being Maj. Gen. David Hunter's unauthorized May 1862 roundup of blacks in the Sea Islands area of South Carolina, then under federal occupation. This effort was disallowed by Lincoln but had little chance for success anyway because Hunter could not pay the troops. Most were sent home in a few months, leaving but one company as a nucleus for a future regiment raised in October 1862, designated the Thirty-third U.S. Colored Infantry, and mustered into U.S. service the following 31 January. Free and slave blacks, officered in part by men of their own race, were enrolled in the First Louisiana Native Guards (later renamed the Seventy-third U.S. Colored Infantry) in September 1862, followed by four more Louisiana regiments by early March 1863. That spring a regiment was formed in Kansas (later the Seventy-ninth U.S. Colored Infantry), and a major recruiting effort began in the Mississippi Valley under the personal direction of the army's adjutant general, Lorenzo Thomas.[3]

The catalyst for the use of blacks in large numbers and in organized military units was Lincoln's acceptance of the inevitability of emancipation. His proclamation of 22 September 1862 promised future freedom for slaves in rebellion states, except for those in some cities that were later to be identified as Union occupied, and counties in Louisiana and Virginia. As for slaves in loyal states, Lincoln promised to recommend to Congress a measure "tendering pecuniary aid" to those states that "may then have voluntarily adopted, or thereafter may voluntarily adopt, immediate or gradual abolishment of slavery within their respective limits." As a further concession to states that believed freed slaves would be a danger or an overwhelming social problem, Lincoln called for support of colonization of freed blacks in overseas nations whose governments might agree to accept them. Although the preliminary proclamation freed few slaves not already considered de facto free, nonetheless, it was seen as the vehicle of liberation by blacks everywhere. The implementing proclamation of 1 January 1863 addressed the question of black soldiers and sailors directly, saying that blacks "will be received into the armed service of the United States to garrison forts, positions, stations and other places"—not exactly granting full equality with whites in terms of promising combat duty but representing a change from simply being given labor assignments. Within the War Department boards were created to examine candidates for officer positions, and the Bureau for Colored Troops was established in the adjutant general's office to govern the raising of black units. Black soldiers, volunteers and later conscripts, were mustered directly into the service of the United States and were not to be assigned as state troops. They were organized and led by officers under U.S. authority. This was unlike most white regiments, militia and volunteer, which had their officers appointed by governors of individual states. Other than two Massachusetts volunteer regiments, and a few others that would retain state identity, each of the 149 black infantry, cavalry, and artillery units was designated or redesignated a regiment or a battery of the United States Colored Troops (USCT), without identification of the state from which its members were recruited. The soldiers were, however, credited to the quotas of the jurisdictions in which they were enlisted.[4]

State authority over one aspect of the U.S. Colored Troops was retained; states were authorized to recruit black soldiers and to provide camps of assembly for their organization into regiments and batteries. The state's incentive was that a black soldier counted the same as a white recruit in meeting a state's Washington-imposed volunteer quota. On the day of mustering in, and after an oath administered by a U.S. Army officer, black units became a federal responsibility. When conscription began in mid-1863, meeting volunteer quotas became more important, since the draft was used only to make up the difference in recruits between the number required to meet quotas and the number enlisted. Exemptions could be purchased, however, and paid substitutes were accepted, thus benefiting the more affluent members of society. The draft itself caused riots among the working class in New York, and numerous assaults on black troops were reported. In Illinois armed resistance to the draft was reported in July and August in Fulton County, Williamson and surrounding counties, Danville, Joliet, and Peoria, the latter unrest, as in New York, attributed primarily to Irish working men. Monumental victories and enormous casualties at Gettysburg and Vicksburg in early July 1863 took the edge off such protests nationally, and they eventually diminished. Of course, declining opposition to black troops may also be attributed to the North's growing sense of reality. As one wartime soldier recalled, tongue in cheek: "Just in proportion as the certainty of a draft increased, did the prejudice against Negro soldiers decrease. It was discovered that Negroes were not only loyal persons and good mule drivers, but exceedingly competent to bear arms."[5]

ILLINOIS ACTS

Illinois governor Richard Yates, a former Whig congressman already earning a reputation as the state's much-admired war leader, may have had the use of black soldiers in mind when he urged President Lincoln in July 1862 to "accept the services of all loyal men," presumably without regard to color. His point was that the rebellion had to be destroyed and that Illinois was ready for the call to total war. His view was shared by others in the state; "a colored company had been started in Galesburg," and many of Illinois's black citizens responded to the call of agents of eastern states, particularly those from Massachusetts. Black interest in military service was not high, but it was encouraged by black leader Frederick Douglass's March 1863 call, "Men of Color to Arms," and was helped by Douglass's active recruiting efforts. His emphasis on the killing of slaveholders did not do much to stir blacks in the North, and the fact that blacks were paid less than their white comrades and were refused commissions made the recruiting job difficult.[6]

A 15 June 1863 editorial in the *Chicago Daily Tribune* described changing conditions in Illinois, noting that opposition to black enlistments was declining in the army and among citizens. The example of Massachusetts showed that blacks adjusted well to military life and duties, and two hundred and fifty Illinois blacks had gone to Massachusetts regiments. It would be better, however, the newspaper observed, if Illinois blacks could enlist "as part of the quota of their own great State," and Chicago alone could supply three to four hundred men. Finally, Secretary of War Edwin M. Stanton was called on to authorize Governor Yates to raise a regiment "that will stand as much hardship, and fight as desperately, and kill as many rebels in battle, as any equal number of men of the purest Anglo-Saxon blood that have gone to the wars."[7]

This editorial was sent by Joseph Medill, the newspaper's editor, to the clerk of the Senate Military Affairs Committee in Washington, D.C., asking the official to talk to Stanton and adding that the three hundred blacks in Chicago ready to join up "refuse to go off to Massachusetts, and I don't blame them." Upon receiving this correspondence, Stanton ordered the army to send Yates the appropriate authority. Nothing appears to have been done immediately, and Yates wired the secretary again on 28 July, asking whether an army officer then in Illinois recruiting black men for units in other states was also authorized to raise black units in the state. Stanton replied the same day, informing Yates that the officer was so empowered but adding, "If you can raise one or two regiments [of black troops], authority will be given to you." A month later the governor answered: "It is my duty to raise a colored regiment in this State," and he requested permission to do so. In late September he was finally "authorized to raise a regiment of Infantry to be composed of colored men, to be mustered into the United States service for three years, or during the war," the order further specifying that no federal enlistment bounty was to be paid to the blacks. Yates was also sent instructions outlining the composition of a colored infantry regiment. The unit would have one colonel, lieutenant colonel, major, chaplain, surgeon (and two assistant surgeons), adjutant (first lieutenant), quartermaster (first lieutenant), and sergeant major and three other enlisted men in the headquarters and ten companies of infantry. There was no battalion organization. A company was authorized one captain, a first and second lieutenant, a first sergeant, three sergeants, six corporals, two musicians, a wagoner, and between sixty-four and eighty-three private soldiers.[8]

Within days Yates was complaining that pay and bounty inequities between whites and blacks would make enlistments difficult. Of course, Washington told the state that it could not and would not correct the condition because the War Department interpreted the law to fix the pay for black troops at ten dollars, including three dollars in clothing, so the scene was set for Illinois to begin recruiting. On 26 October Governor Yates issued his General Orders no. 44, perhaps delaying because of bitter "Copperhead" (antiwar Democrat) opposition to free black soldiers within the state. The first enlistments in the First Regiment Illinois Volunteers (Colored), as the unit was initially named, were made on 1 November: two sergeants, two corporals, one wagoner, and about a dozen privates, all of them signed on at Quincy, where Company A was the first to be organized. Those enlisted as noncommissioned officers had no military

experience but were thought by recruiters to have characteristics or qualifications—such as the ability to read and write—which would be useful in
organizing and running the unit and keeping up with army paperwork.
Recruiting went slowly, perhaps because many black men had already
been enlisted into regiments from other states, whose agents traveled all
over the area, but probably equally because of the difference in pay between black and white soldiers and a deep current of racial prejudice in
Illinois which led prospective recruits to expect discrimination against
them by white soldiers and civilians.[9]

THE RACE ISSUE IN ILLINOIS

The background of race relations in Illinois was not one of tolerance;
many early settlers came from or through the South and had a strong
prejudice against blacks. Although the 1787 Northwest Ordinance prohibited slavery and involuntary servitude, Illinois, when part of Indiana
and later, maintained for twenty-five years a "registered servants" pro-
gram (applied to blacks only) of up to lifetime indenture, allowing slavery
in all but name of supposedly free blacks. Only a year after the state joined
the Union, 1818, it passed the first of a series of "black codes" that continued in effect in various forms until 1865. These laws required blacks to
record at the county seat a "certificate of freedom" and a description of
family members, information allowing overseers of the poor to expel them
from the state when it was thought necessary. Other provisions withheld
court standing and the vote from blacks, allowed flogging of "lazy" or
disobedient blacks, and made harboring of a black by another black a
felony calling for a fine and a thirty-five-stripe whipping. Free blacks entering the state had to post a one-thousand-dollar bond as guarantee against
becoming a public charge, and blacks who could not pay fines could be
sold into indentured service. Furthermore, blacks could not serve in the
militia and were not provided education by law.[10]

There was a two-way traffic in slaves; freed or free blacks were kid-
napped and sent to the South, particularly from the Shawneetown area, a
practice that was not a felony in Illinois. An underground railway of slaves
from border states, most crossing the Mississippi River at Quincy, Alton,
and Chester, ran in the other direction. Tolerance of blacks was greater in
the northern half of the state than in the southern "Egypt" section but not
sufficiently to prevent passage of an 1853 law prohibiting blacks from
entering the state under threat of a fifty-dollar fine. Failure to pay led, as
in similar codes established earlier, to sale of the black at a sheriff's auc-

tion. Asked in 1862 if the state should modify the law making it "a crime for a Negro to set foot in Illinois," 150,000 out of 260,000 voters in a constitutional referendum opposed repeal. In February 1863 six blacks were convicted of living in the state and were sold to the highest bidder in lieu of paying the fine. This law was not repealed until 1864—the remaining black codes were finally abolished in February 1865, almost at war's end; not until 1870, and passage of the Fifteenth Amendment to the U.S. Constitution, were Illinois blacks given the vote.[11]

Illinois's Civil War treatment of blacks was not much different than that of other states. Some were more enlightened in terms of discriminatory laws, but probably most Northerners, regardless of state, shared a common view of the black man which was not much different from the racist, white supremacy views of Southerners. But prejudice was not the entire story, particularly in Illinois. There opposition to blacks was stronger in urban areas because of economic rivalry between unskilled blacks and white laborers, many of the latter being recent immigrants. Farmers were not much concerned economically about blacks, although during the war antiblack sentiment became more acute among farmers of Southern origin. Not all blacks accepted the legal restrictions on their lives in Illinois, but certainly few of them who recognized their subjugation were able to do much about it. In Chicago a group of well-off blacks formed the "Repeal Association" and circulated petitions calling for the end of black codes. In January 1864, just as recruiting for Illinois's black regiment was getting seriously under way, some of the bite was taken out of the black exclusion codes' involuntary servitude punishment clause by a state supreme court decision, but the repeal of exclusion itself had to wait another year. A contemporary writer said of black exclusion that there was "strong public sentiment against it," and, whatever the reason, relaxation of enforcement probably allowed more blacks to drift in from loyal slave states Missouri and Kentucky, from which, it turned out, the majority of the blacks recruited for the Illinois regiment would come.[12]

What incentives encouraged blacks to come to Illinois and remain there? For most of them freedom from bondage was the reason for their migration, and in Illinois they could work for a daily wage. The pay, however, was usually barely sufficient to maintain more than a subsistence existence, and there were no guarantees that it would continue. The body of potential recruits was made up almost entirely of farm and city laborers, few of them with any promise of a future for themselves or their families. Black society, judging from the descriptions veterans recorded in their pension requests, did provide some mutual support and limited social activities, particularly in towns. An army enlistment was attractive to some, however, because it offered regular pay, not as a protection from prejudice or exploitation. It does not appear that patriotism, a desire to serve Illinois, or a wish to help other blacks gain freedom were important considerations.

Prejudice against black soldiers was, as would be expected, strong in the ranks of white regiments, especially among those from Southern and border states, and among the Irish and other groups of recent immigrants. The peak of antiblack sentiment in the army was in mid- and late 1862, and many feared that putting blacks in uniform threatened white supremacy. Other objections were spin-offs of these beliefs, such as the conviction that blacks were not smart enough to soldier. As it turned out, black units were useful and were generally accepted by their white comrades, not because the blacks immediately became outstanding soldiers but because blacks were often used in undesirable fatigue and garrison duties formerly performed by whites. In addition, being able to get a commission in a black regiment was an attractive proposition to many white enlisted men, though there was never universal acceptance of blacks in the military.[13]

The Illinois soldier's reaction to emancipation and blacks in uniform was much the same as elsewhere in the West—initial hostility followed by reluctant acceptance. An Illinois white regiment, the 109th Volunteer Infantry, which had been raised in Anna on the southern tip of the state in September 1862, was disarmed and ordered "into close confinement . . . during the continuance of the war," largely because of opposition in the ranks to the Emancipation Proclamation and the arming of blacks. Another, the 128th Illinois, formed in November 1862, was disbanded because of a high desertion rate, possibly caused by the prospect of white soldiers serving in the army with black troops. The Ninetieth Illinois Volunteers, the "Irish Legion," a Chicago regiment, was also hostile to the government's policy toward blacks as announced by Adjutant General Thomas, and its colonel wrote to a newspaper, saying that he and his men "would not basely stultify themselves and renounce the honest convictions of their hearts." The colonel was "'dishonorably dismissed' by order of the Secretary of War 'for a highly insubordinate statement respecting the Adjutant General of the Army [Thomas] published in the Chicago Times over his official signature.'"[14]

Thomas, on the other hand, reported that, when he addressed Union troops at Cairo in March 1863 on the black troop policy, it "was not enthusiastically received by the troops," with one exception, "the regiment from Illinois." Some white soldiers saw the wisdom of enlisting black troops, a position expressed by an Illinois veteran in a letter home: "I think if a negro could save their lives [whites'] by sacrificing theirs they [the whites] would be willing" to accept blacks. Another wrote that his comrades thought that, "if a negro can stop an enemy's ball, why let him go and do it[?]" Use of black troops as a way of hastening defeat of the rebellion did not overcome prejudice against blacks generally, but it did reduce the aversion to the abolition of slavery and strengthened the promise of black regiments, as far as the army was concerned. Black soldiers had fought in several engagements by early 1864, when Illinois's black recruiting effort was at its peak, and had generally conducted themselves well. In Illinois, however, Copperhead influence was high, and public opinion was generally hostile to black enlistments, despite the sometimes impressive performance of black regiments. This slowed signing up recruits for the Illinois regiment. Well-publicized massacres of black prisoners by the rebels may also have weakened black men's enthusiasm for military service. The most important example of reported barbarity occurred at Fort Pillow on a bluff overlooking the Mississippi above Memphis in April 1864. Here Confederate troops under the command of Gen. Nathan Bedford Forrest shot down a large number of black troops after they had surrendered.[15] This atrocity, occurring at the very time the new Illinois regiment was starting out for war, would be remembered.

The West was rich with candidates for black regiments, and recruiting agents had combed much of it, particularly Missouri and Kentucky, but they did not neglect states with smaller black populations. Indiana, for example, saw it necessary to prohibit agents from soliciting its blacks, "under penalty of being arrested and summarily punished." There the governor had asked to raise a black regiment for reasons similar to Governor Yates's—"not so much because our colored citizens were anxious to enter the service, as for the reason that the State had been and was overrun with agents representing other States, and he had found it necessary, to prevent the men from being enticed away and credited elsewhere." Governor Yates's reaction to the very active agents from outside Illinois, and facing a high October 1863 quota for enlistees, was similar. He proclaimed late that month, "I forbid all recruiting in this State except for our own regiments," a general rule that had particular immediacy with respect to raising the first black companies.[16]

An Illinois citizen who knew Ulysses S. Grant in Galena before the latter's return to the army, Augustin Chetlain, a staunch Union backer and early militia volunteer, was commissioned a brevet brigadier general in 1863 to gather up blacks in Tennessee. He worked for General Thomas, but, since enlistments by such federal officers were credited to the states in which the men were found, no real conflict about his efforts arose with state officials. General Thomas, the primary federal recruiter of blacks, did quarrel a year later with Illinois's adjutant general about the disposition of four hundred blacks at Cairo, most of them contrabands from Southern and border states on the Mississippi. Thomas wanted them sent to Paducah, but Illinois refused, even though the four hundred would be credited to that state. This could have been the result of distrust, given the frequent quarrels between the state and federal governments over recruit counts.[17]

RECRUITING IN ILLINOIS

Within Illinois tension concerning black recruits was high at the end of 1863, in view of the success of prior recruiting drives that had creamed off candidates, Governor Yates's prohibition against recruiters from other states, and the continued presence of these out-of-state recruiters. One of them was Martin Robinson Delany, who, working from his Chicago base, had been raising troops for Connecticut and Rhode Island black regiments. Delany, a black man later commissioned as a major, had subagents in many areas of the state—one, for example, in Quincy. In Delany's view competition between states for the same black recruits could be solved if recruiting in rebel states were permitted and enlistees were credited to the loyal state that signed them up.[18] Permission for this did not come until the following July, and it would only marginally assist Illinois in filling its regiment's ranks and providing later replacements. It is obvious that the pressure on states to meet quotas caused much bad feeling and suspicions. It was in this atmosphere that recruiting for Illinois's black regiment began.

Illinois Adj. Gen. Allen C. Fuller complained to Washington officials that the citizens of the state were not as alarmed about the draft as he was. He likely took this position because of the previous summer's armed resistance to conscription, or he may have been seeking to head off the embarrassment of Illinois failing to find enough volunteers and thus triggering compulsory service. Fuller said he had made appeals to the people "to wake them up to the danger and disgrace of a draft, and yet, with few exceptions, they were as silent as the grave." He told the War Department that he had at least obtained agreement from the principal Democratic newspaper, the *Chicago Times,* and the Republican *Tribune* not to oppose recruiting, but he got little active support, because, he said, the editors thought the quota could not be met anyway. The army officer responsible for recruiting in Illinois later accused "the wicked, reckless, and debauched newspaper press of the State" for all enrollment and draft problems. He went on to say, "And chief among these instigators of insurrection and treason, the foul and damnable reservoir which supplied the lesser sewers with political filth, falsehood, and treason has been the Chicago Times— a newspaper which would not have to change its course one atom if its place of publication had been Richmond or Charleston." The army went beyond talk; Gen. Richard J. Oglesby, later elected governor of Illinois, seized the *Times's* presses at Maj. Gen. Ambrose Burnside's order. Lincoln, however, reversed the action two days later.[19]

Blacks in the state were a small part of the recruiting picture, since at the beginning of the war Illinois's black citizens numbered only 7,628, less than one half a percent of the state's population. Only 3,809 were males, and just 1,622 were of military age, eighteen to forty-five. Though this seems like a shallow pool from which to draw a regiment, particularly after 700 men had already been enlisted by other Northern states, the situation was not as bad as it looked because a large number of blacks from surrounding slave states, many arriving even when entering Illinois was illegal, resided in Illinois, so the pool was actually substantially larger than it might seem. Between 1860 and 1862, for example, 22,000 slaves escaped from Missouri, many of them able-bodied males who went to neighboring states, Kentucky, Indiana, and Illinois.[20] Thus, there were sufficient eligible blacks for Illinois's recruiters, and successfully raising a full black regiment of 900 or more would be useful in relieving the state adjutant general's anxiety about making the federal quota.

The officer charged with this responsibility was Capt. John Armstrong Bross, whom the governor picked to be the new regiment's commander. Bross was born in 1826 in Milford, Pike County, Pennsylvania, studied law in New York, and moved to Chicago, where he practiced law and had been an assistant U.S. marshal and a U.S. commissioner. Early in the war he raised two companies of the Eighty-eighth Illinois Volunteers and was commissioned a captain and commanding officer in one of them. He had a good combat record, his regiment fighting at Perrysville under Maj. Gen. Don Carlos Buell and at Murfreesboro. Bross was a well-known Chicago figure, active in state politics, but he was a Steven Douglas Democrat, not a Republican or an abolitionist. His brother William was an influential Republican newspaperman, co-owner of the *Chicago Tribune,* and later lieutenant governor of his state. Initial announcements that Bross was to command the new black regiment got the attention of opposing politicians, one asking in November 1863: "Who is Col. Bross? Is he some political hack manufactured for the occasion or is he a *'man'* who has been doing yeoman's service in the army[?]"[21]

Bross commenced recruiting in November 1863, concentrating at Quincy, where he set up his headquarters. He was discharged on the first of the month as a captain in the Eighty-eighth Illinois Infantry to accept command of the new regiment and was carried, presumably unpaid, as "on volunteer recruiting service prior to muster." Under army procedures he was eligible for appointment as a lieutenant colonel, when four companies of a minimum of about seventy-five noncommissioned officers and men each were mustered in. Similarly, at company level the first lieutenant was mustered when the unit was half-complete and the captain and second lieutenant when most of the authorized soldiers had been mustered. The regimental major was mustered in after six companies, but the colonel, chaplain, surgeon, assistant surgeons, quartermaster, and adjutant were not signed on until the entire regiment of ten companies was formed, about forty officers and over nine hundred enlisted men. Actual mustering in of soldiers and their officers was accomplished by U.S. Army officers; before this official action, feeding, housing, and transporting recruits were the state's responsibility. Thus, there often was a gap between enlistment and finally being sworn into U.S. service, during which time the new recruits were unpaid. Some states sought permission to muster in soldiers at once, but the army regulation in force since the Mexican War did not allow muster until after a company was organized. It is unclear when that point was reached, and it appears that the pay gap was later avoided through laxity in this matter, mustering in new soldiers at recruitment or soon thereafter. Bross's new regiment was not consistent, some companies swearing recruits in piecemeal, generally within days of each soldier's recruitment, but the first company, A, was to give the oath to almost the entire company at once in April 1864. Some Company A soldiers recruited in December 1863 consequently went unpaid for three or four months. Illinois, however, had a state bounty that, unlike the federal bounty, was paid to black enlistees, and other bounties, county and city, were sometimes authorized, so families of new soldiers were not immediately destitute. Local bounty payment, however, could be contingent on mustering in, so some soldiers and their families depended on public relief. Of course, not all state and local bounties were paid at once—to cut back on "bounty jumping" and help those soldiers with little sense of responsibility to have means to support relatives until they could be regularly enlisted.[22]

State and local bounties varied widely in Illinois, depending mostly on the success each recruiting district had in meeting quotas. The state alone paid bounties from ten dollars to six hundred and nine dollars, but the state bounty seems to have been one hundred dollars when the First Regiment was recruiting. The town of Kewanee in Henry County, for example, in addition agreed to pay a fifty-dollar bounty to single enlistees and one hundred dollars to married ones. A newspaper reported, "Oliver Ward [Company A], Richard Carroll [D], Frank Lewis [A], Archy [Archibald] Hopson [D] and George Bolden [D] immediately volunteered." All these men were former slaves, and each had a different path from bondage to freedom at Kewanee. Ward and Lewis, however, knew each other from youth; they were born on the same plantation near Richmond, Virginia. Both men were sold to a new owner (probably Samuel Olden) in Tennessee before or early in the war. They ran away in 1861 or 1862, but only Ward's story of this is known. A friend (Louisa Washington) wrote in 1889: "On a steamboat in the Mississippi . . . I became acquainted with Oliver Ward, deceased, and Albina, sometimes called Lavina Ward . . . and came with them through Cairo to Kewanee. They were fleeing Slavery in Tennessee where they said they had lived. . . . [T]hey were said to have been married in this county [Henry County, Illinois], 'White folks fashion,' as it was called among colored people. . . . They said they were slaves on the same plantation." Carroll's way to Kewanee and the regiment began near Point Pleasant, Madrid County, Missouri, where he was born in early 1842. He was owned by Mary Mollesby and was a blacksmith on her plantation. He fled in the winter of 1862 and found employment with the Union Army at Point Pleasant as a cook. He was taken to Pittsburg Landing, Tennessee, and finally with other contrabands to Cairo. He was hired as a body servant of the Cairo provost marshal and went with the officer when he was transferred to Kewanee. When his employer resigned from the army, Carroll joined the new regiment. Hopson, like Ward and Lewis, was also born a slave in Virginia but was probably unacquainted with these men, being some years younger. Bolden's background is even more obscure, because he gave different birthplaces to government officials. At enlistment he said he was from New Jersey but in later years claimed Long Town, South Carolina. It cannot be determined how he came to be at Kewanee in late 1863.[23]

The man who would command Company A, Robert Porter, an Illinois resident, was an army enlisted soldier who offered to raise a company of blacks. As was a common volunteer force practice, he no doubt expected to be commissioned captain of the unit when it was up to strength. In past years the governor would have appointed regimental officers, but this was not the approved method of commissioning in black units. All officers had to be examined by federal officers at St. Louis, Cincinnati, or Washington, D.C. The boards of officers were called Casey boards after Maj. Gen. Silas Casey, who established them and their procedures. Qualified candidates were commissioned by the president. In Porter's case those procedures designed to procure better officers than the earlier, sometimes overly political, system may not have been strictly observed. The state accepted his offer in October 1863, two months before the St. Louis army board was asked to examine him for a commission. Porter, a teamster before the war, had prior military service as a three-month volunteer in the Tenth Illinois Infantry, in which he was a corporal and later a sergeant. He reenlisted for three years, was detailed to the "Secret Service," probably operating as a spy behind enemy lines, was captured at Pittsburg Landing during the Shiloh battle in April 1862, and was a prisoner of war until exchanged late that year. That he was afterward assigned to the staff of Brig. Gen. Benjamin M. Prentiss of Quincy, a hero of the Shiloh engagement, likely explains why he was one of the first potential officers accepted for the regiment. Porter was not a commissioned officer when recruiting began in Quincy and, although he could have done so, did not do any active recruiting himself. All Company A's recruits were signed up by T. Jefferson Brown from Toledo, Ohio, who would be mustered in April 1864 as a major and the regiment's second in command. Brown's prewar occupation was as a steward on the Mississippi River steamboat *Black Hawk*, and he had prior service as an officer in the Fiftieth Illinois Infantry. Probably unknown to the officers who decided on his selection as regimental major, he had resigned his earlier commission under rather suspicious circumstances. He wrote that it was "because of private reasons—Unpleasant relations with Colonel," but the details of this conflict are not recorded.[24]

Company A's first soldiers enlisted on 1 November 1863 were mostly farmers, and not one had been born in Illinois. Sgt. Jesse Hazell (or Hazel), age thirty-three, was born a slave in Maryland but was taken west by his owner. His last owner was Louise B. Anderson, and he ran away from her in Missouri and went to Quincy, probably only a few days before enlisting. Anderson, hearing of her slave's enlistment, applied for government compensation for the loss. Her request was honored because the law provided that loyal owners of slaves receive the federal bounty of three hundred dollars allowed to volunteers (one hundred for draftees) which was denied to the recruit himself. Hazell was made the company's orderly sergeant immediately, even though he was unable to write. Asked in later years how he managed, Hazell said, "[Company A Cpl.] Frank Thomas and [Sgt.] George Hazeman [Heithman] did the writing for me." Thomas, who had been a servant—a house slave—in Missouri likely learned to read and write in that environment. As for Heithman, also a Missouri slave (in Monroe County), his literacy may have been gained under similar conditions. Sgt. John M. Perkins, twenty-seven, born in bondage in Kentucky, was moved by his owner to Marion County, Missouri, and escaped to Illinois in 1861. He may have been the first man signed up in the regiment. Perkins could neither read nor write and had been a field hand.[25]

Less is known about the early lives of the regiment's first two corporals, and it cannot be determined from their records what qualified them for immediate appointment as noncommissioned officers. Oliver Tinker, age twenty-six, was born in Missouri and was likely an escaped slave. He claimed that he had been trained as a carpenter. John E. Golden, a farm laborer, ran away from slavery in Marion County, Missouri, to enlist in the regiment. He was age eighteen to twenty-one as far as he knew.[26]

Wagoner George Hawkins, age twenty, was born at Clover Bottom, Kentucky; he knew the bricklaying trade. He said that, along with three other future soldiers—George Burke, Company A; James Jamison, Company C; and Adam Plegatt, Company D—and other slaves, he ran away sometime in 1861 from Ralls County, Missouri. Jamison and Plegatt enlisted a month or two after Hawkins, but Burke did not enter the service until a year later, when he was drafted from Alton. Like other early enlistees, Hawkins was detailed to help find other recruits in Missouri, not an entirely friendly territory for a black soldier. Members of the detail thought it necessary to protect themselves on this duty and purchased pistols; the army did not issue arms to soldiers who were not yet officially mustered. Hawkins, cleaning his pistol at the camp in Quincy, accidentally shot himself in the hand. The injury called for the amputation of his thumb by the acting surgeon, Dr. John Fee, a contract civilian, assisted by Porter, the designated Company A commanding officer. It was because of this disability that Hawkins was mustered as the company wagoner rather than as a private soldier.[27]

Pvt. James Bletcher, twenty-seven, from Pike County, Missouri, was probably a runaway slave. Pvt. Peter Corsey, age eighteen at enlistment, escaped from Thomas T. Phillips in Marion County, Missouri. He said he was accompanied to Illinois by John Wesley Logan and George Washington, both of whom joined the company, but the claim may have been made to support somehow his own postwar pension request. Logan, who enlisted on 15 November, two weeks after Corsey, was born in bondage in Shelby County, Kentucky, in 1837 and was moved to Paris, Missouri, by his owner, Elizabeth Hunter. He said he ran away from her in 1863. Washington was born a slave in the District of Columbia and was brought west to Louisiana, Missouri, by his owner, William C. Hardin. That the three black men were living in three separate Missouri counties when they fled slavery makes it appear unlikely that they crossed the Mississippi River and arrived in Illinois in concert, but Washington enlisted the same day as did Corsey.[28]

The backgrounds of the remaining private soldiers first enlisted in the regiment are similar, and few details survive. Anthony Dudley, age twenty, was a Missouri slave. Benjamin Franklin, eighteen, claimed he was born in Alabama, but he was probably a slave in Missouri just before enlistment. As a slave, James Gilmore belonged to Nancy Gillmore, of Oil Trough Bottom, Arkansas, and he may have been born in Kentucky. How and when he arrived in Quincy to enlist are not known. After the war he took the name of his father and was known as James Johnson. Thomas Johnson, eighteen, was from Marion County, Missouri; likely he was a slave, but nothing more is known about his early life. Andrew Lewis, twenty-nine, was a slave owned by Andrew Lewis, Miller Township, Marion County, Missouri. Lewis's owner, hearing of his slave's enlistment, went to the camp at Quincy in early December 1863 to get a receipt for his property. Such receipts were standard practice and served as a basis to claim the bounty paid to slave owners.[29]

Pvt. Martin Magruder, age thirty, was born in Shelby County, Kentucky. His owner died, and he was taken by the owner's son, Travis S. Magruder, to Clay Township, Monroe County, Missouri. He was working there cutting corn just before he enlisted at Quincy. Richard

Perry, eighteen, was born in Missouri of a slave mother and possibly a free father. Since his mother was a slave, under state law he was also. Perry was owned by Emily Herndon, of Jefferson Township, Monroe County, who got a receipt for him from the army at Quincy and who probably collected compensation. Washington Williams, twenty-one, another Missouri-born slave, was in Quincy long enough to marry before enlistment.[30]

The backgrounds, ages, and fates of these first of the regiment were representative of many other black soldiers enlisted early in Illinois. Sergeant Hazell was captured by the Confederates and survived the war; Perkins was wounded in action; Dudley was captured and died in a rebel prison of "cruel treatment"; Lewis likewise died a prisoner. Magruder, wounded in action, died of disease during the war, and Washington was captured but returned to the regiment at war's end. The others left the service when the regiment was inactivated, but all of them suffered physical infirmities that they attributed to their military duties under harsh conditions.

Company A's first sergeant, William McCoslin, a barber from Bloomington, Illinois—who was to be appointed regimental sergeant major in early 1865, when the regiment reached full strength—and the remaining authorized complement of two sergeants and six corporals all were enlisted before the end of November. McCoslin had some quasimilitary experience; he had worked as a cook with the Thirty-ninth Illinois Infantry before enlisting. McCoslin was wounded at Petersburg in July 1864, injuring his left side and leg, but the wounds do not seem to have troubled him after his service. He lived just ten years after the war, dying in Bloomington of chronic diarrhea and dropsy, according to his death certificate. His widow, who lived until 1917, was pensioned from 1894.[31]

The company's two musicians and most of the rest of its privates were signed on by the end of January and the remaining four by the end of enlistments on 10 February 1864. Among Company A's noncommissioned officers only McCoslin, Sgt. George Heithman, age nineteen, and Cpl. Frank Thomas, age eighteen, appear to have been literate.[32] Officers were slower in arriving, Porter remaining Company A's only officer, acting or otherwise, for several months.

In all seventy-six soldiers below the rank of sergeant were enlisted in Company A before the organization was mustered into United States service in April 1864. Another seventy-eight soldiers were to enlist in the company in late summer and early fall. These men were labeled "recruits," a term covering replacements for losses and men to fill the company up to full authorized strength. Recruits would include soldiers found in Virginia and Maryland, but forty-one were recruited in Illinois. Among them were conscripts, paid substitutes for draftees, and men enlisted by agents of other states promising bounties. The military and pension records of Illinois-mustered original soldiers and recruits read much the same with respect to their lives prior to joining the army. With only a few exceptions the men were slaves or had recently escaped from bondage at the time of enlistment, and nearly all of them identified their former owners to army officials. Background on a few of them is more complete than for most. Pvt. Charles Allen, for example, said that he was born to a slave mother in about 1822 at Hannibal, Missouri, the first of her fifteen children. His father was William Holligsworth, a married white man who had hired her from her owner, John M. Ayres. When he enlisted, the soldier said he was owned by a Charles Allen of Hannibal, who applied to the army for compensation for the loss of his slave. Ayres, however, also claimed the owner's bounty, but it is not known which man was reimbursed. Probably Ayres had the better claim because children of slave mothers were owned by the mother's master. Of course, Allen could have been sold.[33]

Almost every original enlistee in Company A was living in Missouri just prior to enlistment. Many who were shown as being signed up at Quincy could have been found and enlisted by recruiting parties from the regiment, which scoured Missouri's Ralls, Pike, Marion, and Lewis Counties, across the river. Only two privates, William Millander and Lewis Williams, a boatman and cook, respectively, claimed they were born in Illinois; both listed Chicago. About a dozen men had been born in Kentucky but were slaves in Missouri by late 1863, and a scattering of men born in Virginia, Tennessee, and other slave states were enlisted in Missouri. Three men said they had been born free in nonslave states: Pvt. James Rickman, Ohio; Cpl. Samuel Scott, a New York horse jockey; and Cpl. Josephus Turpin, who said he was an engineer from Iowa. An original recruit (signed at Alton) from Maryland, James Needham, gave his age as forty-five, the maximum age for acceptance, but he may have been older. It was not uncommon for recruiters to accept unqualified men for enlistment.[34]

Pvt. Levi Griffin may also have been overage when recruited in November 1863. He said he had been born forty-three years earlier in Fayette

County, Kentucky, and was brought to Palmyra, Missouri, where he was a slave of William Richey. It was determined in March that he had a disqualifying physical disability, scrofula, a lymph gland disorder. Certified as a "rejected recruit," he was released from the army in July. He had never, however, been mustered into the service. Griffin's record became confused because the regiment showed that he had deserted from the hospital at Quincy. Captain Porter wrote from Virginia to the Quincy provost marshal in September 1864, saying that the supposed deserter "has been and is employed in Miller's livery Stable. You will confer a favor" by picking the soldier up. Griffin was not arrested, and after the war he applied for a pension. It was denied on grounds that he had not been mustered in.[35]

Only fourteen of Company A's first soldiers are shown in army records as married, but there were likely more. These fourteen left behind widows who applied for pensions or who otherwise told the army of their marital status for other reasons. Since marriages of slaves or even of free blacks were not recorded in Missouri and other slave states, such unions were frequently informal and difficult to prove. Most of the men married while in slavery and lived with their wives and children until joining the army. A few, however, had their families broken up by slave sales. Willis Johnson and his wife, Permelia, both born in Pike County, Missouri, were married in 1850. They had several children, but all but one of them "were sold as slaves and sent South [to Arkansas]" before the war. Johnson's family was never united because the soldier died of "lung fever" just after the regiment arrived in the East to start war service. Captain Porter wrote to Johnson's widow in a rare surviving letter that her husband "was buried by a platton[sic] of his company in as respectable a way as circumstances would permit. [A]ll of his near-friends were with him and know the spot where he was buried. He was a good and brave man[,] quiet and reserved in his way and Manners[,] always ready for duty when called on and that without a murmur or a word[,] always cheerful, allways [sic] had a pleasant word for everybody—in every respect a soldier and a gentleman." Another soldier, Peter Moss, was married on his owners' (William and Eliza Graves) Lewis County farm and had at least seven children. The entire family was sold in 1851 to Daniel Boone at Palmyra and was still together when Moss enlisted. Two Company A soldiers, Jerry Morris and Washington Williams, found wives at Quincy before the regiment departed for the war. Morris, a forty-three-year-old Virginian and probably a slave in Missouri, married at Quincy in January 1864, two months after his enlistment. Morris died of disease a few months later, but after the war his widow was denied a pension because the soldier had an earlier wife from whom he was not divorced. Washington's marriage seems to have had no impediments, but it was not unusual for slaves to be unclear about their marital status when slave states put no value on its legality.[36]

Just as uncertain were birth dates and even names. Pvt. George Thomas Morgan, although marginally literate, could not be sure about his year of birth, putting it down as somewhere between 1841 and 1843. Born in Marion County, Missouri, he said he was owned by "Fird nan [Ferdinand?] Gill" and that he himself used the name "George Gill in Slavery." Other blacks changed their names when they entered the service as a way of confusing the owners from whom they had fled. The men were naturally distrustful and cautious because, until a 24 February 1864 amendment of the army enrollment act, slaves belonging to loyal owners from loyal slave states such as Missouri had not been freed by emancipation laws, orders, and proclamations and were not freed by their enlistment. That such concealment was not necessary because the soldiers could not be delivered up by army officials was perhaps overlooked by the suspicious and cautious men.[37]

Another uncertainty was the legal status of free blacks and of the few black slaves who hired themselves out on the condition that they agreed to compensate their owners. Pvt. Ferdinand Markell was born at Rear Creek, Missouri, in slavery, although his father had been born free in Kentucky. Children of slave mothers were also slaves, but Markell somehow obtained his freedom shortly before the war and worked as a laborer for wages at Palmyra. It is not known if he was freed by his owner, purchased his own freedom, or was purchased by a family member. Pvt. William McDowell's mother explained, in 1877, her family's unusual status: "she hired her time from her Master [Harvey Wellman, Ralls County, Missouri] in 1863 and her children hired out their time and all went to Quincy." This option available to slaves did not release them from bondage but, instead, allowed them to work as they wished, provided they paid the agreed-on amount. McDowell was a day laborer in Quincy, and he continued to help support his mother after enlistment.[38]

THE "CHICAGO COMPANIES"

Meanwhile, with recruiting for Companies B and C in Chicago well under way, Bross traveled there in mid-November to organize the effort in his hometown. At about the same time, possibly because not many Chicago-area blacks were responding, the *Tribune* made several editorial requests for recruits. The first of these said: "We appeal to the colored men of Illinois to drive home and clinch the reputation of the slanders that have annulled their race and to prove in their own persons, as their brethren have elsewhere done, that beneath black skin rest the great qualifications now needed by the Republic to defend itself against the assaults of its foes."[39]

The next day's follow-up story was certainly upbeat, saying blacks should fill the First Illinois so as to "make room for the second regiment." The newspaper cautioned, however, that many local blacks were paid recruiting agents of other states and to listen to them was "treason to the best interests of the colored race." Recruits should go to the regimental recruiting office at 203 Clark Street and sign up, ignoring all other offers. One questions how effective newspaper appeals might have been because of the low level of literacy among Chicago's black residents, and recruiting went badly, the first soldiers enlisting in late December. Much of this slow progress may be attributed to low army pay in the wartime boom and perhaps equally to pay inequities between whites and blacks. The *Tribune* called for just and equal pay and extension of the federal enlistment bounties then given to white men, making them apply to blacks as well, and a few days later asked for changes in the draft law to allow blacks to serve as paid substitutes for drafted whites, attractive as a way to reduce the chances of white men being drafted.[40]

A Chicago black man, Joseph Stanley, saw the *Tribune*'s 12 November appeal, but, he wrote, the state had no right to call on blacks as long as the shameful black codes were in force. He was sure, he said, that the *Tribune* would not print his complaint because of the newspaper's interest in the First Illinois Regiment, a possible indirect reference to Bross. Stanley said bounty and pay were national problems, but Illinois's situation was worse because laws denied blacks the "most ordinary of rights." Answering this letter, a Quincy newspaper editor said blacks would not listen to Stanley's complaint about the black codes and that the war was an opportunity for blacks to prove themselves to whites so as to reverse the current prejudice against them. Following this same theme of the need for blacks to redeem their race through military service, an officer of a newly raised black Alabama regiment in Tennessee said he had read in the *Memphis Bulletin* about Bross and the regiment at Quincy, and he wanted to tell blacks, "You must go," to vindicate claims to freedom and, by joining up, "sink the opprobrious epithet nigger into eternal oblivion." Meanwhile, some Quincy citizens held a meeting to help the First Illinois Regiment, calling, as might be expected, for equal pay but asking the city and Adams County to offer a bounty in the absence of a federal one, a scheme that may not have been implemented.[41]

It was not very long, however, before the Quincy newspaper that had minimized the importance of the impact of black codes was repeating Stanley's primary complaint. Observing that "recruits are not coming in as fast as they ought to," the paper put it down to the fact that "negroes [from slave states] who come here to enlist, have to do so by stealth, and are often betrayed by Copperhead Illinoisans. Suicidal policy!" The real motivation for this switch was probably belated recognition of what each black soldier meant to draft-eligible citizens of Illinois: "Let the negro-hater remember that every black who enlists in Illinois, counts ONE and takes the place of a *white man*, perhaps himself." By the following month, however, the word was apparently getting out to prospective recruits in Missouri, the *Louisiana* (Mo.) *Journal* reporting that thirty-eight blacks had left for nearby Quincy, induced by promises that their families would be cared for and bounties would be paid, neither of which was law nor policy. A newspaper editor on the other side of the state thought the news good and said he was "glad the darkies have left Pike County and joined the army of the Lord." He hoped every black would follow the example "and take all his relations with him!"[42]

Company B's organization was the responsibility of its designated commander, Hector H. Aiken, age twenty-four. Aiken, a former enlisted man in the Chicago Board of Trade Battery (Capt. James H. Stokes's Independent Battery), joined the regiment in late December 1863 and set to work in Chicago. When the war began, there were but fifteen hundred free blacks in Chicago, and probably twenty escaped slaves passed through the city daily, some staying on, since the exclusion law was not vigorously enforced there. This limited recruiting base, only because it was increased by slave state fugitives and refugee blacks during the war, was sufficient to provide almost all of Company B's minimum requirements of noncommissioned officers and privates, although it took until the end of March 1864 to complete enlistments. The first thirty-four soldiers were signed up in late December, about one-third of the requirement, followed by thirty the following month, and the rest over the next two months. Fourteen of the company's initial recruits were born in Illinois and most of the rest in Kentucky, with a scattering from Missouri, Ohio, Pennsylvania, and several other states.[43]

A number of Company B's recruits claimed to be freemen at the time of enlistment, but some of them may have been concealing their status, fearing that they might be returned to slavery. First Sergeant William Mills was an eighteen-year-old Illinois native born in Galena. He was a barber, a profession that brought standing in the free black community, and it often followed that soldiers who had been barbers had some reading and writing skills. Sgt. Rodney Long claimed he was born in Hopkinsville, Kentucky, in 1843, but it is not known how he came to be in Chicago when he enlisted. He was also a barber and probably literate, which may explain why he was immediately made a noncommissioned officer. Brothers James and Jordan Stewart were born free at Mt. Carmel, Cook County, Illinois, and were both farming at Batavia when they left for the army in February 1864. Neither wore chevrons in the company, but James may have had some education; after the war he took up barbering.[44]

Another freeman was Pvt. Charles Henry Griffin, born in Cleveland, Ohio, where he learned the trade of trunk maker or carpenter. Griffin, just seventeen at enlistment, could read and write. He may have been living in Canada just before he came to Chicago to join the regiment. Another literate free man was Pvt. Willis A. Bogart, who claimed to be a native of England but whose reputation for telling the truth would later be shown to be weak.[45]

Most of Company B's men were slaves or had only recently escaped from bondage. Some of them had made long journeys before reaching the regiment. Pvt. George Brooks was born near Murfreesboro, Tennessee. He was taken by his owner, John Kirk, to Washington County, Mississippi, when the war, Brooks said, "refugeed us." In 1863 he "slipped off" for St. Louis and later reached Chicago, where he enlisted. Pvt. Alfred Grayson, age thirty-six, was born at Maysville, Kentucky. He was a slave of Gideon Pillow, later a Confederate general. Married in bondage, his wife and four children were also Pillow's property. Grayson said he had been a laborer "doing job work" in Helena, Arkansas, in 1860 and 1861 and was in Quincy by 1863. He did not explain the circumstances by which he came to Illinois, but it appears that his wife and children remained behind rebel lines. Pvt. William Graves had an even more complicated background. He thought he was born in 1837 or perhaps 1840 in Lexington, Kentucky. He said he was known as Sanford before the war and had "no surname whatever." His master, William K. Faukoner, moved him to the Kansas City area in 1856. There he was sold to Clay Kimpile (?) of Baton Rouge and taken to Louisiana. Graves claimed he was "in the Southern Army until the summer of 1862—then I went to Chicago Ill." Probably his Louisiana owner hired him out to the rebel army, but the slave would have been a common laborer, not a soldier. Graves left no explanation about how he got in Union hands; he was likely captured as contraband and shipped north. He also did not describe how he chose the name under which he enlisted.[46]

The *Tribune,* in what seems an attempt to put a good face on sluggish recruiting, reported a hundred Chicago-area blacks sworn in during December and in mid-January said a company had already been sent to Quincy and another company was expected to be ready in a week, when, in fact, only a few more than one hundred were enrolled by the end of January. The *Chicago Evening Journal* also put a positive spin on January's showing: "The work of recruiting for the 1st Regiment Illinois Colored Volunteers progresses favorably," forty-six new soldiers being signed up in two days and a total of seventy-two awaiting transport to Quincy. The newspaper reported that enlistments might be further enhanced by the twenty-five-dollar city bounty and a pending increase by the county. These bounties were paid equally to whites and blacks, since both counted toward the state's volunteer quota.[47]

The *Tribune* said the bounty was helping, concluding, "The hundred dollar bounty still paid by the city and county, induces recruits to come here and enlist, thus making them count to the credit of the county in any future draft that might occur." The *Tribune* explained that, once new enlistees were mustered in, the federal government "pays all expenses, and gives them transportation, &c., to Quincy"; however, "to bring recruits [to Chicago], funds are needed to pay railway fare, expenses of recruiting agents, &c., and an appeal must now be made to our benevolent patriotic citizens, who wish to avoid the draft, in order to complete the organization of the regiment." There is no record of how successful this appeal was, but recruiting remained slow. As a further incentive, Chicago increased its own bounty to seventy-five dollars to help secure white and black recruits. At the end of January a newspaper reported that it would be paid for up to two hundred men, apparently the current quota shortage, and said six soldiers of the "1st Illinois Colored" had already received it.[48]

Commander-designate of Company C, the second "Chicago" unit, was James W. Brockway, an Illinois native who applied for a commission directly from civilian life and was approved by a Casey board. (He was not mustered in until 17 June 1864.) Brockway had prior enlisted service with Renswick's Battery, Illinois Light Artillery. Seven privates in his company had been born in Illinois, most in the southern part of the state, and the level of literacy in Company C was not much different than it was in B, only one or two men able to write. First Sergeant Willis Easley, age nineteen, born free in Terra Haute, Indiana, was proficient enough to keep Company C's records. He enlisted in the company with his younger brother David, who was apparently without reading and writing skills. Company C had one future sergeant, Pvt. Samuel Dix, Missouri, who could sign his name, and it also had the youngest (and shortest) soldier in the regiment, Musician (drummer) Logan Davis, age fifteen and four feet four inches tall. All that is known about Dix is that he was a Missouri-born slave. Davis was born in bondage in Holton County, Kentucky, and escaped to Illinois in 1862.[49]

Company C also had its share of older soldiers. Pvt. Napoleon Carr was forty-five when enrolled, a native of Missouri. His records do not show how and when he came to Illinois, but he may have arrived only days before enlistment. He was probably accompanied by the woman he married two days after he was accepted into the regiment. His newly attained freedom gave him the opportunity to be legally married, a status that could not be officially recorded in Missouri. Another older soldier, John Daniels, age forty-three, had been married while a slave, with the approval of his owner, Dr. Morgenther. The soldier was born in Louisa County, Virginia, but was brought to Pike County, Missouri, sometime prior to 1845. His wife was another of Morgenther's slaves, and the couple had eight children. Daniels, his wife, and seven of his children ran away to Quincy on 7 April 1864. That day he went out to find work, and, his wife said later, "He soon came back with Soldier's Clothes on," having enrolled in Company C.[50]

Other Company C soldiers were, like Daniels, well traveled. Pvt. Cato Flowers was born near Trenton, Tennessee, in 1848. With his father, mother, and some other slaves he ran away from his master near Dyersburg (Dyersville?), arriving in Chicago in late 1862. Flowers found work chopping wood at two dollars daily and as a common laborer, contributing his wages to his family. The army must have seemed attractive to him, since he likely was offered state, county, and city bounties. Pvt. Isaac Gaskins was born in slavery on a plantation at Deer Creek (?), Yazoo County,

Mississippi. He was freed by the war and became a servant to a Union officer, Lt. Col. John W. Paddock, 113th Illinois Infantry. Paddock brought Gaskins to Illinois in April 1863. The eighteen-year-old former slave soon found himself out of work, perhaps because his employer left the service, and he enlisted at Chicago in February 1864. Two other soldiers had been born in Virginia and reached Illinois during the war. Pvt. Charles Jones, age forty-four, was moved by his owner, Daniel Jones, from Richmond to Lavaca, Texas, and to Florence, Alabama. He was freed, probably by Union forces, at the latter place and made his way to Quincy, where he worked as a cook, accepting a Chicago bounty for enlisting in January 1864. Pvt. Peter Williams, the other Virginian, could not tell recruiting officers the place or date of his birth, although he thought he was about thirty-nine. He did say he had been married sometime before the war but was separated from his wife "by being sold as slaves," apparently to different owners. He did not describe how he came to be in Illinois, but likely he came from Missouri.[51]

Pvt. John Blakely left an unusually complete record of his life before enlistment. He was born in Oldham County, Kentucky, in late 1824 and, when old enough for labor, worked in a brickyard and stoneyard for his owner, John Lyon. He was later rented out to Charles Fields to drive a hack. Blakely recorded: "I was sold down to Henderson Ky the year the war broke out, then I ran off to St Louis Mo. and thence to Chicago, Ill. where [I] worked in a tobacco factory for [illegible] Freedman & Co. until I enlisted." He also said that when he was sold in 1861 he "was sound as a dollar limb wind and gizzard," but at the time he was trying to show that the army had ruined his health.[52]

Company B and Company C recruits were usually mustered into the federal service within a week of their enlistments, were issued uniforms, and "were quartered in a large hall in McCormick's building," until they could be sent on to the regiment's assembly point in Quincy. New recruits were generally kept under guard to prevent desertion by bounty jumpers and others who changed their minds. The uniform helped identify the new men, but it also created unit pride. Later, some new recruits may have been kept together at Camp Douglas, an army base at Cottage Grove Avenue and Thirty-fourth Street in Chicago, a facility with a twenty-acre garrison area, barracks and other buildings, and a separate prisoner-of-war camp. It is unlikely, however, that Chicago-area enlistees received any military training before arriving in Quincy, and even there not much was available because of a shortage of officers and the fact that not a single noncommissioned officer had any military experience. It is possible that the only consistently given military instruction was reading of the entire Articles of War at mustering in, probably to instill awe if not fear into the recruits by listing the many capital offenses.[53]

THREE MORE COMPANIES

Recruitment of Companies D, E, and F followed, but the area of interest was the entire state. The latter company would be initially filled almost entirely with men recruited primarily in Missouri and Illinois. Most of these recruits were credited to Wisconsin, for state agents could sign up recruits in another state, and these men were counted toward meeting the agent's state's federal levy. Company F's composition reflected the small pool of eligible blacks in Illinois but also showed the effectiveness of Wisconsin's bounty package. That state did not attempt to raise its own black regiment but was able to offset part of its federal quota for volunteers with blacks found outside Wisconsin. Company commanders were, respectively, 1st Lt. (later Capt.) Abner C. Knapp and Capts. William H. Flint and Willard K. Daggett. Knapp, age thirty-three, had been a sergeant in the Ninety-third Illinois Infantry and was wounded at Vicksburg in 1863. Flint, forty-four years old and from Alton, Illinois, was also a former enlisted men approved for a commission by a Casey board; he reported for duty on 10 April but would not be mustered in until more than a month later, when the regiment was outside Washington, D.C. Daggett, who served in the regiment until its disbandment, was a former private in the Twenty-fourth Wisconsin Infantry. Knapp, Flint, and Daggett may have been the only officers-designate on duty while their companies were organizing, but others also awaiting commissions and mustering in joined them in Quincy. One of these, Capt. George R. Naylor, might have been intended to be Company E's commanding officer, but he declined the appointment. Lts. William B. Gale, Company A; Frederick A. Chapman, B; John Gosper, C; and William W. Flint, E, rounded out the officer roster. Although all of these men (and 2d Lt. Isaac N. Strickler, Company A) accompanied the regiment to Virginia, none of them were mustered in yet.[54]

Company D was recruited from all over Illinois, from Ogle County in the north to Shawneetown in the south, and some recruits were enlisted in Quincy and Chicago. First Sergeant Alfred Carroll, a twenty-year-old paper hanger born in Milwaukee, Wisconsin, was induced to enlist at Chicago in January 1864. Born free, he probably had some reading and writing skills, explaining his enlistment as the company's highest-ranking non-commissioned officer. Another man from Wisconsin, Pvt. Edward Hunter, was originally from Virginia. He appears to have escaped from bondage, perhaps in Missouri, before 1856. The thirty-seven-year-old soldier had a wife and three minor children living at Markisan, Wisconsin, when he enlisted and was credited to South Chicago, a locality probably offering an attractive bounty. Another free man, Pvt. Cornelius Elliott, was a native of Eldorado, Saline County, Illinois, where his family, unusually well propertied, owned a 120-acre farm on which they raised tobacco and corn. Elliott, just eighteen, probably enlisted because his family was self-sufficient and possibly for the adventure and a Shawneetown bounty.[55]

One of Company D's musicians, Edward Charles Liggons, was just sixteen. He had been owned by John Finney in St. Louis, but he was freed from or fled slavery and went to Chicago, where he was employed as a bellboy in the Sherman House hotel. Being the company's oldest soldier, Pvt. James H. Patton was free before the war. He was born in Tennessee but had been living in Eldorado for five or six years when he enlisted. He was forty-four and had a wife and four children. Brothers Cpl. Frank Gash and Pvt. Jefferson Gash had been slaves of Jeremiah Stropshire of Liberty Township, Marion County, Missouri, but they ran away to Galesburg, Illinois, in 1862, and both men enlisted at Chicago in January 1864. Because the company's initial recruits were mostly residents of Illinois for some time before enlistment, most of the soldiers seem to have had little concern that their former owners could track them down and somehow force them back into bondage. There was no real reason for them to change their names, but many had variations in spelling and other mistakes caused by the recruiters' haste in completing processing of new soldiers, abetted by a common inability of recruits to distinguish their names in writing. Of course, soldiers, once enlisted, were not libel to be returned to or penalized by their former owners, but not all of them trusted in that assurance. Pvt. Charles David Logan, born in Kentucky, was in slavery in Missouri before the war and escaped to Quincy in late 1863. He enlisted under the name Charles David, he said, "to prevent others, former owners from knowing where he was and obtaining his pay."[56]

Company E's recruiting was concentrated in the southwestern part of the state, and the initial complement of enlisted men was secured by late March, the last two soldiers being added on 2 April. First Sergeant John F. Perryman was born in Fayette County, Kentucky, in 1836, presumably a slave. He was married in 1850 and was living with his wife at Edwardsville, Illinois, before enlisting. Perryman was marginally literate, a surprising accomplishment for a farmer and laborer. He may have been assisted in his army duties by Sgts. Edward B. Milion and Wiley Sexton, who seem to have had comparatively substantial educations. Another possibly literate soldier, Sgt. John W. Riden, a nineteen-year-old laborer, was born in Green County, Missouri, but not in slavery. He was, he claimed, "a Freeborn negro." His family had moved to Alton, Illinois, because it had been, obviously uncomfortably, the only black family in that part of Missouri. Riden would be promoted to first sergeant of Company C a year after enlistment, First Sergeant Easley being absent and temporarily demoted for medical reasons.[57]

Company E's soldiers were the usual mix of a few native Illinois-ans and many escaped and former slaves born all over the South. Four of the former were Pvts. George Singleton, from O'Fallon, a plasterer; George Smith, of Gallatin County, a carpenter; and Soloman M. White, of Locust Grove; and Musician Charles Hunter, from Adams County. White had no recorded work experience—he was just shy of his six-teenth birthday when enlisted—and Hunter was seventeen. Pvt. Moses Alexander recalled that he was born in St. Charles, Missouri, in 1839, a slave of Henry Copes. Copes sold Alexander's father to a new owner, who took him to California, and Alexander, then ten, never saw him again. Copes went south when the war began, leaving his slaves in the charge of Bob Parks, who rented them out for farm labor. Alexander said, "I ran off from St Charles and went to Alton & worked about a year for Bill Chamberlain on his farm about six miles from Alton" before entering the army.[58]

Pvt. Andrew Brooks had an unusual road to the regiment. He was born in Maryland in 1829, and his master, William Pentacord, took him to Clay County, Missouri, two or three years before the war. Pentacord became a Confederate soldier, likely an officer, and Brooks accompanied him to Vicksburg. When Vicksburg was captured by General Grant in July 1863, Pentacord was taken prisoner. Brooks, now a "contraband" former slave, made his way to Alton and found employment as a cook. He was attracted by the bounty offered by Collinsville, and he enlisted in March 1864. Pvt. Minor Gardiner, although only eighteen at enlistment, also had a tangled history. He, his mother, Rena, two brothers, and a sister were living at Alton, and the young Gardiner was helping to sup-port his family by chopping wood and doing odd jobs for several local farmers. Apparently tiring of this, he went off to join the regiment with Wiley Sexton. All Gardiner's family used the surname Hawkins, but he preferred his father's name. The family had been owned by Joshua B. Sharp, of Montgomery City, Missouri. Some years later, in connection with a pension claim, Sharp, for no apparent reason, was asked whether he had given Rena and the children their freedom before or after the Emancipation Proclamation. The old man replied: "I can safely say that I did not at any time either before or after the Proclamation of the president freeing the negroes, voluntarily grant the colored persons named herein, their freedom. Minor the son of Rena left my House, without my consent, and went with some other negroes to join the army as I then understood. This was in the Fall of 1862. Rena and her daughter Ellen left, a short time after Minor left me." Another soldier with a similar story was Pvt. John Jackson, known for no obvious reason as Jack Hamilton after the war. He was born a slave of Hamilton Hughes in St. Louis County, Missouri, in 1836. He was sold in 1855 to Barton Bates, Louisiana, Missouri, and was married in the following year. He ran away in September 1863 to the American Bottoms area near Alton. There he supported his wife and himself cutting wood, hard work that he escaped by joining the company in March 1864.[59]

Pvt. Jackson Batty, age thirty-three, was brought to Louisiana, Missouri, from Overton County, Tennessee, by his owner, a man named Webb. After the war Batty preferred the name of his owner and called himself Robert Webb, perhaps because the spelling of Batty was written Bady, Badley, Bayty, Baty, and other variations, a matter that caused the soldier problems in the service and later complicated pension applications. Batty himself was not much help in straightening out the confusion because he had never learned to read or write. He said he had been living in Louisiana, as a "slave on Bates' place," when he was recruited for army service. It is not clear if Bates was his owner or if the future soldier was hired out. Bates was also thought to be Pvt. John Jackson's master.[60]

Seven related men, all named Arbuckle, enlisted in the regiment, five of them in Company E. While the relationships of these soldiers are not very clear, some links can be made. The patriarch appears to have been Cpl. Conrad J. Arbuckle, age forty-three, who enlisted at Alton in February 1864. Born free in Anderson County, Illinois, Conrad was married and had six children. His twenty-year-old son, Pvt. Robert S. Arbuckle, enlisted the same day. Conrad's son and Robert's half-brother, Joseph C. Arbuckle, twenty-one, was enlisted as a sergeant in the company. He was born in slavery near Lexington, Ray County, Missouri. Sgt. Arbuckle was known as Big Joe to distinguish him from another Joseph (Little Joe), twenty-three, also born in Ray County, who enlisted at the same place and on the same day as Big Joe. How they were related is not known. Pvt. William Arbuckle, five years older than Little Joe, was also born in Ray County but enlisted a few days before the others, and his connection to them is obscure. The last two Arbuckles to enlist joined Company I a year later than the other soldiers. John P. (or C.) and Samuel A. Arbuckle are thought to have been sons of Conrad and brothers or half-brothers of Big and Little Joe. One of them was born in Ray County and the other at Alton.[61]

Company F was recruited at the same places in Missouri and Illinois as were the other companies. Ninety of its initial recruits, noncommissioned officers and privates, are shown by Illinois's adjutant general as being from Wisconsin (just twelve gave Illinois residences), but only a handful ever saw Wisconsin and fewer were living there when enlisted. Acceptance of soldiers raised by Wisconsin's agents, mostly in Illinois, represented a failure of Illinois's recruiting efforts and incentives, as soldiers credited to Wisconsin—which paid them a $100–150 state bounty—did not help meet Illinois's quota. Wisconsin did not seek to form its own black regiment, probably because the state had few black residents and, not being adjacent to any slave states, was seldom a destination for those fleeing bondage. Because Illinois was having difficulty recruiting beyond the minimum number of soldiers needed for the first five of the regiment's ten companies, adding the Wisconsin-recruited men was accepted, even if it was not useful in meeting Illinois's manpower quota. Wisconsin's bounties may have been seen as a new incentive for black men in Illinois not previously attracted to military service, or perhaps Wisconsin was more effective in reaching possible recruits than Illinois had been. Company F was not to be fully manned or mustered until the beginning of July 1864, several months after the regiment was ordered to join the Army of the Potomac in Virginia. Only twenty-two soldiers were mustered in and were at Quincy by the time that the regiment departed Illinois for war service.[62]

Half of the Company F noncommissioned officers had been recruited earlier in Illinois in anticipation of future need and were excess to Company A through E requirements. First Sergeant James L. Williams, thirty-five, was born at Chatham, Canada West (Ontario), where there was a substantial community of African Americans. Two of the four other sergeants were recruited early and counted against Illinois's quota. The two others were signed on in March and April 1864 and were recorded as Wisconsin men. In fact, the latter two men, Alfred Weaver and Peter Stark, were born in North Carolina and Pennsylvania, respectively. Weaver, a former slave, was living in Vernon County, Wisconsin, by 1858, where he worked as a carpenter and laborer before his March enlistment at Madison. Little is known about Stark's early life. Another sergeant, Tennessee-born John Walmslee (sometimes Walmsley), a butcher, enlisted at Dixon, Illinois, in December 1863, and, except for his age, forty-five, little else about him was noted on his military records.[63]

The minimum number of soldiers was not immediately available for Company F, even with the Wisconsin men. Of the small total of early enlistees in the company few had distinctive backgrounds. Pvt. Primus Long had little knowledge of his date and place of birth, but he did recall that he was first the slave of Halsey White in Canton, Missouri. In 1861 he had been sold to John C. Kelly in St. Louis and sold again the following year to Samuel Scotton, Louisiana, Missouri. Sometime during these wanderings he was married to another slave. He and his wife ran away in January 1864. Long said he fled because "my master cursed my wife," and he remembered the date "for the snow was deep, and we crossed the Mississippi River on the ice." Long spent two weeks at Quincy but went to Chicago to enlist because he heard that the city was paying a one hundred dollar bounty to recruits. He was soon sent back to Quincy to train with the regiment. Another early enlistee, thirty-year-old Pvt. James Taylor, knew Primus Long in slavery in Missouri. He ran away from his owner, Burdine Owsley, of Palmyra, Marion County, in the summer of 1863, was recruited by Company A's Sergeant Perkins in December at Quincy, and was counted as from Milwaukee, though he had never been there. Although enlisted, Taylor was not immediately mustered into U.S. service, as was the early practice at Quincy. There he lived in barracks and performed the duties of a soldier. He also was married during this period. Taylor became ill on guard duty in March and was sent to the hospital for treatment by Dr. Fee. He remained in care for the rest of the month, was returned to duty, and was immediately sent back to the hospital. Consequently, he was left behind when the regiment departed for Virginia. His record reads, "rejected by Mustering officer at muster in of the company July 8, 1864, because of 'Chronic Rheumatism.'" Technically, Taylor was never officially a soldier, but in later years he claimed that the rheumatism that disqualified him was a result of his military duties after enlistment and before muster. In 1882 Taylor successfully convinced the government that he should be pensioned for his disability, but in 1926 a conscientious examiner reviewed the case and concluded that Taylor never had a legal entitlement. The examiner, sensibly deciding that it was too late to do anything about it, allowed Taylor's widow (he had died in 1887) to remain pensioned.[64]

Company F recruiting dragged on through June, some soldiers being signed on by regimental officers, but most of the requirements for new men were met by agents of Wisconsin. As will be seen, the required minimum number of privates for the company would be enlisted and forwarded to the company in Virginia. These almost completely untrained soldiers arrived just in time to participate in the regiment's bloody baptism of fire. No immediate attempt was made to organize the last four companies in Illinois. To Bross this was a serious problem because he preferred enlisting men in Illinois or from elsewhere in the North, where there were free blacks, so as to get "a more intelligent class of men than by accepting companies of contrabands from the government."[65] It was clear that recruiters from several New England states had already skimmed off many of the more literate and patriotic free black men in the Old Northwest before Illinois began recruiting for its regiment. Because of the depleted manpower pool, Bross had no choice but ultimately to agree to accept four companies of former slaves recruited primarily in Virginia and Maryland, but they did not join the regiment until after its battle testing. Consequently, Bross had not been promoted to colonel when the troops faced this test. The last four companies did receive some enlisted men from Illinois, many of them paid substitutes for others and draftees. Recruiting replacements for the original six companies was a continuous process in the state over the next year, but those companies would also look for contrabands in Virginia and Maryland and would receive a large percentage of substitutes and draftees among them.

The regiment was considerably handicapped by the lack of company officers. Governor Yates attempted to do something about it in a telegram to Secretary of War Stanton in late January 1864. He said, "I respectfully ask that I have the power to appoint officers for the negro regiment." He concluded, inaccurately, "We have four companies, and no officers." Of course, Stanton reminded him that "the system . . . requires that the officers be appointed by the President," but, he continued, if the governor would make suitable nominations, "they will be appointed on your recommendation." Some officers had already been secured, although none were mustered in, and others were in the pipeline. In December newspapers had printed General Casey's instructions on how to apply through army channels for a commission in a black regiment, and this information was generally available throughout the army. A candidate with his commanding officer's recommendation had to appear before one of Casey's examining boards, where he was examined on his knowledge of army procedures and company paperwork. To many of the enlisted men aspiring to wear shoulder straps this was a formidable obstacle, because men in the ranks had little experience with such matters. Partly because of General Thomas's difficulties finding soldiers qualified for commissions, private citizens of Philadelphia set up and paid for the Free Military School for Applicants for Command of Colored Troops, to which soldiers could be sent by their commanders for a thirty-day course. Those completing this instruction did well seeking commissions, and at least nine of the school's graduates were assigned by the army to the First Illinois Infantry. Since most officers for black units were appointed centrally, only a few from Illinois found their way to the regiment.[66]

It should have been that officers in black regiments started their commissioned service with qualifications many volunteer officers in white units did not have—military service as an enlisted man, a recommendation from a serving commanding officer of the army, and having passed screening by a board of impartial officers. There is no way, however, to determine if this gave them an advantage, and probably most new officers had very little prior experience to transfer directly to their new jobs leading black troops. The colonel of the first South Carolina black regiment said volunteers such as himself had civilian qualifications directly applicable to military life, just as peacetime service's pacifistic pursuits helped to round out West Point–educated regulars. New officers and their men had to learn soldiering as they went along. An officer, observing somewhat condescendingly a black unit in his brigade, wrote: "I should think the black troops would become demoralized. Their officers are generally of a wretched class." A more serious problem than officer qualifications was likely the very low level of literacy in the ranks, particularly among the noncommissioned officers. A historian suggests that the troops were unwilling "to work amicably with the non-commissioned officers of their own race." An officer in an early black regiment thought training duties "were increased a hundred fold with colored troops," and the job must have been made extremely difficult without experienced noncommissioned officers. The officer said it was not enough to teach just military duties but that soldiers should learn everything: social, educational, and sanitary. The army took some notice of the low level of education among blacks, commissioning General Casey to prepare a training manual for the new units, *United States Tactics for Colored Troops,* which clarified complex maneuvers and eliminated others. Generally, however, black troops seemed to progress well when time, training facilities, and a sufficient number of qualified officers were available, but Illinois's regiment had none of these.[67]

Troops who enlisted in the regiment were all sent to Quincy, where facilities were sparse. The new soldiers and some of their families were housed in old Mexican War barracks on Twelfth Street and at the Mission Institute on Twenty-fifth. Apparently, rations were also in short supply, reportedly inducing former Illinois senator Orville H. Browning, a Quincy attorney, to complain to the secretary of war that the army should properly support the troops. Practicing law in Washington, D.C., in early 1864, Browning represented an Illinois ration provider whose contract had been canceled by the army's commissary general, so any protest he might have made could have been more business than principle. As early as January 1864, citizens of Quincy were asking that the army supply clothing, food, and shelter for "a large number of women and children, at present about 200, and constantly increasing, without any means, helpless in condition and character." The petitioners added that recruiters promised that families of soldiers would be taken care of, and these people, "mostly being escaped from slavery in some of the states," were "utterly destitute." Other conditions were also poor; Bross asked the army early in the new year, for example, to provide a hospital for the troops. Some attention had to be paid, however, to the health of the men, and no medical officers were authorized until the regiment reached full strength. The civilian contract surgeon, John Fee, remained responsible for examining new recruits when they arrived at Quincy and taking care of the regiment's health needs. Fee would soon be complaining that recruiters were sending him too many plainly unfit soldiers, likely because of the difficulty finding recruits.[68]

TO THE THEATER OF WAR

While the new soldiers learned basic squad and company drill, mostly marching in ranks, not much other training was available to them. The time spent at Quincy was used primarily to issue clothing and equipment from the Quincy quartermaster depot, but no arms were supplied. Nonetheless, these troops were needed for the Army of

the Potomac in Virginia to support newly appointed Union commanding general Ulysses S. Grant's plans for the decisive offensive against Lee's
army, and in March the regiment received orders assigning it to the Ninth
Army Corps, then at Annapolis, Maryland.[69]

That the regiment was untrained and only partially manned counted
for little in light of the army's need for infantry, that April marking the
end of what a historian calls "this hysterical period of recruiting." Bross,
who received his commission as lieutenant colonel on 7 April, must have
been disappointed that he would take his regiment to war unready and
shorthanded. On 25 April 1864 the unit, except for Company F, was for-
mally "mustered into service of the United States by Charles C. Pomeroy,
Capt USA," the Chicago-based recruiting officer, and the First Regiment
Illinois Volunteers (Colored) officially became the Twenty-ninth United
States Colored Infantry. On hand for the ceremony were about four hundred and fifty enlisted men—over two hundred of whom had been sworn
in the previous day—and a dozen officers, most of the latter still waiting
for their commissions and so not mustered in. Companies A, B, C, D, and
E had the minimum number of privates, sixty-four. Company F had but
fourteen, too few for company muster. Each company had nearly all its
authorized requirements of noncommissioned officers, musicians, and
wagoners, except F. As for officers, all companies were short two or even
three; the regimental staff consisted of Lieutenant Colonel Bross, Major
Brown, and perhaps a handful of enlisted men borrowed from the companies. Two days later the ranks were further thinned by three desertions
and the death of Company A's Cpl. Oliver Ward of "lung fever." Two of the
deserters were from Company B. Pvt. James Freeman was a seventeen-
year-old Virginian, and Pvt. James O. Hawkins, eleven years older, was
born in Kentucky. It is possible that they were together as slaves in Missouri, but their records are incomplete. The other deserter in Illinois was
Pvt. A. McGarthy (or Gaity), of Company E, who also missed the movement to Virginia. A fourth soldier, Pvt. James I. Winyard deserted in March,
but he was apprehended and returned to his company a week before
it left Quincy. Winyard, born in Jefferson County, Kentucky, was
twenty-seven years old at enlistment. He was a farmhand at Ottawa,
Illinois, when he married in May 1861, apparently freed in the war's
early days. Throughout his military service he continued to be a disciplinary problem. The other three men were never returned to duty. An
apparent deserter was Primus Long, who had escaped from Missouri
with his wife over the ice on the Mississippi River in January 1864.

Long had become ill and was not considered fit enough to be mustered in until late June. He was ordered east on 8 July to join the regiment in Virginia, along with a number of new Company F recruits, but he deserted. Long remained absent until he turned himself in or was apprehended in April 1865. He was then sent to join the regiment at City Point outside Richmond. He may have heard of President Lincoln's 11 March amnesty proclamation that allowed his return to duty without penalty. Perhaps, however, he had just been sick at home in Quincy from July on, and the company had lost track of him.[70]

The morning following muster the regiment was ordered to cook six days' rations and to be prepared to depart Quincy on 27 April. That afternoon, after speeches by Brig. Gen. Benjamin M. Prentiss, Quincy's Shiloh hero, and others, the regiment boarded twelve coaches of the Chicago, Burlington, and Quincy Railroad, bound for Chicago on the first leg of the journey east. Left behind were Major Brown and Captain Daggett, who continued recruiting, and a few sick soldiers.[71]

The regiment arrived in Chicago, in the words of one report, "safe—without accident," early in the morning of 28 April, the troops proceeding to the soldiers' rest on the lake shore near Dearborn Park. There "the generous and patriotic ladies [of Chicago] had in readiness a bountiful repast to which the regiment did full justice." The regiment was formed up before a crowd of several hundred citizens at about 11 A.M. for a ceremonial presentation to Bross of a horse and accoutrements, a gift paid for by a number of his friends. The horse, a cream-colored Gold Dust Morgan, a well-known Kentucky breed, was a war veteran, having been ridden in two Virginia campaigns by an Illinois cavalry officer. Chosen to make the presentation was Col. F. A. Eastman, who said:

> Permit me to remark, that your moral courage, as shown in your taking the Colonelcy of the 1st colored regiment of Illinois volunteers, is as creditable to you as honorable to our State. Regeneration is going on here; here, in Illinois, whose constitution and statutes are disgraced by the infamous "black laws," light is breaking in. And the evidence of it is before me. A white man of good family, of culture, and of social position, does not hesitate to place himself at the head of a regiment of blacks, recruited in Illinois, to go forth to fight for the honor and freedom and unity of our great country.

Eastman also spoke about Fort Pillow, calling on Bross to protect his men, who "are ennobled by their sentiments to liberate their race from bondage—they are made like unto ourselves by the uniforms they wear." Continuing the Fort Pillow emphasis, he concluded, "These colored troops should take no prisoners until the massacre at Fort Pillow is avenged," an invitation that can be seen as having encouraged offsetting atrocities.[72]

Colonel Bross followed with brief remarks, in which he continued Eastman's theme: "When I lead these men into battle, we shall remember Fort Pillow, and shall not ask for any quarter." Pillow was, of course, current news; the engagement there was described in the Quincy *Daily Whig and Republican* a few days before muster and was a front page *Tribune* story, "Inhuman Brutality," on the morning of the day Eastman and Bross spoke.[73]

Rebel treatment of black soldiers had probably been a factor in slowing recruiting, and it continued to be an important issue among the Twenty-ninth Infantry's officers and men. It was known that incidents such as Milliken's Bend and Fort Pillow appeared to have the approval of the Confederate government. President Jefferson Davis, for example, had proclaimed in December 1863 that commanders of some black troops should be "reserved for execution," but seeming to be more serious was the Confederate Congress's joint resolution that "stipulated that white commissioned officers of colored troops when captured should be put to death or otherwise punished at the discretion of the military court before which they should be tried." While it may appear that organized rebel revenge for using blacks against the South was directed only against officers, reported incidents had uniformly included killing of ordinary soldiers, and some captured blacks, whether free or in bondage at the war's start, were made slaves.[74]

Lincoln reacted to early atrocity reports, announcing that the government had a duty to protect its citizens, particularly soldiers, regardless of color, and that abuse of captured persons was contrary to "the laws of war [and] a relapse into barbarism and a crime against the civilization of the age." "It is therefore ordered that for every soldier of the United States killed in violation of the laws of war a rebel soldier shall be executed, and for every one enslaved by the enemy or sold into slavery a rebel soldier shall be placed at hard labor on the public works and continued at such labor until the other shall be released and receive the treatment due to a prisoner of war."[75] There is no evidence that Lincoln's order was ever implemented, and it may not have been noticed in the Confederacy.

The Fort Pillow murders were not denied in the South. The *Richmond Examiner,* for example, recommended: "Repeat Fort Pillow . . . and we shall bring the Yankees to their senses, and, what is even better, our government will rise to a proper sense of its position as an organ of a nation." But, despite Confederate legislation and orders and other official and unofficial support, atrocities were scattered and, except for a few of the more egregious, not widely known. Nonetheless, federal use of black soldiers was a serious political question in the South because of its implications regarding white supremacy and slavery. A Richmond newspaper later said, "It is a deadly stab which they are driving at our institutions themselves, because they know that if we were to yield on this point, to treat black men as the equals of white, and insurgent slaves as equivalent to our brave soldiers, the very foundation of slavery would be fatally wounded." The Twenty-ninth USCT's officers and men had reason to be apprehensive about what they would face in Virginia, and their colonel's remarks must have brought home to them that they should not expect to be treated as soldiers by the enemy. As the *Tribune* put it, "Let it be understood that they are to expect no quarter, and they will give none."[76]

The "gallant regiment of 'black and *Blue* boys'" departed from Chicago's Madison Street depot in late afternoon, 28 April, on cars of the Pittsburgh, Fort Wayne, and Chicago Railroad, bound for Pittsburgh. A cynical and biased observer wrote that the regiment was followed to the depot "by a vast throng of especial admirers, including a large number of females of African descent of all shades presenting a practical result of the theory and practice of miscegenation." He said: "At the depot the officers commanding experienced great difficulties keeping the shades on board the cars. The guards at the doors tried in vain to prevent an escapade, for whenever the Ethiops could not find an excuse sufficient to obtain permission to pass out, they leaped from the car windows, and, dodging outside of the fence, started rapidly up the street. Officers with drawn swords and revolvers thereupon set out in hot pursuit, thus affording bystanders occasion for considerable merriment." The observer revealed the reason for his fanciful view of what he judged to be inferior humans: "White women were there in attendance, to bid farewell to black husbands, around whose necks they clung long and fondly! Black women, too, and men almost white, were locked in each other's arms, some weeping while others were shouting, praying, or singing." Possibly the only accurate part of this display of vicious racism was a description of some soldiers pursuing a recruiter named Ishell, who was accused of failing to pay over bounty money due to the recruits.[77]

Arriving at Pittsburgh at nine the following evening, the troops were fed at a soldiers' rest, Sergeant McCoslin writing about the "splendid supper" and the kindnesses shown to the troops by the ladies of the city. The regiment left the city at midnight on the Baltimore and Ohio Railroad for Baltimore; McCoslin noted that the black soldiers were "in generally good spirits, feeling proud of the treatment we have received, being the same if not better than some of the white soldiers received." Still, according to McCoslin, "crossing the mountains was quite an undertaking, especially when we went through the tunnels"[78]—many of the men, after all, had never been far from home.

Chapter 2

CAMPAIGNS IN VIRGINIA

By early May Maj. Gen. Ambrose E. Burnside's Ninth Army Corps, which had been at Annapolis, had marched through Washington and on to Virginia, where it was preparing for the major campaign. Burnside had organized the corps into three white divisions and one black one and was concentrated at Manassas Junction south of the national capital. The Fourth Division, composed of black troops, was commanded by Brig. Gen. Edward Ferrero, who had only five of his promised nine regiments, the rest, like the Twenty-ninth, en route or not ready for active service. Ferrero was a volunteer officer whose civilian occupation was as a dancing instructor at West Point. Long active in the New York state militia, he had been colonel of the Fifty-first New York Infantry and had commanded a division under Burnside at Knoxville.[1]

The Twenty-ninth USCT was directed to proceed from Baltimore to Washington, D.C., arriving in the latter city late on 1 May, spending the night in another soldiers' rest. Bross's telegraphed orders directing him to report to Maj. Gen. Silas Casey, who commanded the Provisional Division made up of new troops, at his Long (now Fourteenth Street) Bridge headquarters, somehow were lost or misunderstood, so the regiment went on to the soldiers' rest in Alexandria, Virginia. Company C Pvt. Jordan Thomas's military service was cut short by an unusual accident during the march. Thomas, probably a free man from Kankakee, Illinois, fell through the deck of a bridge—variously described as Long Bridge or the one crossing "Trestle Creek." He dropped about six feet onto lower timbers and was taken to the hospital at Arlington Heights. The soldier was thereafter not fully fit for duty, and he returned to the regiment for a few short periods between hospital stays at Portsmouth, Point of Rocks, Portsmouth again, and Fort Monroe, until his discharge.[2]

The day after the regiment's arrival at Alexandria, Casey complained to the War Department that Lieutenant Colonel Bross had ignored orders. The general was undecided what to do with the regiment—order it to Manassas Junction or not—apparently because Bross had not provided him with a report on the Twenty-ninth regiment's readiness. The matter was somehow resolved, and the unit marched in a heavy rain, retracing its steps to Camp Casey near Fort Albany, one of the installations built to defend the capital (not far from where the Pentagon now stands), reaching the camp in the evening on 2 May. Camp Casey was a training and gathering point for newly arrived units later to be sent to the brigade organization of the army. Obviously not ready to send on to Ferrero's division in the field, the Twenty-ninth stayed for almost a month with another new and unready regiment, the Twenty-eighth U.S. Colored Infantry, which had just reported in from Indiana with six companies.[3]

The morning following the regiment's arrival at Camp Casey, Bross was ordered to take command of the post, and he appointed Company B's commander, Captain Aiken, as acting commanding officer of the regiment. Second Lieutenant Isaac N. Strickler, who had been assigned just before leaving Quincy, was detailed to take over Company B, but on 20 May he declined appointment and was dropped from the rolls. Bross laid out the regiment's daily routine at Casey soon after arrival. Reveille was to be at 5 A.M., guard mount at 8, and company drill from 9 to 11 and, after lunch, from 2 to 4 P.M. At 5 a parade was scheduled; supper was at 6 and taps at 9. A week after arrival at Camp Casey the regiment was issued arms, the .58 caliber Springfield Rifle Musket, Model 1861, and one might imagine that weapons and combat training followed. Yet instructional camps, such as Camp Casey, gave troops little more than proficiency "in close order drill and parade evolutions . . . but that this type of training might not be the best to prepare troops for combat never occurred to the high command." The Twenty-ninth Regiment's soldiers were apparently delighted to receive their rifles, and their enthusiasm about testing the weapons led to issue of General Orders no. 4, prohibiting casual discharge of weapons in camp. Five days before the order, Private Winyard, the soldier who had earlier deserted his company and been returned by the provost marshal, was shot in the hand, but the circumstances were suspicious. The soldier said another soldier on guard duty had accidentally wounded him, but some comrades thought his wound was self-inflicted. In any case it was disabling, and Winyard did not return to his company; he was finally discharged in November 1864.[4] That there were not more such incidents is surprising given that the soldiers received no firing instruction; they were given some familiarity training, however.

However inadequate the camp of instruction stay was for the Twenty-ninth regiment, Bross appeared satisfied with it, writing: "My men are improving rapidly in their duties. Captain Aiken is all I can desire in his conduct as [acting] commanding officer of the regiment." Not all was going well; Bross issued this order in late May: "The commanding officer has witnessed with pain and mortification the prevalence of gambling among a portion of the non commissioned officers & soldiers of this command and more particularly in the 29th regt U.S. Col Troops." He added that the troops should not descend to "the low level of the black leg and scoundrel." Drill and ceremonies continued as part of the daily routine, culminating in a 23 May review of all the black troops at Camp Casey by Lt. Col. Charles S. Russell, commander of the Twenty-eighth Colored Infantry. Russell, a Boston native, entered the army in Indiana, and he fought at Antietam and Chancellorsville, earning brevet promotions to major and lieutenant colonel "for gallantry and meritorious service."[5]

Meanwhile, recruiting to bring the unit to strength was not overlooked; Major Brown and Captain Dagget, who had remained behind in Illinois to oversee the operation, continued their work, the primary objective being to fill up Company F. They were not immediately successful, obtaining only nine more qualified recruits in May. Rather, their efforts and the work of other agents were more effective in the longer term, because in June another thirty-nine joined, but it was not until 8 July that the majority of the new recruits, sixty-six of them (and Major Brown), were mustered in. All but one soldier was listed as a Wisconsin acquisition. The following day Brown and ninety-four men were reported to have left Chicago for the Twenty-ninth USCT, then in the field before Richmond. Over two dozen of these men were not headed for Company F but were soldiers of other companies left sick in Illinois and soldiers destined for other regiments of U.S. Colored Troops.[6]

The new Company F soldiers had profiles very much like those of their comrades in the other companies. Pvt. John Christine (Christian), thirty-six, was born in slavery at La Grange, Missouri, and he enlisted at Quincy, attracted by the Wisconsin bounty. Pvt. Anthony Foggey (sometimes Foggery or Foggy) also enlisted at Quincy for the same reason. He was just nineteen when he ran away from his owner, John Edward Forgey, of Paynesville, Pike County, Missouri. Generally, most of the "Wisconsin men" were Missourians from Pike County, where they had been signed up by agents. (One of these recruiters was future regimental lieutenant Nimrod G. Ferguson, a native of Louisiana, Missouri.) Cpl. Julius Rice explained how his enlistment came about. "I got on a steam Boat with lots of other men at Clarksville pike county Missouri and we all went up to Quincy," where they enlisted "and went soldiering." Rice was originally from Prince Edward County, Virginia, and was brought to Missouri by his second owner, James Hicks. A few Company F men were actually recruited in Wisconsin. Pvt. Henry Sink escaped from slavery in Arkansas and was living at Green Bay in 1861. Another with a similar background was Sgt. Alfred Weaver, born a slave in Orange County, North Carolina, and brought west by an owner. He escaped from bondage and made his way to Vernon County, Wisconsin, by 1858, where he worked as a carpenter and laborer until his enlistment. Cpl. William (Pitt) McKenney's trip from bondage to the regiment is better known. He was born a slave of William Irvine, who lived seven miles from Jackson, Mississippi, but he was raised in New Orleans. He ran away in 1860 and went to Cincinnati and on to Madison, Wisconsin, arriving there at the start of the war. He was hired by Lt. Col. Charles A. Wood of the Eleventh Wisconsin Infantry to be the officer's servant in the field. By the summer of 1862 the Eleventh Infantry was posted near Helena, Arkansas. In June 1863, when the officer completed his period of enlistment, McKinney returned with him to Madison. Being now unemployed, McKinney went to Chicago and was signed on by a Wisconsin agent.[7]

While Brown was raising needed men for Company F, the other five companies—and a handful of Company F men—continued organizing at Camp Casey. Further recruiting for the original companies appears to have been suspended, although in early June three new men joined the regiment in Virginia. They may have been thought of as replacements for losses, but losses were more numerous than were new men. In May five soldiers, one each from Companies A, D, and E and two from C, died of disease, four at Camp Casey and another in the Claremont (later L'Overture) Hospital for black soldiers in Alexandria, Virginia. Pvt. Willis Johnson, the Company A soldier, died of "lung fever" just after the regiment's arrival at Camp Casey. He left behind his widow, Permelia, and son, then living in the barracks at Quincy "prepared for the freed men who cam[sic] from Missouri." She applied at once for a pension but had difficulties—as did many dependents from slave states—because marriages of slaves or even of free blacks were not recorded. Lacking documents, a widow had to produce affidavits from persons who could certify that the couple had lived together for at least two years prior to the soldier's enlistment. She and the child were finally pensioned effective the day of Johnson's death. Company C's losses were Cpl. William Wood, twenty-five, born in Maryland, and Pvt. James Baldwin, twenty-one, originally from Alabama, both of whom died on 16 May 1864. Pvts. Lewis Phoenix, eighteen, of Company D, and James R. Phillips, twenty, of Company E, also died in May; they were not married. Their mothers filed for pensions as dependents, the first in 1878 and the other in 1901, but neither was approved.[8]

A shortage not made up was officers, and that was worse than it seemed because the understrength regiment was not authorized regimental staff. In mid-May only Bross, Aiken, both Flints, and Gosper were mustered in, but Porter, Knapp, Strickler, Chapman, Fee, and another prospective officer, George R. Naylor, were present but not mustered. Porter and Knapp received their discharges as enlisted men in a few days and were sworn in. Strickler and the otherwise unknown Naylor declined appointment, and Fee remained a contract surgeon. Despite vacancies, regimental duties still had to be performed, so existing company officers were appointed to do essential jobs. Gosper, for example, was made acting regimental quartermaster officer on 3 May, and Chapman was acting adjutant by mid-June or earlier. On the plus side 2d Lt. Thomas N. Conant of Warren County, New York, a former enlisted man in the West, joined the regiment and was assigned to Company C. With active field service likely, a critical shortage was medical officers; although Fee was still with the regiment, no army surgeons were authorized or assigned. It is possible that other officers were available for company duties although not yet commissioned or mustered in. The casual personnel records of the time do not say, but in any case there were too few.[9]

WITH THE ARMY OF THE POTOMAC

At the end of May, after only a few weeks of training and being equipped, the regiment was ordered to join the Army of the Potomac in the field. The bloody Battles of the Wilderness and Spotsylvania in early May had cost Grant thirty thousand casualties, but Grant, unlike earlier Union Army commanders, was willing to press on against Robert E. Lee's Army of Northern Virginia, regardless of losses or even defeats. Therefore, it was important to replace casualties, and even ill-trained black troops would be useful. The regiment marched from Camp Casey to Alexandria on 30 May, spending the night at the soldiers' rest. The next morning the soldiers boarded the steam transport *George Weems* for the trip to join the army at White House Landing, Grant's supply center on the Pamunkey River. Arriving on 3 June, "after a pleasant sail from Alexandria," the regiment was put to work building fortifications to screen the concentration point.[10]

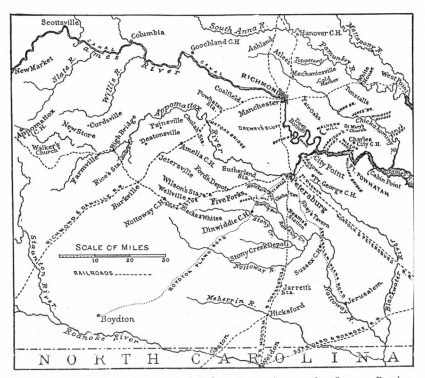

Map of the area of the Twenty-ninth Infantry's wartime service. Source: *Battles and Leaders of the Civil War.*

One important addition was made to the Twenty-ninth USCT on 10 June: Surgeon David Mackay, an experienced army doctor from New York, was assigned to the regiment, even though it was understrength. Mackay, age thirty-two, born in Scotland, had been an assistant surgeon in the Seventy-ninth New York Infantry, "The Highlanders." He was with that regiment at Jackson, Vicksburg, and Knoxville, and was discharged when the regiment's enlistment expired in June 1864. Soldiers were then given an opportunity to reenlist, the incentive being a thirty-day furlough home, during which they could recruit others. Mackay thus could have rejoined the Seventy-ninth regiment, now designated a veteran unit, but going to a black regiment as surgeon was a promotion. Mackay's background had been left behind in Scotland, and it was not revealed until after his death in 1904. In Glasgow he had been employed as a cotton spinner and had married in August 1856. His wife, Mary, filed for a separation in October of the same year, before the couple's son was born. She cited grounds as "on account of his ill treatment, brutality and general abuse." The ruling the following June by the Sheriff Court at Glasgow granted a separation, not a divorce, and Mackay was ordered to pay seven shillings a week for support of his wife and son. Apparently, Mackay fled to the United States to avoid this obligation and in 1861 was qualified in medicine, having received his M.D. from the Hygio-Therapeutical College in New York.[11] Contract Surgeon Fee also accompanied the Twenty-ninth Regiment to the field, since it was short two assistant surgeons.

Routine labor duties continued until 8 June, when the regiment received orders to move. The following day the regiment joined Ferrero's Fourth Division at Old Church Tavern on the Pamunkey River, a few miles above White House Landing. Sergeant McCoslin wrote about the undisciplined state of the regiment on the forced march: "Many of the men had to throw away nearly all of their baggage, so as to keep up." The stay at that position was uneventful for the Twenty-ninth U.S. Colored Infantry, although some Company B soldiers came under fire from enemy cavalry near Haw's Shop on 10 June, the company recording "pickets driven in, some confusion." The Twenty-ninth USCT remained at Old Church Tavern until 12 June, when it broke camp and headed for the James River as part of the army corps' rear guard. During these movements several more men became casualties. Pvt. Henry Clay Todd, twenty-one, a former slave of Harriet Matson of New London, Missouri, injured his ankle and was sent to Alexandria to recuperate. His recovery took some time because he also had to be treated for rheumatism; he remained absent from Company A until the following March. Company A's Sgt. Samuel White, a native of North Carolina brought to Kentucky about ten years before the war, escaped to Quincy with his new wife early in the war. He became ill at White House Landing and was sent to L'Overture Hospital in Alexandria on 10 June. He was to die there of inflammation of the lungs in September, leaving behind a widow and two children. Richmond-born Pvt. Edward Carter, a recruit signed up at White House on 6 June, was reported by Company B's First Sergeant Mills to have been ill from "heavy marching," but he continued under Mills's urging, in a few days to be hospitalized for about a month. Another of those few Virginia recruits, Pvt. John Dotson, twenty, who enlisted at the same time and place as Carter, was listed as missing on the day he joined. Although the circumstances behind his absence are not explained, he was captured by the enemy and was carried missing in action by Company B until May 1865, when he was returned to the regiment.

Coincidentally, Carter was captured almost two months after Dotson was made a prisoner and likewise survived the war.[12]

Pvt. John Carter, age eighteen, Missouri-born, was one of Company A's first recruits. His military service was cut short by his hospitalization for bronchitis just after the march from White House Landing. He was moved to several hospitals, arriving at West Point, New York, in early 1865. Carter never rejoined the regiment and was discharged in late May. Another Company A loss was Pvt. Jerry Casey, nineteen, a former Missouri slave, who was hospitalized at the same time as was Carter. Casey, however, died in the field hospital of chronic diarrhea on 29 June. The same malady was the cause of death of Alabama-born Pvt. James W. Couch, twenty-seven, who did not make the march but was sent sick from White House Landing to Mount Pleasant General Hospital in the District of Columbia, where he died in September. Finally, Pvt. Edward Hunter, born in Virginia, also died as a result of the march. He succumbed to pneumonia on 14 June in an ambulance at New Kent Court House, leaving behind a wife and three minor children at Markisan, Wisconsin. Other soldiers were ill during and after the movement from White House Landing to the James River, but no others died immediately.[13]

While the Twenty-ninth USCT was performing support activities, the Union Army was engaged in heavy fighting. Grant's tragic frontal assault on Lee's forces at Cold Harbor from 1 to 3 June had raised Union casualties for a one-month period to sixty thousand, just about equal to Lee's strength. Trench warfare continued until 12 June, Grant by then planning a change of his base from White House to the James River in an attempt to seize Petersburg, outflank Richmond, and force Lee to retreat or accept a siege of the Confederate capital. The Twenty-ninth USCT's part in this operation was restricted to guard duty in the Army of the Potomac's rear areas.

Ferrero had organized his Fourth Division in two brigades in early May, preparing to support Grant's newly begun offensive operations. The division had been encamped since late April at Manassas Junction, the last unit in the Ninth Corps. Ferrero lacked four of the nine black regiments earmarked for him, so, because it was understrength and unproved, the division's initial part in the campaign consisted of covering the rear of the Army of the Potomac and escorting supplies. The supply train was made up of wagons, carrying ten days' rations and ammunition, and cattle on the hoof. For this support duty the division was detached from Burnside's Ninth Corps, and Burnside did not see it again for a month.

The division took up positions generally covering Germanna Ford, the principal crossing of the Rapidan River, until early June and then moved south, picking up the Twenty-ninth Regiment on the way. The division arrived at New Kent Court House on 13 June, the day after the Army of the Potomac began its successful movement to the James River.[14]

On its way south Ferrero's Fourth Division had aroused the interest of soldiers in the Army of the Potomac because black troops had not been seen before. A staff officer described his impression in an 18 May letter:

> A five this morning a novel sight was presented to the Potomac Army. A division of black troops, under General Ferrero . . . marched up and massed in a hollow nearby. As I looked at them, my soul was troubled and I would gladly have seen them marched back to Washington. Can we not fight our own battles, without calling on these humble hewers of wood and drawers of water, to be bayonetted by the unsparing Southerners? We do not trust them in battle. . . . They have been put to guard the trains and have repulsed one or two little cavalry attacks in a creditable manner; but God help them if the gray-backed infantry attack them![15]

Another who observed the Fourth Division at New Kent Court House, however, was more impressed, reporting that the veteran cavalry command he was with cheered the blacks: "No brigade ever made a better appearance or a better impression upon those who for the first time saw colored troops." An officer of the Fourth Division's Thirtieth U.S. Colored Infantry, writing of one of these first encounters, said, "Our men, aware that they were objects of criticism, closed up their ranks, brought their guns to right shoulder, and presented a credible military appearance." He continued: "The white soldiers were not about to let them pass without some 'chaffing,' to which the black men were quite equal. One colored soldier, with a clear, mellow voice, raised the song 'Will you, will you, Fight for de Union?' Instantly the whole line took up the chorus: 'Ah-ha! ah-ha! We'll fight for Uncle Sam.'"

The blacks had a few minor skirmishes similar to the brush at Haw's on their way south, mostly involving cavalry raids on the trains. They did not run, an important quality in their gaining acceptance by white soldiers. One of General Grant's aides wrote, "The display of soldierly qualities [shown by the blacks] won a frank acknowledgement from both troops and commanders, not all of whom had before been willing to look upon negroes as comrades," but he may have been exaggerating the importance of these minor, early tests of the black soldier in the Army of the Potomac.[16]

The parent Ninth Army Corps, from which Ferrero's division was temporarily detached, apparently did not have much of a reputation. Grant's chief provost marshal reported following the Ninth Corps's supply train: "And such a train. . . . There is any quantity of straggling on these marches, from 9' Corps—which is in very bad discipline & its Staff Departments worthless." This lack of discipline may have been partly the result of General Burnside's dispute over his seniority in the army. He was senior to Army of the Potomac commander, Maj. Gen. George Meade, but had a subordinate command. Grant initially kept the Ninth Corps reporting directly to him, finally placing it in Meade's army on 24 May, three weeks into the advance on Richmond, after Burnside agreed to serve under Meade.[17] Further, the corps had only lately been transferred from Tennessee, many of its new regiments and replacement troops were untrained, and Burnside had just assumed command. Disorganization, which might be expected under such circumstances, would cost the corps dearly in July.

The Twenty-ninth USCT was assigned to Ferrero's Second Brigade, under Col. Henry Goddard Thomas, the first regular army officer to accept command of black troops. Born in Maine, he became a lawyer at age twenty-one, enlisting as a private in the Fifth Maine Infantry at the start of the war. Within months he was commanding a company and was appointed a captain in the Eleventh U.S. Infantry, a regular army regiment. He had been colonel of the Seventy-ninth U.S. Colored Infantry and was then commanding the Nineteenth Colored Infantry, one of the regiments in the brigade. Regiments in the Second Brigade were, in addition to the Twenty-ninth and the equally shorthanded Twenty-eighth from Indiana, Thomas's Nineteenth, the Twenty-third, and the Thirty-first U.S. Colored Infantry Regiments. Leading the First Brigade was Col. Joshua K. Sigfried, commander of the Forty-eighth Pennsylvania Infantry, a white regiment in the Ninth Army Corps. His regiments were the Twenty-seventh, Thirtieth, Thirty-ninth, and Forty-third Colored Infantry.[18]

To the Twenty-ninth Infantry's soldiers, however, brigade commanders and assignments were less significant than the regiment's move toward more active service. Spending the night of the twelfth at New Kent Court House and following the wagons via Statesville, Cole's Ferry, and Charles City Court House, the Twenty-ninth USCT arrived on the north bank of the James River on 16 June. Ferrero's division relieved units of the Sixth Army Corps which had been assigned to protect the remarkable 2,200-foot pontoon bridge just built by the engineers over the James between Fort Powhatan and Windmill Point. The Fourth Division crossed on the seventeenth, proceeding to Wilcox's House, still protecting the army's supplies. This duty was finally completed on the nineteenth, and the division was returned to Burnside's corps.[19]

ON THE LINE BEFORE PETERSBURG

The Ninth Corps's position on the developing front before Petersburg was initially the left flank of the Union line. After some early tactical failures the whole Army of the Potomac settled down to static trench warfare by 22 June, two other corps having extended the line further left in an unsuccessful attempt to outflank Lee. The Fourth Division's posting was not firmly established, the black units first going to Bailey's Creek near Old Court House and on to other secondary positions in the works. The division was constantly moving for a month, beginning on 27 June, when it was posted at Prince George Court House. It was later deployed along the Jerusalem Plank Road, then to the Second Army Corps, and on 2 July to the Old Norfolk Road covering Sixth Corps. It was back under the Second Corps a few days later and shortly afterward was ordered to cover the Fifth Corps. The division returned again to the Ninth Corps on 22 July, the First Brigade scattered among the corps' trenches and the Second stationed in reserve. Company B Pvt. Charles Griffin wrote home on 10 June that he had not yet seen any battles but that pickets had come under some fire. He said he thought he knew why the black troops were being left alone: "One thing the rebels is afraid of [is] the nigers[;] they may be fighting all day with they White soldiers but as quick as the Collard soldiers come up they fell back." As he was writing this, however, his position came under fire—"The rebbels is coming"—and he took cover. He resumed writing later, saying, "I have been in now six months and have not come near going into a battle as I did a little while ago." Union troops, however, "drove them back." He concluded with the comment: "We expect an attack here pretty soon but I see no danger."[20]

The Fourth Division was not holding its own section of the line, although small units were sometimes deployed among the white regiments in the trenches. Ferrero's troops did not, therefore, receive the same unusual punishment as that reported by the three white divisions. One veteran wrote: "The rebs always alluded to the Ninth as 'the_ nigger corps,' from the fact that the Fourth Division [was] composed of colored troops. They always knew where the Ninth lay, and annoyed us accordingly." The annoyance was constant random shelling and sniping, which was to cost the white divisions sorely over the next month. An officer wrote, "The appearance of the wooly heads never failed to draw a lively return fire from the vigilant Johnnies." He also said that the corps had orders to fire a hundred rounds per man on the line per day, and this may have been responsible for rebel retaliation. Along the rest of the front line soldiers fraternized with the enemy during quiet periods, exchanging tobacco, newspapers, and other items and even warning one another of impending attacks, but "absolutely no such socializing or swapping, let alone warnings, took place in front of IX Corps' stations." The three white divisions, not fighting a single major engagement, lost 12 officers and 231 enlisted men killed and 44 officers and 851 men wounded before the end of July, a total of 1,150 casualties, a loss rate that caused a serious decline in morale. (Only twelve men were missing, however, a low number had any battles or skirmishes occurred.) It may have been to bolster his men's spirits that Ferrero ordered one-half a "gill of whiskey be issued to each of the men of this command each day until further notice."[21]

The Fourth Division was not the only black organization on the front. Accompanying Maj. Gen. Benjamin Butler's Army of the James's 5 June move from Yorktown and Gloucester Point to seize City Point and the Bermuda Hundred on the James below Richmond, as part of Grant's strategic move, were twenty regiments of black troops, one division of two brigades each in the Tenth and Eighteenth Army Corps.[22] Black troops were growing into a substantial part of Grant's armies before Richmond, but they were still scattered among several commands, in which they were not always welcome. They were not organized in units of a size large enough for significant military accomplishment on their own, nor were they trusted to perform to a standard commanders had come to expect from white units. They were, of course, useful as labor troops, and when sometimes called on to take part in hazardous attacks they performed bravely and with perseverance.

The Twenty-ninth and its sister regiments in the Fourth Division were selected to lead an important corps operation that promised to penetrate the Confederate line and allow occupation of Petersburg. If accomplished, this could force the rebels to abandon Richmond. The division was not chosen because of confidence in its fighting capability but primarily because it had over four thousand men and had not suffered the casualties and morale decline sustained by the Ninth Corps's other three divisions since the last half of June. The Ninth Corps also happened to be in the position on the line where the operation would be undertaken, and it would not be easy to substitute another corps. Its job should not have been too difficult, providing all went as planned.[23]

The plan was centered on an unusual idea, tunneling under and mining a salient in the Confederate lines relatively close to federal positions, but the shaft would have to be more than five hundred feet long, a formidable engineering feat. The operation was suggested by Lt. Col. Henry Pleasants, a civil engineer and acting commanding officer of Col. Joshua K. Sigfried's Forty-eighth Pennsylvania, a unit made up largely of experienced miners. Pleasants obtained Burnside's reluctant permission to begin the tunnel, and on 25 June he set to work with his regiment and with little logistic support or encouragement.

Ferrero's black regiments were withdrawn from other duties one at a time to learn the maneuvers they would employ in the planned attack. Colonel Pleasants was pleased with the choice of the fresh black troops for the follow-up to his mine's explosion and thought the troops showed commendable enthusiasm when "put through the drill in the tactics that were to be employed." Not much time per regiment could have been spent on this training, and ordinary drills and parades were continued, perhaps to instruct new recruits in routine practices. Lincoln visited Grant's headquarters at the City Point supply center in late June and reviewed some black troops in the Eighteenth Corps. He told Grant that he had been hearing many objections to black troops, but "it was just as well to be a little color-blind." While not asked to parade for Lincoln, an unspecified Fourth Division regiment was on hand for a 1 July review by a delegation of French officers. Their escort wrote:

> I took advantage of the propinquity of the nigger division (which had come to fill part of the 6th Corps' line, during its absence) to show the unbleached brethren to my imperial commissioners. We rode first to General Ferrero's Headquarters. . . . There was turned out for them a regiment of darks. The sun was intense and the sable gents looked like millers, being quite obscured except when they stood perfectly still. They did remarkably well. . . . [The] Frog officers . . . were in ecstacies over their performance.[24]

That French officers were so entertained seems odd, since Secretary of State William Seward, who accompanied Lincoln to City Point in late June, spoke with Grant about the threat to Texas from French troops supporting Maximilian's Mexican regime. Grant allowed that the United States might have to "make a demonstration on the Rio Grande" when the war was over. He later ordered such an expedition, and the Twenty-ninth Colored Infantry, along with most of the black regiments under his command, became a part of it.[25]

The records of the Twenty-ninth Regiment do not specify day-to-day positions or routines; paperwork seems to have been neglected during this active period. The regimental history says simply: "Left rifle pits in front of Petersburg Va. June 27, marched five miles to the rear to Prince George C. H. Va. . . . During the month of July the Reg't was in the front of Petersburg on various parts of the line engaged in throwing up earthworks and fortifications."[26] Sergeant McCoslin thought the regiment was "not in good fighting trim . . . on account of an insufficiency of officers":

> We are expecting every day; to be sent to the front, but it is or-
> dered otherwise, probably for the best. Our regiment has built two
> forts and about three miles of breastworks, which shows we are not
> idle, and that we are learning to make fortifications, whether we
> learn to fight or not. We are now [26 July] lying in camp, about a
> mile and a half from the city [Petersburg], resting a day or two. It is
> quite a treat for the boys to get a rest after working day and night,
> four hours on and four hours off. We have worked in that way for
> eight or ten days, without stopping. But my opinion now is, that the
> laboring work is over, so that we have nothing to do but watch the
> rebels.[27]

Despite the hard labor to which they had been put, the men probably shared their brigade commander's pride in being selected for a mission, the nature of which was not told to them. They knew they were training for some kind of an assault. As Thomas wrote later: "Both officers and men were eager to show the white troops what the colored division could do. We [the officers] had acquired confidence in our men. They believed us infallible."[28]

The regiment did not alter its composition in the month it spent be-fore Petersburg, and not one casualty was caused by enemy action. There were other reductions before the end of July: five deaths from disease. Two of these soldiers, both privates, were from Company A. Moses Por-ter, twenty-one, died of an unspecified illness at the City Point hospital on 14 June, leaving no survivors. He was among the first of the regiment's soldiers who had entered as a paid substitute for a drafted man (Benjamin

Anderson), a practice that became common in the fall. Jerry Morris, a blacksmith born in 1821 in Virginia, probably escaped from slavery in Virginia. He died of pneumonia in the Third Division's field hospital near Petersburg on 14 July while under Dr. Mackay's care, having been ill only a few days. Morris had married in Quincy in January, but it was later discovered that the soldier had another wife from whom he was not divorced. A third Company A man, Virginia-born Cpl. George S. Williams, died at City Point in late June, leaving no dependents. The fourth death was Pvt. William McGrundy, eighteen, who died in Alexandria on 9 July, and the fifth was Pvt. Charles Lee, Company F, who "died in camp near Petersburg Va July 28 - 1864" of unknown causes. Kentucky-born Lee was eighteen and left no dependents.[29]

Accidents leading to injury which disqualified soldiers for service seem to have remained rare during the first months in Virginia. Pvt. General Houston, a Tennessee-born twenty-four-year-old former slave, had enlisted in Chicago in February 1864. Assigned to guard duty in a quartermaster warehouse when the regiment was at White House Landing, Houston was pinned under a bale of blankets, which had fallen on him. He was discovered by Company A's Pvt. John Carter, taken to the dispensary, and sent on to the L'Overture Hospital in Alexandria. Although he eventually rejoined his company, Houston did not recover fully from his injuries, and he was discharged in the field for his disability early in 1865.[30]

These losses, while seemingly few, did not give the whole picture about the condition of the six companies of the Twenty-ninth Colored Infantry in July 1864, on the eve of battle. Certainly, the regiment's officers were concerned about the general health of the troops, particularly as some of the men were ill or injured and many others were detailed away for divisional duties and were unavailable to their company commanders. Counting Company A's sick, in addition to the men who had died in hospitals, eight were not present for duty. Pvts. Peter Bernard and Martin Campbell, both eighteen-year-old former Missouri slaves, were hospitalized, the first with smallpox and the second with an undetermined illness. Cpl. John E. Golden, one of the first enlistees at Quincy, was injured in a log fall while building fortifications on 24 July. It is not entirely clear that he was immediately hospitalized, but it seems likely. He was in the hospital several times, however, for typhoid and other maladies, and he spent little time on duty. Musician Thompson Kay, age eighteen, the company fifer, was hospitalized for heat exhaustion or sunstroke in June and was in the Alexandria hospital by early July. He never returned to his company because the doctors diagnosed him as having "distortion of the chest," probably a preservice condition that should have disqualified him for enlistment, and they discharged him early. Cpl. Samuel Scott, the forty-five-year-old horse jockey claiming birth in New York, was sick from early June in the hospital in Alexandria, where he stayed well into the winter. His complaints seem to have been bladder trouble and a hernia, and, when he returned to Company A, he was given the relatively easy duty of cook. Cpl. George M. Washington's injuries are not clearly defined in his records. He said he received multiple minor wounds to his head, wrist, arm, and heel in late July, but he may have been injured in an accident rather than by enemy action. He remained in the hospital for treatment of chronic diarrhea until September. Pvt. Guss (Augustus Thomas) Williams's injury, like Golden's, seems to have been the result of a fort-building accident; his knee was struck by a pick, disabling him until October. Pvt. Washington Williams, like Golden an original enlistee, was detached from the company for teamster duty at the brigade or division. Because medical records are often incomplete and lists of detached soldiers not often included in morning reports, other Company A soldiers were likely elsewhere, rather than on the line preparing for battle. The other companies had fewer deaths than did Company A, but all of them suffered severely from sickness in that hot summer, and all of them were subject to calls for men to be detailed for brigade and division activities.[31]

While regimental records for June and July are incomplete, they do show that the Twenty-ninth Colored Infantry, which should have had on duty a minimum of four hundred and eighty noncommissioned officers and private soldiers, probably could count on just over half to two-thirds that number, plus a handful of officers. Regimental headquarters was made up of Colonel Bross, Major Brown, Surgeon Mackay, and Acting Assistant Surgeon Fee. No other regimental staff officers were authorized or assigned, so from time to time company officers were detailed for essential duties, further reducing leadership in the companies. Company A's First Sergeant McCoslin, although not officially assigned to the job until several months later, was acting regimental sergeant major. Only one enlisted man was actually assigned to Bross's staff, Musician Lewis T. Wood, a bugler, who was transferred from Company B in late June. Wood, about whose early life and arrival in Chicago little is known, was born in Mexico in 1829 and may have been able to read and write. It cannot be confirmed that the two soldiers later assigned as regimental quartermaster and commissary sergeants were informally working in headquarters, but it is plausible that they were chosen early for the critical jobs. Both of these men, Joseph N. Scott and James H. Brown, were in the regiment officially in Companies E and C, respectively. Scott, age twenty-seven, was born in Harrisburg, Pennsylvania, and Brown in Maryland, the latter a former slave; both enlisted in Chicago, were barbers, and had writing skills. Brown was not officially assigned as commissary sergeant until November and was Company C's orderly sergeant, the senior noncommissioned officer under the first sergeant, in the coming battle.[32]

Discipline does not appear to have been a major problem in the regiment, but Company E's Sgt. Joseph C. Arbuckle was reduced to private by sentence of a court-martial on 15 July 1864. Charges and specifications on which he was convicted were brought by Captain Flint, including that he was "never ready and willing to execute an order," and he was "constantly finding fault with and disputing his superior officers and attempting to defy their authority." Arbuckle was only temporarily demoted; he would be appointed first sergeant of Company I when it was organized the following December.[33]

At least two new officers, both awaiting commissioning and mustering in, joined the regiment in July, possibly accompanying Major Brown, Captain Dagget, and the Company F recruits from Chicago. They were 1st Lt. Nimrod G. Ferguson and 2d Lt. Michael J. Hassler. Ferguson had been a Missouri cavalryman, his experience primarily in "bushwacking affairs"; he was assigned to Company E. Hassler, a Missouri militiaman, went to Company B. First Lieutenant Samuel A. Johnston, late of the 140th Pennsylvania Volunteers and with a long combat record, was on duty with Company A but was also not mustered.[34] Apart from adding a few officers and Company F and its Wisconsin-credited recruits, the regiment had much the same composition as when it arrived in Virginia from Illinois. A change would come, however, on 30 July.

Chapter 3

TEST OF BATTLE

Doubts about the ability and soldierly qualities of black troops continued, despite examples of their courage and competence in combat. Few noticed that most feats of arms by black regiments were in unsuccessful military operations, such as Milliken's Bend, Port Hudson, Battery Wagner, and Olustee; accusations against blacks were most often that they lacked the bravery shown by whites. The question of winning or losing battles was not as important in the public perception of this issue as was steadiness under fire. An early July 1864 letter to the *Army and Navy Journal* decried a *New York World* editorial disparaging black soldiers, claiming the troops were "perfectly docile, anxious to do their duty well, [and] . . . only require officers to appreciate their peculiarities and encourage their aspirations," listing most of the failed engagements in which blacks participated. Just for taking part in the war, blacks deserved thanks. A rebuttal letter the following week pointed out that blacks did not need such friends as the earlier writer and that in their most prominent defeats, Battery Wagner and Olustee, the blacks were not properly supported by white troops or were responsible for saving the defeated white units. Blacks deserved to be appreciated for their actual contributions to the war, not just their casualties or conduct under fire.[1]

Blacks were in the army because every man was needed in the routinely casualty-intensive operations, so their use in more than the secondary roles, mostly wagon guarding and hard labor, they had held before Petersburg was inevitable.[2] Race was not an issue from the perspective of federal commanders, although some officers may have had egalitarian agendas that favored using blacks. Black unit participation in the mine assault was decided on by General Burnside for purely military reasons. Simply, the black regiments were fresh and strong in numbers, and they were being asked to perform what seemed to be an important but relatively risk-free part in a nevertheless unusual operation. There was no reason to believe that their lack of combat experience would be a critical factor, because, although leading the attack on the Confederate lines, their role would be closely supported by the Ninth Army Corps's veteran white divisions, which would seize advanced positions and perhaps go on to Petersburg. As it would develop, however, politics changed the operation in a way that would turn opportunity into yet another bloody failure.

The plan for following up the explosion of Colonel Pleasants's mine as outlined by corps commander Burnside was not complex, but the leading division's duties might have been difficult for raw troops. The first regiments of the two black brigades of the Fourth Division would leave the federal lines in columns and expand a corridor for the troops following behind by moving right and left in the breach along Confederate lines, this maneuver being the one practiced by the USCT units. Black regiments not required for holding open the way were to move on to Cemetery Hill, the high ground behind rebel lines, followed by the three white divisions "as soon as they can be thrown in." Burnside also thought that the attack might succeed in going beyond Cemetery Hill, in which case he would "throw the colored division right into the town." He told his superior, Army of the Potomac commander Meade, that the chance of success was "more than even."[3]

There was some apprehension about the leadership qualities of Fourth Division commander Ferrero, but it was not sufficiently grave to cause his superiors to consider replacing him. Colonel Pleasants said of him, "Ferraro [sic] had not distinguished himself particularly in any part of our former campaigns, but he had come through certainly experienced in military offensive tactics." He had, however, shown signs of cowardice at Knoxville. There he had hidden in a bombproof shelter for the entire battle, but Burnside, who was commanding there, chose to ignore his conduct. The doubts among officers in the USCT regiments did not concern Ferrero and the brigade commanders as much as the inexperience of the troops and the shortage of companies. The Forty-third U.S. Colored Infantry—which would have been the first regiment in the attack—had only seven companies, and its commander was therefore reluctant to lead the division. Colonels Bross and Russell were similarly short companies but did not record their concerns. In all, at least on paper, the First Brigade had about two thousand troops and the Second twenty-two hundred, each somewhat better than half of full strength. Even if these totals inaccurately included men sick and on other duty, the Fourth Division had considerably more men than any of the white divisions.[4]

Tunnel digging continued until 17 July, firing chambers under the rebel positions were completed less than a week later, and eight thousand pounds of powder brought in and the fuse set by 28 July. Security was maintained by keeping information on the mining activities from the troops, and telltale earth was moved away from the line for disposal. Such a large-scale project could not be completely concealed, and rumors of it were common along the Union line. A lieutenant wrote home on 4 July: "Genl Grant may pursue the same course that he did at Vicksburg. *Under mine* them and blow them up. I understand that something of that kind is realy under way *good if true.*" The enemy had suspicions that its positions were being mined, having heard rumors from pickets, prisoners, and deserters; plans had been "discussed and accepted by the troops" all month.[5] Rebel countermining did not lead to discovery of the shaft, and it ended, after 23 July, when no more Union digging was heard. Even with this knowledge, where the blow would strike was uncertain, and no redeployments, other than to counter federal diversionary activities elsewhere on the front, were undertaken by the rebels. Confederate forces defending Petersburg numbered only three divisions, eighteen thousand men.

Burnside's superiors, Meade and Grant, had improved the chances of success as the digging went on by assigning new units to protect and follow up the assault and to stage diversions elsewhere along the trench line. Maj. Gen. Gouverneur K. Warren's Fifth Corps and Maj. Gen. Edward O. C. Ord's Eighteenth Corps were to attack behind the Ninth Corps, Maj. Gen. Winfield S. Hancock's Second Corps would support the right flank, and other forces would put pressure on Lee north of the James River. All seemed to be ready in late July to spring the mine and attack enemy positions, but on the afternoon prior to the attack the situation changed. General Meade, who had been kept informed of Burnside's plan, objected a few days before to some parts of it but, after hearing Burnside's protest, agreed to let Grant decide. Burnside, hearing nothing from Meade, assumed by late morning of 29 July that Meade's changes were not going to be approved. Consequently, as he was about to brief his division commanders, Meade showed up at Burnside's headquarters accompanied by a large staff and other corps commanders and told Burnside that Grant had approved Meade's changes: replacement of the Fourth Division by another and alteration of the corridor expansion tactic to a full effort at the point of the mine's explosion. Burnside, whose relationship with Meade was not good, protested again, but Meade insisted, explaining that the black division was untried and that such an important operation should be headed by the most experienced units. The problem may have been that Meade was concerned that the rebels had a secondary line of defense along the Cemetery Hill line which could jeopardize Burnside's plan. There were, however, no such backup defense positions; they existed only in the "imagination [of some newspaper correspondents], inflated by the stories of stragglers and coffee-boilers," proclaimed *Harper's Weekly*. The real reason might have been somewhat different. Grant later testified that, were the attack to fail, using black troops would leave the army open to criticism. It may have been more directly political than Grant would say. With Lincoln's campaign for his second term just beginning, Grant and Meade were unwilling to risk helping the Democrats: "It must not be said that Lincoln the emancipator was careless with black lives."[6]

Meade's order for the assault was clear enough. It outlined the duties of the three army corps commanders, Burnside, Warren, and Ord. Burnside had important initial responsibilities, one of them being that at dark the evening before the mine's explosion he was to "prepare his parapets and abatis for the passage of the columns." This responsibility was critical because the area between the lines was purposely cluttered with obstacles to slow enemy attacks. Furthermore, the trenches were up to eight feet deep to protect frontline troops, too deep for easy movement of attacking columns over the parapet. Burnside was specifically directed to explode the mine at 3:30 A.M. on 30 July and immediately to "seize the crest in the rear," where Meade expected to find Confederate defenses that would not be disrupted by the explosion. He also clearly ordered all participating forces to avoid the crater itself, correctly believing that it could be a distraction for the troops and occupation of it of little military value. Meade specified that the "headquarters during the operation will be at the headquarters of the Ninth Corps," but Burnside was not given authority to give orders to the other corps commanders involved in the battle, a breakdown in normal military procedure which would prove important in determining the coming battle's outcome.[7]

Burnside had twelve hours to alter the plan, shuffle his units, and bring off the operation before dawn on 30 July. Considering the conditions of his three white divisions—they were uniformly weak and tired—he let the division commanders draw straws for the honor of leading the attack. The First Division, commanded by Brig. Gen. James Hewitt Ledlie, was selected, an unfortunate choice, as was known to many in advance. A civil engineer before the war, he had been a major in a New York artillery unit that mutinied, many of its soldiers having been sent to a Dry Tortuga prison. He was promoted through the ranks to his present grade, was discharged, and was later reappointed, in October 1863. His assignments from then until he joined Grant the following May were commanding garrisons. An officer commanding one of Ledlie's regiments expressed his dismay at Ledlie's selection, recalling finding him drunk during an engagement a month earlier and noting that the general had offered his resignation, but it was not yet accepted: "The officers and men were discouraged at having to lead, as we had heard all along that the negroes were to do this, and we had no confidence in Ledlie. He had failed on several occasions." The officer was even more frank in later years, writing: "In every fight we had been in under Ledlie he had been under the influence of liquor. . . . It was an absolute crime to let such a man head so important an undertaking." He added his regret about having not preferred charges against the general. Another soldier remembered years later that his regiment had longed for its earlier division commander (Brig. Gen. Thomas G. Stevenson, killed in May by a sniper), and Grant's aide said of Ledlie that he "was by far the least fitted [of the divisional commanders] for such an undertaking." As for the First Division, an officer of the First Rhode Island thought Ledlie's division the best one for the assault, not having received the same punishment in the trenches as had the other white units, but a newspaper correspondent wrote a few days after the battle: "The worse troops in the army led the line of assault—troops who heretofore had acted badly on various occasions." That Burnside was unaware of Ledlie's already demonstrated shortcomings—more of them were to be revealed—is difficult to believe; he irresponsibly allowed the attack to be headed by his least capable division commander, anyway.[8]

As Meade had done, Burnside issued his order for the attack, specifically directing Ledlie to avoid the crater and continuing, "*if possible,* [to] crown the crest at the point known as Cemetery Hill, occupying, *if possible,* the cemetery." The Ninth Corps's Second Division was to head to the left of the crater to protect the left flank along the Jerusalem Plank Road, which ran generally parallel to and behind the rebel front line. The Third Division's job was much the same on the right flank, and Ferrero's Fourth Division was to go forward "immediately" behind the others, following Ledlie's path.[9]

Ninth Corps troops were relieved on the front line by black units of the Eighteenth Corps on the night before the attack. Ledlie, meanwhile, was briefing his brigade commanders, Brig. Gen. William F. Bartlett and Col. Elisha G. Marshall, both experienced soldiers. As he explained the operation, the First Brigade was to go to the right of the expected crater, the Second to the left, and the division would be followed closely by the other three divisions, the Second more toward the right, the Third left, and the Fourth up the middle, to Cemetery Hill. As it happened, however, Colonel Marshall misinterpreted these instructions, confusing his left with the Confederate left. Consequently, both of Ledlie's brigades were to angle off to the right. Ledlie, however, would not be there to sort out his regiments. But perhaps more important was that Ledlie's instructions, which were not written, did not emphasize the ridge behind the front line as the division's objective, describing it as the responsibility of the Fourth Division. Meade spoke with Burnside's division commanders—except for Ferrero—the evening before the attack, but Meade did not say later what he had told the generals. The plan had to have been discussed, so Ledlie's changes to Meade's written order are even less excusable.[10]

The Fourth Division's holding position for the next day's combat was at the foot of an abandoned railway embankment in the rear of the Union lines near Fort Morton, a strong point where the line bulged toward the Confederate positions. Morton, which was to be Burnside's battle headquarters, was about eight hundred yards from the mined Confederate position known as Elliott's Salient or Pelgram's Salient—the former name for the brigade with sector responsibility and the latter for the artillery unit there. Ledlie's division was concealed just behind the picket line, the most advanced Union positions. The other two white divisions were on the forward slope of the railroad cut. The Twenty-ninth Regiment received its orders to march to the front at 9 P.M. and was in position among some pine trees an hour later. A newsman wrote, "The colored regiments, on their way to the front, were unanimously cheered by the white troops with such cries as, 'Go in bully boys!' 'Give them h——l!' 'Remember Fort Pillow!'" but this seems unlikely. Colonel Thomas was not notified that his brigade and the rest of Ferrero's division would not lead the assault until 11 P.M., and he told this to his soldiers. Whether the disappointment or the impending danger was the cause, Thomas said the troops sat around in groups "'studying,' as they called it":

They waited, like the Quakers, for the spirit to move; when the spirit moved, one of their singers would uplift a mighty voice, like a bard of old, in a wild sort of chant. If he did not strike a sympathetic chord in his hearers, . . . he would sing it again and again, altering the words, more often the music. If his changes met general acceptance, one voice after another would chime in; a rough harmony of three parts would add itself; the other groups would join them, and the song would become the song of the command.

> We-e looks li-ke me-en a- a-marchin' on,
> We looks li-ike men-er-war.

Shortly half a thousand voices were upraised extemporizing a middle part and bass. It was a picturesque scene—these dark men, with their white eyes and teeth and full red lips, crowding near a smoldering camp-fire, in dusky shadow, with only the feeble rays of the lantern of the first sergeants and the lights of candles dimly showing through the tents.

Thomas added to this colorful account that his regiments had often sung this song but, after the battle, never again. The Thirtieth USCT's regimental commander wrote that when he briefed his officers about the plan they had made light of the possibility that the rebels would execute them for leading black troops. Uniformly, these company officers had told the soldiers themselves that they should remember Fort Pillow. This was done not to arouse them not to give quarter but, rather, to impress on them that defeat and capture meant death, as it had for the troops at Pillow. He did not say, however, whether these briefings made the men more anxious or more warlike.[11]

Other preparations for the attack were also under way, particularly to take care of heavy expected casualties. An officer of a Maine regiment, who was himself seriously wounded the following morning, described the scene: "A large number of surgeons arrived from City Point to render their assistance; amputating tables and bandages seemed to be the order of the day among the surgeons. Near our brigade quartermaster's tent could be seen a wagon with picks and shovels to be used in burying the dead." In the Twenty-ninth U.S. Colored Infantry these matters might have seemed far away from the regimental camp. Surgeon Mackay ate supper the evening of 29 July with Colonel Bross and other officers. He reported that all were relatively calm, though they were facing an uncertain tomorrow. Bross, for reasons not explained, had shaved his full beard, leaving a "Burnside cut"—a shaved chin and what are now known as sideburns. Bross was also in full lieutenant colonel's uniform for the first time, his baggage having just arrived. Four officers not yet commissioned or mustered in asked to go into battle, and Bross accepted this courageous offer. Three of the four, future lieutenants Ferguson, Hassler, and one other not identified, were among the few regimental officers not killed or wounded in the engagement. Bross had, in all, Major Brown and eleven company-grade officers, plus the unmustered volunteers.[12]

THE CRATER BATTLE

It was a short night; the regiments were awakened at 3 A.M. and issued a breakfast of raw salt pork and coffee, after which they waited. The mine was due to be exploded at 3:30, but nothing happened. Grant was ready to order Burnside to attack anyway, but Colonel Pleasants's men discovered a faulty fuse, which they repaired at great personal hazard. At 4:44 the four-ton charge went off with a tremendous roar, throwing huge chunks of the clay-like soil into the air, along with a battery of Confederate field guns and scores of rebel soldiers. This was followed by concentrated fire from all the artillery that the Union army could bring to bear on the rebels in the area, 164 guns. There was some understandable confusion caused by the noise of the explosion and artillery barrage among First Division soldiers ready to leave the Union trenches, but by 5 A.M. Colonel Marshall gave the order to climb over the parapet. Few ladders and other equipment had been brought forward to the frontline trenches, however, so the troops improvised their exit. With difficulty, and the help of sandbag steps and bayonets stuck into the logs lining the trench fronts, Ledlie's men climbed out and began the advance. Formation of battle lines was difficult because Burnside had decided that clearing various obstructions in front of Union lines, abatis, chevaux-de-frise, and wire, might alert the enemy and would not be a serious obstacle to his infantry, so the brigade's regiments moved in groups, each finding its own way forward, rather than in a broad front. The advance also went more slowly than it should have because of obstructions, no easy ways out of the trenches, and narrow, restricted approaches to the front line. General Bartlett's brigade followed Marshall's, virtually unopposed by the Confederates, who were still in shock. Reaching the crater, both brigades bunched on the right, some occupying deserted rebel positions, but most could not resist seeing and entering the crater that measured fifty to sixty yards long, twenty yards wide, and ten to fifteen yards deep. A rebel officer wrote that the soldiers, "with the stupidity of sheep, followed their bellwethers into the crater itself." No immediate attempt was made by the mingled and disorganized regiments to go on to Cemetery Hill, a little more than five hundred yards distant, but Ledlie's brigade commanders had not been told that was the division's primary objective. The other two white divisions followed within fifteen or twenty minutes, channeled by uncleared Union and Confederate obstructions along the same paths taken by Ledlie's division. The divisions attempted to protect the flanks according to plan, but many of the men were also drawn to the crater.[13]

The Twenty-ninth and its sister regiments had been arranged in four-abreast columns from 4 A.M. and continued to wait in this formation for several hours at the head of covered trenches connecting the rear of the railway embankment with the forward positions, while the rest of the corps was engaged. The plan for the Fourth Division to follow close behind the other divisions was delayed because of limited access to the front. It was impossible to advance because of by now heavy Confederate artillery fire and the inadequate capacity of the protected "covered ways" to the front line. These passages allowed men to move without being exposed to fire, but they had to handle two-way traffic. By now returning wounded and panicked unwounded soldiers from the white divisions, some accompanying Confederate prisoners, were causing congestion. A wounded white sergeant being carried past the waiting black troops told them to go in "with a will. . . . There's enough of you to eat 'em all up." A black is said to have replied, "Dat may be all so, boss; but the fac' is, we habn't got jis de bes' kind ob an appetite for 'em dis mornin'."[14]

Burnside was meanwhile receiving battle reports from aides, and, despite his orders to the commanders of his three engaged divisions to move their units out of the crater, his influence on the fighting was small. Meade, who was kept informed partly by Burnside and partly by his own aides on the scene, gave what Burnside said later were "preemptory orders" to "throw in all my troops and direct them against the crest [Cemetery Hill]." Burnside, however, thought it was too late to send in the Fourth Division because of crowding in the approaches to the front line and in the vicinity of the crater itself, but he obeyed the order at 6:00 A.M. It was not until 8:00, however, that the Fourth Division was able to join the battle, Ferrero explaining that his troops were blocked by other units, and by then the affair was going very badly.[15]

If the battle plan was failing almost from the start, it was not apparent to the Confederates. Brig. Gen. William Mahone, commanding a division behind the line, wrote later that the Union army was on the edge of success:

> If the mine . . . had been followed up by a vigorous attacking column . . . it may not be too much to say that the retreat would have been unavoidable and most likely on the order of d——l take the hindmost. After the explosion there was nothing on the Confederate side to prevent the orderly projection of any column through the breach that had been effected, cutting the Confederate army in twain, rendering the rescue of its artillery quite impossible, the retirement of its infantry, now in the trenches, to chance, and opening wide the gates to the rear of the Confederate Capitol.

In other words, Confederate secondary defenses behind the front line which worried Meade and other reserves did not exist. Furthermore, "at least three hundred yards of our lines were deserted by their defenders, and left at the mercy of the attacking column." The Union objective was in reach, but the condition of an "orderly projection" was already impossible. It was obvious to Mahone that the rebel army faced a large force—he counted eleven flags at the crater's edge—so he ordered his two brigades forward and sent for others.[16]

The First Division's initial muddle, its troops moving into the crater and vacant Confederate works to the right of it, was not easily corrected because Brig. Gen. Stephen Elliott Jr.'s South Carolina brigade slowly recovered fighting capabilities after the initial shock of the explosion under some of its positions and brought the Union troops under increasingly heavy fire. Although rebel infantry was not able to counterattack immediately, Confederate artillery was, the first guns being brought to bear on the crater and approaches to it only a half-hour after the explosion. General Ledlie, however, was not on the scene to reorganize his units because he remained in a protected bombproof shelter, the Third Division's medical station well behind the Union front line, for the first four or five hours of the battle. Furthermore, he persuaded the surgeon at that position to provide him with "stimulants" in the form of rum. Ledlie told the doctor that he was suffering from malaria and, at some time during the action, added that he had been hit by a spent musket ball. According to the surgeon, Ferrero also got "some stimulants." All the regiments, brigades, and divisions, confined to a relatively small area, were hopelessly mixed and confused. Officers on the scene, such as Colonel Marshall and General Bartlett, tried without success to reorganize and continue the advance. One participant in the battle summed up the situation: "For the ground covered, there were too many Generals and by far too many men."[17]

The Fourth Division, the corps' only remaining resource, was still stuck in Union lines two and a half hours after the action began. Although division commander Ferrero's orders were to "advance at all hazards, and if necessary lead them [the Fourth Division] in person," he had decided that his presence on the field was unnecessary and had joined Ledlie in the bunker about half an hour after the mine explosion. The Thirtieth U.S. Colored Infantry, First Brigade, led the Fourth Division's tardy assault, running across the hundred and fifty yards of relatively open ground toward the crater, taking immediate casualties from rebel rifle and cannon fire. Following were the Forty-third, Thirty-ninth, and Twenty-seventh Regiments, in that order. According to one eyewitness: "[the] colored division moved out from our works in fine order, which promised us success. Growlers were put to shame, and then most of the [white] men fell into line, to go forward. Some few declared that they would never follow 'niggers' or be caught in their company, and started back to our lines but were promptly driven forward again." Sgt. Harry Reese, who had spliced the faulty fuse earlier in the action, also observed the long-delayed charge of the Fourth Division: "It made me frantic to see the useless destruction; and when the assault had failed, it made me still more furious to see a division of colored soldiers rushed into the jaws of death with no prospect of success; but they went in cheering as though they didn't mind it, and a great many of them never came back."[18]

The black regiments, under fire for the first time, also felt the lure of the crater. General Bartlett succeeded in diverting some of the leading Thirtieth Regiment into a honeycomb of Confederate rifle pits, entrenchments, and covered ways toward the right, but most of the men mixed with the white troops sheltered in the pit. Confederates reported shouts of "Remember Fort Pillow!" as the Thirtieth and Forty-third Regiments advanced. Those units of the First Brigade which heard and obeyed the order to disperse captured about two hundred Confederate troops in the enemy's works near the crater. Some rebels fled the assault by the blacks, a Confederate captain explaining "that we could not expect the sons of Southern gentlemen to fight 'niggers.'" A Union officer wrote that rebels were told by their major that they should "die," rather than run, "but never surrender to niggers," the black troops bayonetting the holdouts. Another said that the black soldiers, "thinking of Fort Pillow," had "a half determination . . . to kill them [the prisoners] as fast as they came to them," but were prevented by their officers.[19]

The Second Brigade had followed the First closely, the Thirty-first U.S. Colored Infantry leading the Nineteenth, Twenty-third, Twenty-eighth, and Twenty-ninth Regiments. A First Brigade witness said of the advance:

> We saw the Second Brigade going in fine shape over the line of the First Division, over the bomb-proofs out into the open field on our left and their front. Instantly the batteries on Cemetery Hill and [Capt. Samuel T.] Wright's Battery turned on them, and a sharp infantry fire reached them from the ravine in their front. We could see great gaps made in their lines as the grape tore its way through. They reached a covered way that ran diagonally across the ravine and stayed there.[20]

Apparently, only the Fourth Division followed its orders in its initial advance. The Second Brigade, in particular, was directed toward Cemetery Hill, moving "well closed, perfectly enthusiastic" some distance beyond the crater and in a position to assault the high ground. Company A Musician Sidney Northup wrote of the charge, "It was a memorable sight to see our dusky sons marching to destruction that hot July morning." One of Meade's aides recorded the black "troops would not go up with any spirit at all." A Confederate officer disagreed: "To the credit of the blacks be it said that they advanced in better order and pushed forward farther than the whites." The lead regiment lost most of its officers, and its troops were "mowed down like grass." The first officer casualties of the Twenty-ninth USCT also occurred at this time. Captain Aiken, Company B's commander, was seriously wounded and died two days later, and Captain Flint, commanding Company E, was killed, as were, in Colonel Thomas's words, "hundreds of heroes 'carved in ebony.'" In the face of these serious losses Thomas soon ordered the brigade to scatter and fall back into the First Division's positions forward of the crater.[21] The entire corps was now immobile.

Ferrero forwarded an order from his bunker: "The General commanding directs that you at once charge the battery in front of you." Responding to the order at about 9:15 A.M., Thomas organized part of the Twenty-third, Twenty-eighth, and Twenty-ninth Regiments, placing Lieutenant

Colonel Bross and the Twenty-ninth Regiment in the lead. Accounts of events at this critical moment in the Twenty-ninth USCT's action on 30 July do not provide details about individual officers and soldiers, but casualties associated with the regiment's United States colors were recorded. Customarily carried into battle in the Civil War, they attracted enemy fire.

The best soldiers were usually named color-bearers, and, when they were wounded or killed, others took on the task. Two of the bearers were killed—Cpls. Isaac Stevens and Frederick Bailey, of Companies B and C, respectively—and three others were wounded. Stevens, thirty-eight, had claimed to have been born free in Pennsylvania. Nothing more is known about him. Bailey, seven years younger, left a widow and a minor child or children, but they were not pensioned. Company B Cpl. Joseph Brown was wounded in the right hand and wrist, the damage done by splinters from a shot that hit the flagstaff. Brown's thumb was amputated at City Point hospital, and he was sent on to Alexandria to recuperate. Brown was discharged for disability after some months. He successfully applied for a pension, claiming that his injury did not permit him to reenter his prewar profession of stonecutter. Cpl. John Maxon, Company C, a mature twenty-nine-year-old, was seriously wounded by a rifle ball through the neck. The injury never healed properly, but the soldier was returned to duty anyway. He was bothered by an open wound the rest of his life, and his death certificate says he died of it. The pension bureau did not agree that the fatal abscess was service related, so his widow received a lower pension than she might have. Company C commander Captain Brockway, the fifth man to carry the flag, was severely injured in the ankle, eventually losing his foot. Colonel Bross seized the colors after Brockway fell, Lieutenant Chapman writing, "Standing upon the parapet he said, 'The man who saves these colors shall be promoted.'" He was fatally shot moments later, his last words being, "Forward, my brave boys." Confederate men saw "a gallant Union officer, seizing a stand of colors, [who] leaped upon their breastworks and called upon his men to charge." Another wrote of the gallant colonel who "seized his colors, [and] sprang over the protective ditch," before he was shot down. Despite this heroism by officers and men, the Twenty-ninth Regiment left its colors at the crater, and they did not turn up later in rebel hands.[22]

The troops obeyed Bross's last command, but the timing was bad because, at that moment, "[Col. David A.] Weisiger's Virginians [one of Mahone's brigades], inflamed by reports that the 'nigger' troops facing them were giving whites no quarter, burst screaming out of the ravine that had sheltered them." The brigade had arrived on the field just in time to meet the charge after making its way along covered ways and trenches under heavy federal artillery fire. Confederate Col. Fitz William McMaster, who took command of the wounded Elliott's depleted brigade early in the action, wrote that the blacks were "welcomed into hospitable graves at 9 o'clock A.M., At about 9:30 A.M., Old Virginia [Weisiger's brigade] with eight hundred heroes rushed into the trench . . . and slaughtered hundreds of whites and blacks, with decided preference for the Ethiopians." The shock of the counterattack was too much for the Second Brigade; a ragged First Brigade charge had just minutes before been repulsed. Hit by the enemy, Thomas's command was "after a struggle driven back over our rifle pits. At this moment a panic commenced. The black and white troops came pouring back together." Thomas claimed that one group of black soldiers did not break and continued fighting until he ordered the men back. A First Brigade officer wrote, "Looking to the left we saw the Second Brigade coming back faster than it went over, and with it many of the white troops, and between us and them the 14th N.Y.H.A. [New York Heavy Artillery Regiment, fighting as infantry] were stampeding for the Crater like a flock of sheep." The broken three black regiments had carried with them white soldiers of other divisions in positions outside the crater, Weisiger regaining almost all this ground, but he was unable to advance further. This may have partly been because some black soldiers did not follow the lead of their Fourth Division comrades, Burnside recalling, "Some held the pits behind which they had advanced, severely checking the enemy until they [the blacks] were nearly all killed." Whatever rare examples of steadiness under fire in an impossible tactical situation untrained and inexperienced black troops may have demonstrated, one should not have expected them to be more than, as one of their officers said, "wholly unmanageable, and totally demoralized in their defeat." The disorganization was surely increased by rebel soldiers killing blacks after the latter had surrendered. A Confederate wrote of one murder, "It was a brutal, horrible act, and those of use who witnessed it from our position in the trench, a few feet away, could but exclaim: 'That is too bad! It is shocking!'" The incidents were caused, he said, because the rebels "seemed infuriated at the idea of having to fight negroes." "As a forlorn hope, [the Fourth Division] was dispatched to do what the other three had failed to do"; it did what it could without support and finally broke.[23]

The stampede, as it would be called, of the Ninth Corps could not be controlled. Some soldiers ran for the Union lines, their officers unsuccessfully attempting to rally them, and others fled into the crater, where there were already several thousand dead, wounded, and sound soldiers confined in a steep-sided, one-quarter-acre space. A few were observed "running up the gentle slope toward Petersburg, voluntary prisoners." Thomas's brigade, except for about two hundred retreating soldiers, who went into the crater, and much of the Nineteenth Regiment already there, fled all the way to the Union lines, where they were soon reformed behind the front. These troops would take no further part in the battle.[24] The stampede marked the end of organized resistance by Union forces and the beginning of the siege of the crater itself; it did not end for almost five hours.

MOPPING UP

General Grant, who had ridden out to the front line, arriving when the Fourth Division and the others broke, thought the day was lost and told Meade to terminate the engagement. Following up, General Meade sent Burnside another "preemptory order," this time to withdraw his troops from Confederate positions and the crater, giving Burnside discretion about when this should be done so as to preserve lives. Burnside protested the decision, going to Meade's headquarters to plead his case, perhaps thinking that the situation now, despite all evidence, favored the Union forces, but more likely because he was incapable of taking prompt action and also resented being ordered about by his former junior, Meade. Burnside kept up his pressure on Meade until noon, but the latter would not back down. Finally, at 12:20 P.M. Burnside notified his division commanders, not one of whom was actually on the battlefield, and they passed word on to the brigade commanders remaining in and around the crater, leaving it up to them to decide the best time to retreat. The delay had deadly consequences for the Ninth Army Corps.[25]

Only a small number of the troops in the crater could defend themselves from the still limited Confederate attacks, but, aided by Union artillery, they did a good job keeping the rebels at bay. Only those at the lip of the crater, lying nearly vertically on the steep sides, could fire, others below passing up loaded rifles. According to a survivor, "A full line around the crest of the crater were loading and firing as fast as they could, and the men were dropping thick and fast, most of them shot through the head." When the units in advance of the crater broke and ran back, this fire helped slow the Confederate advance and soon stopped it. But for some of the retreating blacks there was no place to go, because, a witness wrote:

> The bravest lost heart, and the men who distrusted the negroes vented their feelings freely. Some colored men came into the crater, and there they found a fate worse than death in the charge. It was believed among the whites that the enemy would give no quarter to negroes or to the whites taken with them, so to be shut up in the crater was equal to a doom of death. It has been positively stated that white men bayoneted blacks who fell back into the crater. This in order to preserve the whites from Confederate vengeance. Men boasted in my presence that blacks had been disposed of, particularly when the Confederates came up.

Another soldier recorded his view of the situation: "Worse still the 13th Indiana white . . . deliberately shot down many of the retreating soldiers. When I say there is a fearful mortality among the dusky heroes you will readily understand how it happened." (The Thirteenth Indiana Infantry was a Tenth Army Corps regiment that had advanced behind the Fourth Division on the right of the crater; some of the black troops retreated over the Thirteenth's position.)[26]

Surgeon H. E. Smith, of the Twenty-seventh Michigan Volunteers, a dispenser of General Ledlie's alcohol during the battle, said Ledlie left his bombproof shelter well behind the Union front line "about the time of the stampede of the darkies," possibly so he could order reorganization of those First Division troops that stampeded with them. Colonel Pleasants wrote that he observed Ledlie at about this time, noted that he was drunk, and called him a coward. As for General Ferrero, Ledlie's companion during the action, no one reported his activities. He himself described the retreat, ending with a comment that the "troops were rallied" at the Union front line, but did not claim a role for himself in the reorganization of his Fourth Division regiments.[27] Although Ledlie and Ferrero would later be singled out—but not uniformly punished—for their actions or lack of them on 30 July, the other two Ninth Corps division commanders, Brig. Gens. Robert B. Potter and Orlando Willcox, never ventured forward of the Union lines either, but they were not criticized.

Confederate attackers were handled severely while clearing their positions of occupying Union troops and pushing survivors back to the crater and were unable to advance without reinforcement. This was coming, as Mahone's call was answered by forces hurrying from other parts of the Confederate line. Arrival of Brig. Gen. Ambrose R. Wright's Georgia Brigade helped to increase pressure on the crater-bound soldiers, closing the circle on all but the rear of the Union positions. Rebel forces were still not sufficiently large to complete the encirclement, and the stalemate continued. In the crater itself conditions rapidly grew more and more intolerable, the day being "fearfully hot." By 10:30 A.M. ammunition and water were running out, and it was impossible to bring up new supplies from Union lines because Confederate artillery could not be silenced by counterbattery fire. In fact, rebel cannon fire increased; two Coehorn mortars arrived and commenced dropping high-angle projectiles into the masses. The mortar shells did not do the damage they might have because they buried themselves in the soft earth in the pit before exploding. A New York newspaper, which early on recognized the engagement for the disaster it was, described the scene in the crater vividly: "[The rebels had time] to train upon the fateful pit all the artillery, to rain into it a fire of musketry, grape and canister, that tore remorselessly, and without the possibility of error of aim, the solid mass of wriggling, heaving, twisting, crawling, helpless soldiers, black and white, that, inextricably intermingled, defied all attempts to tactically extricate them."[28]

Brig. Gen. John C. C. Saunders's Alabama Brigade entered the action and took up positions so close to the crater that the troops "could hear the Yankee officers in the fort trying to encourage their men, telling them among other things to 'remember Fort Pillow.'" The Confederate officer who wrote this explained the meaning of the Pillow reference: "In that fort Forrest's men had found whites and negroes together. History tells what they did for them." At half past twelve, before Burnside's retreat order was received in the crater, Mahone directed a coordinated charge by his brigades, Elliott's Brigade (led by Weisiger), and other troops. This attack put the Confederates on the rim, but they were forced back, digging in a few feet short of the edge. From here they could not fire directly down into the pit but were able to keep the pressure on by such measures as throwing muskets with bayonets into the crater, "harpoon style." Within the crater, an officer wrote:

The white troops were now exhausted and discouraged. Leaving the line, they sat down, facing inwards, and neither threats nor entreaties could get them up into the line again. In vain was the cry raised that all would be killed if captured with negro soldiers; they would not stand up. From this time on the fire was kept up, mainly, by the colored troops, and officers handling muskets. . . . The troops seemed utterly apathetic and indifferent. The killing of a comrade by their very sides would not rouse them in the least.[29]

The Confederate forces prepared for a final assault, their officers' orders being clearly heard in the crater. General Bartlett, the senior Union officer, had considered waiting until nightfall to withdraw, but the situation now did not allow it. He directed surrender of those unable to return to Union lines and told the others to make a run for it in one rush, so as to reduce casualties crossing between the Confederate and Union lines. Retreating forces were to be particularly hard hit because Union artillery had stopped firing on the Confederate batteries and advancing troops, probably because of Meade's order to retreat. Thousands joined in yet another stampede for safety in friendly trenches, and a small number determined to resist. An officer on the scene said that, as the rebels entered the crater, some of them bayoneted wounded blacks, causing other black soldiers to resist. At last Union forces stopped fighting, but rebel killings continued for some time; acoording to one Alabama Brigade officer: "This slaughter would not have been so great had our men not found negro soldiers in the fort with the whites. This was the first time we had met negro troops, and the men were enraged at them for being there and at the whites for having them there." Another wrote, "Our men, inflamed to relentless vengeance by . . . [the] presence [of the blacks], disregarded the rules of warfare which restrained them in battle with their own race, and brained and butchered the blacks until the slaughter was sickening." As might be expected, Southerners did not think the blacks resisted effectively in the last fighting in the crater. When rushed with the bayonet, "they did not show the stubborn power of endurance for which the Anglo-Saxon is preeminent, nor do I believe they ever will in any field." Finally, after a short resistance a thousand whites and blacks surrendered in the crater, but the killing of black soldiers was not yet over.[30]

Company C Pvt. Isaac Gaskins, an eighteen-year-old soldier born in Yazoo County, Mississippi, was liberated by the Union Army and came north as a servant of a Union officer, Lt. Col. John W. Paddock,

113th Illinois Infantry, and he enlisted several months later at Chicago. Gaskins wrote that he was captured unwounded in the battle:

> After I was made a prisoner I was shot by a rebel guard and my cartridge box entirely carried away and my hip severely injured. Just before firing at me he, with an oath, called me a damn nigger, and said if he had known I was a nigger he would have never taken me prisoner, and I had so much of that damn Yankee blood over my face that he couldn't tell what I was. He said he did not recognize any damn negro as a prisoner of war and that I would never get back to my brother Yankees alive.[31]

As it turned out, however, Gaskins survived captivity but not before much hardship and further injury.

A Union colonel came out of a shelter in the crater with a black soldier to surrender: "The negro was touching my side. The rebels were about eight feet from me. They yelled out, 'Shoot the nigger, but don't kill the white man'; and the negro was promptly shot down by my side." Later, as he was being escorted to the rebel rear area, the officer "saw the rebs run up and shoot negro prisoners in front of me. One was shot four times." A Georgia soldier remarked in a letter home, "Some four negroes went to the rear as we could not kill them as fast as they passed me." A Southern soldier thought all blacks "would have been killed if it not been for gen Mahone who beg our men to Spare them." Mahone "told him for God's sake stop," but the soldier replied, "Well gen let me kill one more, whereby he deliberately took out his pocket knife and cut one's throat." Another rebel also credited Mahone with preventing further killing of black prisoners, claiming that his intervention had spared as many as one hundred and fifty of them (but possibly four hundred "wounded and disarmed" blacks "perished by the bayonet"). "I should not have taken any of them," he said, "Especially after they shouted 'No quarter' which they did when they mounted the breastworks." A current historian writes that Mahone's men "privately . . . admitted to having bayoneted men in the act of 0surrender, and they were by no means ashamed of the act, considering their provocation," which he suggests was the mine explosion itself rather than the presence of blacks.[32]

The notion that the blacks somehow brought on their own murders because of their actions and shouts during the initial part of the battle was a prevalent one initially in the South. The Richmond *Daily Dispatch,* for example, described the two charges by blacks: "The Yankee negroes and their white coadjutors came forward, exultant with pride and hope, mainly protected by strong potions of whiskey, crying, 'No quarter! Remember Fort Pillow!' . . . [Bodies showed] how the cry of 'Remember Fort Pillow!' was responded to by our Spartan braves." And a day later the newspaper said blacks were placed in front, "and our men, enraged by the cry of 'No quarter,' slaughtered them like sheep. Comparatively few were taken prisoner, while hundreds were slain." A Virginia Brigade veteran recalled years later that his comrades "spared the white men as best they could, but negro skulls cracked under the blows like eggshells. They begged pitifully for their lives, but the answer was, 'No quarter this morning, no quarter now.'" A Petersburg newspaper more clearly associated the cries of blacks on the charge with their subsequent murders, saying "this favorite arm of the Yankee army is no match for Confederate soldiers. The negroes rushed wildly forward immediately after the explosion, with the cry of '*no quarter.'*—At a later hour of the day, the time for the Confederates came, and our brave boys took them at their word and gave them what they had so loudly called for—'*no quarter.*'" The *Daily Richmond Enquirer,* printing the Petersburg paper's account, affirmed that no quarter had been given and noted that General Mahone, "sickened at the spectacle, . . . ordered the work of death to cease." In an editorial the same day the *Enquirer* blamed Grant: "His war cry of 'No quarter,' shouted by his negro soldiers, was returned with interest, we regret as not as heavily as ought to have been the case, since some negroes were captured instead of being shot." The writer said blacks were dangerous because they would, if they had the chance, kill Confederate wounded, so Mahone should not have stopped the murders, concluding:

> We beg him [Mahone], hereafter, when negroes are sent forward to murder the wounded, and come shouting "no quarter," shut your eyes, General, strengthen your stomach with a little brandy and water, and let the work, which God has entrusted to you and your brave men, go forward to its full completion; that is, until every negro has been slaughtered.—Make every salient you are called upon to defend, a Fort Pillow; butcher every negro that Grant sends against your brave troops, and permit them not to soil their hands with the capture of a single negro.

Northern newspapers were curiously silent about these atrocities, the *Army and Navy Journal* commenting mildly, "What treatment the black soldiers received from the victors, there is too much conflicting testimony to determine."[33]

COUNTING THE COST

Seventy-nine officers of all four divisions were captured by the Confederates, and those among them who led black troops no doubt expected to be executed for that association as the rebel government had ordered. Consequently, many concealed their correct regimental number. Two Thirtieth U.S. Colored Infantry lieutenants, however, "decided to face the music," gave their regiment, and "saw the words 'Negro officer' written opposite [their] names." A Confederate soldier wrote that some white officers had torn off their shoulder straps designating rank, "so we should not recognize them as officers; but the fresh marks showed plainly on their sun-burned jackets." An officer "nearly scared the life out of them by standing them apart from the negroes, and impressing the fact upon them that they were to swing instanter. How they begged!— and, without exception, said 'they had been forced in; they could not avoid commanding the blacks,' and all that. They were sent to the Libby [prison in Richmond]." There is no evidence, however, that these USCT officers were treated significantly different from other officers, at least after a time. They were publicly humiliated, however, the rebels marching the prisoners through Petersburg, General Bartlett on a horse (he had lost a leg in an earlier battle), "without saddle; then four wounded negroes, stripped of everything but shirt and drawers; then four officers," and so on. Black prisoners were first "corralled at Poplar Lawn in Petersburg," where some of them were claimed by their former owners. The Confederates at first confined black soldiers with white officers and men, a newspaper remarking, "Our authorities will not be so cruel as to separate such bosom and deeply sympathizing friends in their captivity." While the Confederates no doubt thought they were humiliating the officers, the action was the cause of hardship and, as some claimed afterward, unnecessary death and suffering. A captured and later paroled surgeon reported that Brig. Gen. Henry A. Wise, commanding the First Military District, ordered crowding of wounded white soldiers in prison, not all officers, between wounded blacks against the advice of doctors, "a cause of destroying the life of our soldiers." One of the captured officers explained why he thought that Union army outrage was not apparent; a majority of officer prisoners from white regiments, he said, "would have been glad to see the officers of the Fourth Division hanged or shot, if thereby they could be relieved from the terrible humiliation of marching through Petersburg with negro soldiers." He went on to say that the bad feeling inspired by "deep-seated hatred and prejudice" continued for a long time in prison camps.[34]

The day after the battle Ferrero reported casualties of over sixteen hundred officers and men, of which just over half were listed as missing. Obviously, there was something wrong with the preliminary count, and it would take some time before the numbers could be verified and many of the missing moved to the killed column. In addition, the numbers of wounded were undercounted because records of such matters were kept at several treatment points and were often incomplete. Ferrero's reported Twenty-ninth USCT casualties were probably those forwarded by the regiment, and they were undoubtedly wrong, because most of the company officers were incapacitated as a consequence of the battle. His numbers for the Twenty-ninth Infantry were one officer and eleven men killed, eight officers and thirty-nine men wounded and two officers and eighty-six men missing. Illinois newspapers reported the battle but did not make prominent mention of the state's regiment's role in it. One journal did say of the Twenty-ninth USCT that it was "of Chicago (Colonel John A. Bross, commanding), eight officers and about 275 men killed, wounded and missing." It was not immediately known that Colonel Bross was dead, William Bross in Chicago being notified as late as 2 August that "I could not learn positively that your brother, Colonel Bross, was among the captured. He may have been killed in the heroic charge he led, but I believe not." Later the same day, however, Lieutenant Gosper, who may have been slightly wounded early in the battle, also wired William Bross: "Colonel John A. Bross is dead and buried inside the picket line." In addition to Capts. William H. Flint and Aiken also killed in action or dead from wounds, almost every other officer was wounded, some seriously, except Major Brown and the not-yet-commissioned lieutenants. Brown, who was now regimental commander, was not available for full service because during the battle he was partially paralyzed from sunstroke, and the junior officers departed for their homes to wait for their commissions. Captain Brockway, who was to lose a foot, did not return to the regiment, but others with serious injuries did, including Captain Daggett (hip wound) and newly promoted Captain Knapp (back injury). Captain Porter was wounded in the leg, but he neglected to seek treatment for three days because he was preoccupied helping to reorganize the shattered regiment.

Porter was cared for off and on by Dr. Mackay over the next six months, but he was in discomfort for the rest of his days. Others with slight wounds—Chapman, William W. Flint, and Gale—were all apparently granted leave. Soon brigade commander Thomas turned to Ferrero for assistance, because "the 29th U.S.C.T. is now without an officer, and [I] would ask if three or four of the officers who report for duty to the 43d to-day cannot be assigned, temporarily, to this (29th) regiment." Five lieutenants were loaned to the Twenty-ninth Infantry on 3 August, one of them acting as commanding officer, and later that month Lt. Col. Charles E. Wright, of the Thirty-ninth USCT, was temporarily detailed to command the regiment, allowing Major Brown, being unfit for duty, to go to his home on leave. Wright, however, stayed only a few days, being replaced on 15 September by the partly recovered Captain Porter.[35]

Although the enlisted men of the regiment had suffered equally in the battle, unlike the officers, not many of them were furloughed. A large number were taken from the battle line field aid stations to what was termed a hospital for black troops at the nearby major support base at City Point, and many were sent on to Fort Monroe, Portsmouth, Alexandria, Philadelphia, and other general hospitals. An officer visiting two days after the attack wrote, "I was over at the Hospital of the 4' (Colored) Division, of 9' Corps—There had come in between 600 & 700 wounded—They bear their wounds & pain very patiently." He also said he sent "a Mrs. Moore & her daughter professing to belong to the Sanitary Commission" to help the black wounded and sick. A physician on the scene called conditions appalling. "It was . . . in no sense a hospital," he said, "than it was a depot for wounded men," where "mortality was frightfully large." The doctor worked with a remarkable young woman from Massachusetts, Helen L. Gilson, who had begun in June to organize, with little official recognition, a "modern hospital for the colored troops" and for the army's black washerwomen and families of black soldiers. Miss Gilson accomplished a great deal at City Point with very little assistance but could not do much to reduce the death rate.[36]

Resistance in the crater and a few close-by trenches ended about 3:30 P.M. on the day of the attack, but the suffering by the wounded not returned to Union lines did not. The Confederates may have left some seriously injured black troops, who had survived the killing just after surrender, in the crater and elsewhere within rebel lines to die. Hundreds of other Union soldiers had been shot down between the lines in the advance and several retreats. Burnside estimated that a hundred of these—badly wounded and incapable of helping themselves—were stranded beyond the reach of the Union forces. A local truce was requested after the battle so that the wounded could be assisted and recovered, but the Confederates refused this normally granted request, bucking the question to General Lee in Richmond. An officer in a white regiment explained what might have been the reason for the newly rigid policy: "A 'flag of truce' was sent out this AM to exchange wounded prisoners with the Johnnies and they drove it back. All on account of the 'darkies.'" The following day, while awaiting Lee's answer, some assistance was given to the wounded by the Union party parlaying with Confederate officers, but it did not go "beyond supplying water and whisky to the wounded between the lines, and passing whisky in to our wounded in their lines." A four-hour armistice was agreed upon for early morning, 1 August, but by then most of the suffering was over, and the wounded, except for a handful, were dead from wounds, heat, thirst, and further gunfire. Colonel Thomas described the scene that morning; long rows of bodies were laid out by work parties. "There is no distinction in color now. The Virginia summer sun has shone two days on these brave men and has turned them all a purplish black." A Confederate soldier wrote, "A long trench was dug in front equidistant between our works and the enemy's, and the negro prisoners were made to carry the dead bodies to the trench and throw them in." The burial pits—there were two of them—each forty yards long and ten feet deep and wide, were filled close to the top with dead "thrown in indiscriminately." Use of black captives for this burial work (and to repair rebel works) was seen by an aide of General Meade as "meanly employing" them, but no protest is known to have been made.[37]

From the perspectives of rebel and Union officers the burial operation took on some aspects of an outing. Ferrero, Potter, and Brig. Gen. Julius White, Burnside's acting chief of staff, were said by a Confederate to be "very courteous and chatty, and brought out buckets of lemonade and other refreshments in profusion." Not all Confederates had the same view: one Union officer offering to introduce a Confederate officer to Ferrero was told that "we down South were not in the habit of recognizing as our social equals those who associated with negroes." Colonel Thomas, commander of the Second Brigade, disguised himself in a private soldier's coat and a broad-brimmed straw hat and, posing as a member of the Christian Commission, which was gathering the dead, set out during the truce to inspect Confederate positions. He was arrested and brought to the local Confederate commander's headquarters, where he admitted he was a colonel, worrying about whether he would be shot for leading black troops. He was released the next morning, his adventure a farcical footnote to the tragedy.[38]

The body count between the lines on 1 August was reported as 180 blacks and 155 whites. In the crater itself the reoccupying rebels reported that they buried 54 blacks and 178 whites during their late 31 July cleanup, exclusive of burials in trenches. Confederate corps commander Ambrose P. Hill, in his 30 July report of the action to Secretary of War James A. Seddon in Richmond, claimed 74 officers and 855 enlisted men captured and said 500 of the enemy were killed in the trenches, but it is unclear if the latter number included the crater itself. These reports total about 1,100 killed, which is probably accurate and does not include a significant number who died later.[39]

In all the Ninth Corps lost 3,828 officers and men killed, wounded, and missing, about 20 percent of the force engaged, but a disproportionate share of these casualties, almost 35 percent, were in the Fourth Division. Black regiments had 209 killed, 697 wounded, and 421 missing when the counts were remade after the war to account for those who had died of wounds or in rebel hands; the source gives counts of 21, 56, and 47 in the same categories for the Twenty-ninth U.S. Colored Infantry. Another source claims twice as many officers and men in the Fourth Division were casualties, making their total more than that of all three white divisions. After the war 669 bodies of white and black soldiers were found buried on the battlefield (and another twenty-nine in 1931), close to the highest estimates of whites and blacks killed, probably because many reported missing were actually slain in the action but were not immediately identified. Of course, many others died of wounds and in rebel prison camps. Whatever the correct numbers, even the low counts, "to anyone familiar with the extent of regimental losses in action, . . . tell a heroic story."[40]

The Twenty-ninth Regiment's morning reports should indicate casualties, but the records are incomplete, partly because of officer losses in the battle and also because paperwork was not kept current at the front. Information on Companies B and D is the only contemporary battle count surviving, and it does not agree with other records, probably because of uncertainties concerning missing soldiers just after the battle. Company B reported four killed, ten wounded, and six missing and that seventy men and one officer were present for duty. Actually, eight men had been killed, the extra four perhaps explained by wounded who died shortly after. In addition to Captain Aiken and color-bearer Stevens, Cpl. Jesse Crawford and Pvts. James Green, William Lee, George Simpson, Jordan Stewart, and James Watts were the casualties. Simpson was known to have died on the battlefield; Sgt. William Alexander certified that he was with Simpson when he was shot and that he had "held his hand until he died." The soldier was Missouri born but was living in 1858 in Chicago, where he married. His widow was pensioned at once because a marriage between blacks in Illinois was recorded. Watts, a former Virginia slave, was likewise married in Illinois. He left a widow with four children born between 1856 and 1863. While the widow Watts should have also been speedily pensioned, the award was delayed because she thought her husband had been killed at Vicksburg. Another man, Richmond-born Pvt. Edward Carter, age twenty-four, who enlisted in the regiment at White House Landing in June but was not mustered in until two days before the battle, was reported killed. He turned up at war's end, having been a Confederate prisoner of war. Taken to Fort Monroe hospital to recover, he was discharged there in April 1865, "under special circumstances," his "services no longer being required." Another of the early Virginia recruits, Pvt. John Datson, was also thought missing in action, but he was returned at the end of the war. Datson was mustered in by Captain Flint on 28 July at the front before Petersburg, so, like Carter, he too was officially a soldier only two days before his capture. Born in Caroline County, Virginia, twenty years before his army service, Darson was likely a former slave. Major Brown declared him dead a few days after the action at the crater, but he was later carried on company rolls as absent without leave. This was resolved on 23 May 1865 after he rejoined the regiment. Sgt. Rodney Long was wounded in the foot and left behind on the battlefield. He was captured, imprisoned at Danville, and exchanged in March 1865. Records of wounded are not complete, but Pvt. Nathan Hughes was seriously injured, and Pvt. Henry B. Carter spent several months in the hospital recovering from unspecified wounds. These men were former slaves from Kentucky and Missouri, respectively. Private Griffin, the Ohio-born soldier, was also a casualty, his a rather unusual problem: he was hospitalized in Philadelphia for what he called "fatigues, nerves and everything unstrung."[41]

Unlike any of the other five companies, only Company B had its full complement of officers on 30 July. The company reported one officer present the following day, but it is uncertain who this could have been. The commanding officer was dead, and the first and second lieutenants,

William B. Gale and Frederick A. Chapman, both mustered in on 22 July, were wounded. Gale went home to New Hampshire on 4 August on a twenty-day sick leave, complaining that he was disabled by a concussion of the brain and spine which had left him partially paralyzed. He never returned to the regiment, resigning his commission in the middle of September. The lightly wounded Chapman was appointed acting regimental adjutant from 30 July. The officer on hand might have been acting lieutenant Michael J. Hassler, the Missourian waiting for his officer's appointment, who went into action with the company and emerged uninjured, but he soon went home to await commissioning and do some further recruiting.[42]

Company D's after-action morning report shows one killed, ten wounded, and seven missing among the eighty men in the action. Only Cpl. George Asher was mortally wounded on 30 July, but one of the injured, Sgt. Michael D. Duffin, died of loss of blood and infection at L'Overture Hospital in Alexandria on 30 August. His knee had been severely damaged by a gunshot, and his leg was amputated from the lower third of his thigh, presumably at the field hospital or City Point. Duffin, only twenty years old at his death, was born free in Ogle County, Illinois. His father, with whom he had worked sawing wood near Galena for two years before enlistment, had been a slave of Denny Wagoner, Boonsboro, Maryland, but had gone to Illinois—escaped or freed—in 1838. Duffin's father asked for a pension on grounds that his son had given his father his earnings before the war and had promised to send half of his army pay home. The father said that the sergeant did not remit money, though he wrote several letters promising that he would. Although those letters had been lost, the father was pensioned.[43]

Eight—not the preliminary count's seven—were missing in action, but only one, Cpl. Thomas H. Burnett, was exchanged late in the war. Burnett, age twenty-one, a waiter born in Galena, Illinois, and living in Oshkosh, Wisconsin, suffered a serious gunshot wound in the shoulder before his capture, and he later claimed a saber wound on his back and said that he had been struck on the head with a rifle by a rebel soldier. After exchange, he was sent from Camp Parole, the recuperation center near Annapolis, to St. Louis but was somehow left by the train at Grafton and went on to Wheeling, Columbus, and finally Cincinnati. There he was hospitalized for seven weeks. Released, he went to Chicago on furlough but, when he was due to return, missed his train and lost his ticket and papers. The provost marshal returned him to the regiment under arrest, but he was not punished. One soldier is known to have died in rebel hands, but the other six missing men were left dead on the battlefield or were killed after they surrendered. One of them, Pvt. Joseph W. Jordan, an eighteen-year-old former Maryland slave, had less than three weeks' service when he was killed, having enlisted at Cold Harbor on 8 July. The other missing later declared dead were Pvts. Shedrick Boston, thirty-six, born in Kentucky; Charles Green, eighteen, from Missouri; John Maloney, twenty-five, from Kentucky; Charles Sidnor, forty, from Virginia; Jackson Summerfield, thirty, from Missouri; and Charles Williams, twenty-two, from Mississippi. Boston, who had lived in Missouri most of his life, was a slave of John G. B. Geery, of Ralls County, and had been married by a slave minister at his master's farm in 1850. Because such unions were not recorded in Missouri before the war, Boston's widow had to prove she had lived with the soldier as his wife. Gerry, the slaves' owner, helped her by providing a deposition. Such assistance by former masters to freed slaves was not unprecedented, but it was certainly not common. Furthermore, the deposition was not written until 1872, well after the war. Green left a mother and a father at Quincy, but the couple had been separated by slavery in Palmyra, Missouri, before the war. A pension examiner explained the breakup as caused "by being sent to different sections, the father yielding the children to the mother and finally abandoning her and their support." Green's mother received one letter from him in 1864 reporting that he had been in a battle but was unharmed. The soldier was captured at the crater, and he died in rebel hands at Hospital 21 in Richmond on 3 November 1864; the cause of death was shown as chronic diarrhea but was probably dysentery. Green's mother received his three hundred dollar bounty and back pay, but the still estranged father was pensioned in 1892. Summerfield left a widow and three children at New London, Missouri, where he had been a slave. No record was found showing he had been captured, so he was one of the unknown dead on the battlefield.[44]

Captain Knapp, the only Company D officer in the action, said he had been knocked down by a shell at the crater and had been trampled by his own men in the stampede. His spine was injured, "paralyzing lower extremity of body." Knapp was treated by Dr. Mackay for four months for "paralysis of bladder, resulting in incontinence of urine," and he was discharged for the disability in March 1865. He was not pensioned for this but did receive eight dollars and fifty cents monthly for loss of a toe in June 1863 at Vicksburg, when he was an enlisted man in an Illinois regiment. Of probably a half-dozen other wounded, only one, Sgt. Levi Marlow, seems to have had critical injuries, chest and thigh gunshot wounds, spending the next sixteen months in the L'Overture Hospital in Alexandria. His pension was three dollars monthly from the date of discharge.[45]

Casualties in Company A were particularly heavy. Four men were known to have been killed on 30 July, but eleven were missing in action and a large but indeterminate number wounded. The known dead were early enlistee Richard Lewis and Pvts. James Lancaster, James Markell, and Thomas Thornton. Kentucky-born Lancaster was thirty-five when he died. He had been the slave of James H. C. Phillips in Canton, Missouri, who was paid the bounty when his slave entered the army. Thornton was at first thought to be missing but was very soon declared dead, perhaps because his body was identified or fellow soldiers certified his death. He left a wife and child, who were pensioned as of 30 July. Twenty-year-old Markell was a slave freed shortly before the war and was working as a laborer at Palmyra, Missouri, before enlistment. His dependent mother was pensioned. Thornton, age thirty-five, had been a slave of Caleb Taylor in Marion County, Missouri, who was paid the bounty. Thornton had no apparent survivors.[46]

Pvts. Charles Allen and John Brown took different paths to the regiment, were captured together, and, finally, were linked posthumously. First thought to have been killed at the crater, Allen, forty-one, died on 20 January 1865 of what was described as dropsy in the rebel prison at Farmville, Virginia. Brown, twenty-five, was also first reported missing but died in a Richmond prison—probably of poor treatment—in October 1864. Although both had been slaves in Missouri, they were from different parts of that state and did not enlist at the same time. Thirty years after the war Allen's aged mother, Martha Harris, applied for a survivor pension, but a rival claim was made by a Charlotta Allen, also representing herself as the soldier's mother. The conflicting claims delayed matters somewhat, but the second claimant was found to have applied also for a pension as the needy mother of Private Brown. Reaching the conclusion that Harris had the legitimate case, her claim would have been honored but for another complication—a deposition from Sergeant Perkins, who said that Allen did not die in the war but was murdered afterward by bushwhackers at Palmyra. Other soldiers disputed Perkins's information; former Company A Pvt. George Morgan said he did not hear of such an ambush, and Daniel Parker, a former soldier of the Thirteenth U.S. Colored Infantry, who was apparently a prisoner too, certified that Harris had died at Farmville. Mrs. Harris was finally pensioned in 1894, but Brown has no pension file, so the allegation that Charlotta Allen applied as his mother is unsupported. Two soldiers, both among the company's first enlistees, Jesse Hazell, promoted to first sergeant in place of promoted William McCoslin five days before the battle, and Pvt. George Washington, were prisoners but were exchanged late in the war. Hazell was wounded when captured and may have been wounded again while, he said, trying to escape from a rebel work detail. After exchange he returned to duty in the company and finished the war as first sergeant. He was later pensioned for a gunshot wound in his right arm. Washington was turned over to Union forces at North Ferry, North Carolina, in March 1865; from there he was sent to Annapolis and then to Benton Barracks in St. Louis, Missouri. Washington was hospitalized with typhoid in the U.S. Marine Hospital at St. Louis until he left without permission for Quincy. He was not missed by the army until he wrote to military officials in Illinois asking for back pay and a discharge certificate. This triggered an investigation to determine if Washington should be tried for desertion; he was found not guilty of that offense "but guilty of absence without leave from October 2/65 to Mch 30/66, the date of his application for muster out." Because the board found Washington to be confused about his status and generally ignorant about procedures, the sentence was mild. He received no pay for the period he was absent. The former soldier likely died soon after this, and no pension application was made by survivors.[47]

Two of Company A's first sixteen enlistees, Anthony Dudley and Andrew Lewis, died "of cruel treatment" at the Danville, Virginia, prison within two days of each other in early November. Pvt. Ransom Green, a thirty-three-year-old Missourian, also died at the same time and place, his death attributed to "bad treatment." Pvt. Edward A. Dyer died "of starvation" at Salisbury, North Carolina, six months after his capture. He had enlisted from Frankfort, Pike County, Missouri, where he and his wife were slaves of William Pitt. Pitt had purchased Dyer (for $920) in Virginia in 1856. His wife and two minor children received a pension in 1866. Another casualty of bad treatment was Pvt. George Jamison, who succumbed at Farmville in January. Just eighteen when he died, the Kentucky-born soldier had been the slave of John Roth, of Roselea, Missouri.[48]

Pvt. George Williams, a Missouri-born former slave, was married in Quincy a month after his enlistment in December 1863. He died at Richmond in Confederate hands in January, leaving his widow, Mildred, and a young daughter who were living in Melrose, Illinois. Louis Williams, no relation to the other man, was thought to have been born free at Chicago, but very little more is known about him. He died a prisoner on 10 August, ten days after the battle, probably of wounds received in the engagement. Finally, Pvt. Peter Corsey, another of the first enlistees, may have been the twelfth Company A soldier to be captured. He said that he escaped from the rebels a few days later, but he may have just made his way back to Union lines from the battlefield. The army had no record of this claim.[49]

As might be expected, the number of Company A wounded was proportionally large, but only the more disabling injuries are found in soldiers' military records. In the quest for pensions many former soldiers reported being wounded and even disabled, and sometimes the pension bureau approved awards based on examination of these claims by a doctor. Some claims were found fraudulent, such as that of Pvt. John W. Logan. The army found that Logan was unwounded at the crater but that the injury he presented was caused by him accidentally cutting off his finger with an ax while building a mud chimney when the regiment was in winter quarters in early 1865. The Kentucky-born former slave of Elizabeth Hunter was living in Paris, Missouri, when he ran off to the army at Quincy. Logan went back to Quincy after the war and was eventually pensioned for the effects of sunstroke in the summer of 1864. A soldier with truly disabling wounds was Cpl. William Millander, a freeborn Chicagoan, whose shoulder wound was too severe to allow further service, and he was pensioned as three-quarters disabled for work. Pvt. Sandy Johnson's record shows he was seriously injured at the crater, a shell explosion damaging his left shoulder, side, arm, and fingers. Many years after the war he asked for a pension based on these injuries, but it was denied. The regiment's mustering out records show him as "absent without leave since October 19th 1865—no discharge furnished." The soldier apparently deserted the company and was never apprehended and punished. He ultimately received a discharge dated the day he left, probably under one of a number of postwar amnesties, but he was never pensioned.[50]

A number of Company A soldiers said they had been trampled in one of the stampedes on 30 July, but none of them could make a plausible case of injury. Of somewhat more merit are the wound claims of other men, but a number of them are suspect, and the records of others are incomplete. Pvt. Harrison Doolin, born at Hannibal, Missouri, a slave of Harriet Halsey, was married in 1863 at age eighteen. He said he was wounded in the groin by a bayonet thrust while engaged in carrying off the wounded during the crater battle. The pension bureau accepted this, even though Doolin claimed that his only witness—another soldier whom he could not name—had been killed in the action. Pvt. Thomas Fonsey, one of the trampled soldiers, also claimed a gunshot wound in the side, and indeed the army thought he was in the hospital until September. Fonsey, a native of Nashville, Tennessee, was a slave owned by Dr. Jacob Tipton of Philadelphia, Missouri. He never applied for a pension, but his widow and two children did—not, however, until 1910. While the widow Fonsey's claim is not unusual, the fact that it was still being considered in 1916 is. Furthermore, she was able to get depositions from ten of her husband's former comrades, all of them well along in years. Sergeant Hazell, for example, was a hundred years old. Other wounded with weak claims to verified injuries were Pvt. Benjamin Franklin, unspecified; Cpl. James H. Rickman, head and leg gunshot wounds and trampled; Pvt. Daniel Rogers, trampled; Pvt. Robert Smith, unspecified; Sgt. William South, gunshot wound in shin; and Cpl. George M. Washington, flesh wounds head, wrist, arm, and heel. Pvt. Martin Magruder, was injured in the foot in the battle, but the wound may not have been serious. He developed some complications and was sent in mid-August to Summit House General Hospital in Philadelphia. He died there of general debility and diarrhea a few days later. A woman named Caroline, claiming to be his widow, was pensioned in 1866. It seems that she never collected regular payments and was probably the victim of fraud by a pension subagent, James McGindley, who would later be sought for prosecution. A second woman, also claiming to be Magruder's widow, turned up in 1877. The record suggests that the mixup was because the soldier had a brother, Henry, whom one or both wives confused with Martin. While the second wife appeared to be the legitimate claimant, she was not admitted, and the first wife was not paid.[51]

Company C's casualties were not as heavy as A's. Five soldiers were killed, and seven were listed as missing. Four of the latter turned up alive in the waning days of the war—Isaac Gaskins, the soldier wounded after capture, Pvts. Peter Williams, James Bibb, and Henry Mosely. Gaskins wrote:

I was imprisoned at Danville, Va., and the second day after my imprisonment there, while passing a rebel guard, he seeing I was colored, struck me with a musket in the left side, causing very severe internal injuries from which I have never recovered.

I never knew what it was to get anything respectable to eat while in prison, and there was not one third enough of the vile stuff that was given us. We were marched out every morning about 8 o'clock to build breastworks, and without anything to eat.

Gaskins was exchanged in late February 1865, suffering from frostbitten feet, the result of the rebels taking away his shoes at capture, "running sores all over my body," and general emaciation. The Union army sent him to the hospital at Camp Parole for six weeks; gave him a thirty-day furlough home to Kankakee, Illinois; returned him to Fort Monroe hospital; and discharged him there in November. He never rejoined the regiment but was in it long enough to earn a bad reputation. First Sergeant Easley wrote, in 1884, "Private Gaskins from the time of his enlistment seems to have a wish to shirk duty—would Happen as often as twice a month that He was sick or lame in order that he might get on the sick list." Gaskins tried years later to be pensioned for injuries from the rifle stroke by the guard; he said it showed the "spite he had against the negro race as it was the custom of Said guards to treat myself and other negroes worse than if we were dogs." The plea was unsuccessful, but he was pensioned for other maladies dating from his imprisonment, and he died in 1900, outliving two wives and all his children.[52]

Williams, another Company C surviving prisoner, reported that he had been confined at Danville, Libby prison in Richmond, Castle Thunder, Andersonville (for just three days), and then Cumberland, where he worked on entrenchments for five months. He several times described his prisons and movements with numerous variations of places and dates, but Confederate prison records in his file are inconclusive on this matter. Williams said he escaped on 3 April 1865, when he and twenty-five other black prisoners were taken into the woods to be shot but were allowed to run off by a Colonel Booker of the rebel army. The soldier was at once returned to duty, apparently not much affected by his time as a prisoner.[53]

Bibb received a gunshot wound to his right ankle at the crater and was left on the battlefield. He had been born in Kentucky, was married "slave fashion," and had two children. He reported that one day, while he was at work, his master sold the children, and Bibb never saw them again.

He became so troublesome that his owner sold him to another man in Louisiana. He remained unruly and was sold several more times over a number of years, ran away to Canada (via the underground railroad), and went to Chicago early in the war. Bibb was imprisoned at Danville and was in the hospital there several times for treatment of his wound. Sent to Andersonville after a rebel doctor removed the bullet, Bibb soon was returned to Danville and was exchanged on 17 April 1865. He did not rejoin the regiment and was discharged. He was pensioned in 1880 at six dollars monthly for the wound, drawing back payments to 1864. Mosley, at thirty-nine four years older than Bibb, was also a Kentucky native, but he spent his early years in Nashville, Tennessee, where he was a slave of B. Emery. How he came to enlist at Quincy in late December 1863 is not known. Confined by the Confederates at Richmond, he was freed (at Burkesville, Virginia) the same day Bibb was exchanged and was sent to Fort Monroe hospital to recuperate. He was eventually discharged, not returning to his regiment. Of the other missing men, Pvts. William H. Rue, Richard Robertson, and Rollin Richardson, only the first had a dependent survivor, his mother pensioned in 1887, and the circumstances that brought them to the regiment from Missouri, Kentucky, and Virginia, respectively, are not recorded. Rue was born to a family of slaves owned by Moses D. Bates in Palmyra, Missouri. Being twenty when he enlisted, he was confined by the rebels at Richmond after his capture. Transferred in November to the Salisbury, North Carolina, prison camp, he died there on 2 January of "debility." Probably the two other men were among the unknown dead on the 30 July battlefield.[54]

Company C's dead, in addition to Corporal Bailey, the color-bearer, included Cpls. Kitchen Butler, nineteen, born in North Carolina; and Joseph Broaddy, twenty-nine, born in Coles County, Illinois. The corporals were unmarried, but Broaddy had a dependent mother, who unsuccessfully applied for the pension. The other dead, Pvts. Alfred Jones and Napoleon Carr, were Missourians, and both left wives and children. Pvt. Jones, forty-four, was a slave of Janus R. Dudley, Marion County, Missouri, before his escape to Quincy early in the war. He left behind two or possibly three women, each claiming to be his wife. Resolving this matter was to raise still further questions. Carr, age forty-five at enlistment, died in the hospital a day after the battle. He had married in Quincy a few days after he enlisted and had one child. The wives of Jones and Carr were finally pensioned, as were children under sixteen.[55]

Apart from Captain Brockway's serious injury, the company's records are unreliable with respect to the wounded. Brockway, after some time in the City Point hospital, was given leave to go to his home in Chicago. The ankle did not heal, and the captain's foot was amputated at Camp Douglas. Consequently, Company C's commanding officer did not return and was discharged on 2 March 1865. He became a Chicago businessman, operating a restaurant at 154 Clark Street, and sometimes encountering veterans of the regiment after the war. The company's first lieutenant, Gosper, was not in the battle, as he was still occupied with duties as acting regimental quartermaster. Second Lieutenant Conant, lightly injured, was the remaining company officer, but for some reason he was not immediately able to lead the unit.[56]

Pvt. John Blakely, the articulate soldier from Kentucky, described his wound:

> I was jarred all up by the explosion [of the mine]. I was knocked insensible and I was in the field hospital for a week or so and then Corporal Smith [probably Henry Smith, Company B] and Sergeant Maxwell [Cpl. John Maxon] and I were sent to Alexandria. We staid some time. We three were mustered out at one time. Corporal Smith was ruptured and Sergeant Maxwell was shot through the neck and had a silver tube put in his windpipe. We got through tickets [in November 1865] to Chicago and I went there with them and then came down to Louisville.

Medical records verify Maxon's wound but not Blakely's. Indeed, his file shows that he was discharged for "injury to spine and left hip [the] result of a fall from the cars while being transported from one field of duty to another." Furthermore, Blakely was in the Alexandria hospital from 26 May, was discharged on 6 January 1865, and was never in battle. He was nonetheless pensioned—but not until 1900 and then for prostate trouble and diarrhea.[57]

Company C had another imaginative soldier, Sgt. Brown, who would soon be promoted to regimental commissary sergeant. He said that he had been wounded in the left thigh by a rebel soldier with a bayonet but claimed that he treated the injury himself and did not report to the hospital. Brown made a pension claim twelve years after the war, and it was impressively supported by Lieutenant Conant and a substantial number of Company C noncommissioned officers and privates. Consequently, he was awarded two dollars monthly backdated to his date of discharge in November 1865. It took the pension bureau ten years to discover that the depositions were almost entirely forged and that Company C had not engaged in any hand-to-hand combat. Brown had wrongly collected his pension for ten years and twenty-seven days, $241.80 in all, but could not repay it, and the statute of limitations precluded his prosecution for fraud. Not discouraged, Brown applied again a few years later and was pensioned at twelve dollars a month for rheumatism and heart disease.[58]

Company E had no men missing in the crater action, although a few were temporarily listed as such before being declared dead. Nine were killed, and two, including company commander William H. Flint, died of wounds, Flint the next day and a soldier a month later. That soldier, Pvt. Reuben Wilson, was born in 1822 in Amherst County, Virginia; he was probably brought west by a slave owner. It appears that he was free in 1844, when he married in Madison County, Illinois. His leg was amputated after the crater battle, and he was sent to Alexandria. He died there of his wounds on 20 August, leaving a widow and five minor daughters, the youngest, Henrietta, only eleven months old. Wilson is buried at the Alexandria National Cemetery.[59]

The remaining seven Company E dead were Cpls. Julius White and Hiram D. Route; Musician Robert Walker, twenty-eight, from Illinois; Wagoner Thomas Scott, twenty-nine, from Kentucky; and Pvts. John J. Brown, nineteen, from Tennessee; Henry Higlon, thirty, from Kentucky; Samuel Hammons, eighteen, from Tennessee; George Perkins, thirty, from Virginia; and Cyrus J. Parker, thirty-nine, from Pennsylvania. White had been born and raised in Illinois and was never a slave. He enlisted at Alton and was made a corporal probably because he had some education. Married before the war, or perhaps in 1863, he left behind a widow and daughter. Route joined the regiment at Alton when he was twenty-four. He was born in Missouri, the slave of Charlotte Massey, was married about 1856, and had three or four children. His wife explained: "Mr. George Massey [son of owner] told Hiram Route, that he must take me for his wife, and told me that I must take him for my husband, this was the way slaves were married and all the Ceremony there was to it." Route went to Illinois about a year before he enlisted and worked (possibly as a mason) for a Dr. Hull in Alton. This one-year gap proved a problem for his wife's pension claim because it might have appeared that she had been abandoned. The widow received her eight-dollar monthly payments beginning after 1886, and she was awarded a lump sum, in arrears from the date of Route's death. Musician Walker was a Tennessee native, living before the war in Madison County, Illinois, following his escape from slavery. He and his wife had seven living children when he enlisted, four of them born free in Illinois. Walker's wife, however, had no trouble receiving the pension that was awarded her in 1866, eight dollars for herself and two dollars for each child, since all were less than sixteen years of age. Perkins and his wife had been slaves at Fulton, Calaway County, Missouri, and were married in 1852, "after the manner of slaves." They remarried in Illinois in 1863, so the widow was easily able to show a legal relationship with the soldier. Kentucky-born Scott was also married in slavery in Tennessee, and he and his wife had five children, the first born in 1854. Scott's wife had little difficulty collecting her pension, except that she was required to prove that her husband died at the crater. For this she relied on a deposition from Capt. William W. Flint, who said the soldier had been "shot through the body" on 30 July. Higlon and Parker were the only dead Company E soldiers without wives, children, or dependent mothers.[60]

One of the most seriously wounded men who survived the battle was Pvt. Lewis Martin, a Missouri-born slave who enlisted at Alton in February. He lost his right arm at the shoulder and the left leg below the knee. Martin recovered at Harewood General Hospital in Washington and was discharged for disability in December. As was customary at Harewood, Martin was photographed in order to illustrate the wound; this picture is the only extant wartime image of an enlisted man in the Twenty-ninth U.S. Colored Infantry. Solomon M. White was wounded by a bullet in the shoulder at the crater and was under treatment at L'Overture Hospital in Alexandria for six months. White was born a free man at Locust Grove, Williamson County, Illinois, and was living at Edwardsville when he enlisted just shy of his seventeenth birthday. He was a good soldier and was promoted to corporal and sergeant. Although he eventually returned to duty with the company, he remained partially disabled from the wound and was pensioned at four dollars monthly from the date of discharge. First Lieutenant Flint's wound, the nature of which is unspecified, was serious enough that he did not return to the company, in which he was the only surviving officer. Flint was promoted to captain but did not serve on duty in that rank; he was mustered out at Varina, Virginia, in mid-March because of his injuries. Lieutenant Ferguson, who fought on 30 July even though he was not mustered in, was not wounded, but he left the company, anyway, to return to his home in Missouri awaiting orders and to recruit more men for the regiment. A soldier who claimed a 30 July wound later narrowly avoided prosecution for fraud. Sgt. Wiley Sexton, age twenty-four, born in St. Clair County, Illinois, applied for a pension based on a gunshot wound in the left hand, but it was discovered that the injury dated from before the war. In February 1861 he had been hunting at Ridge Prairie and had stopped to visit a school, putting his shotgun under the building stock first. When he withdrew the gun by its muzzle, it fired the entire load through his hand. Sexton was ultimately pensioned for other maladies common to old veterans at the time, rheumatism and heart trouble, but never for the gunshot.[61]

Casualties of Company F were eight killed, two wounded who died of wounds, and one missing. The missing soldier was Pvt. Frank Odin, an eighteen-year-old born in Maryland, who was captured at the crater and was exchanged many months later. The fatally wounded men were Jackson Mackay, who died at the City Point hospital for colored soldiers on 14 August, and John Jackson, an eighteen-year-old private from Missouri who died a short time after the battle. Seven killed in action were Pennsylvania-born Sgt. Peter Stark and Pvts. Jefferson Allen (nineteen, Tennessee), Benjamin E. Price (twenty-nine, Illinois), William C. Ross (twenty-five, Colorado), Richard Robinson (eighteen, Arkansas), Sanford Strander (twenty, Arkansas), and Charles Tinsley. The eighth man killed was Cpl. John Thrasher, but he was thought to be a prisoner. That soldier was likely a displaced Missouri slave when he enlisted in Chicago in early 1864. He was living in Quincy and probably went to Chicago for that city's bounty. Thrasher was married, and his widow petitioned for a pension in 1866; she was told, however, that Company F's rolls showed her husband as a deserter from 1 January 1865, and she was consequently not eligible. She unsuccessfully tried twice more, even though she obtained depositions from five of Thrasher's comrades, who swore they had seen the soldier's body on the crater battlefield. The pension bureau finally agreed that he had been killed in action, but what caused this change was not the testimony of illiterate former soldiers. It was a letter from the officer who replaced the fallen regimental commander, Bross. The officer, Col. Clark E. Royce, wrote that he was unfamiliar with the facts of Thrasher's case because he had not reported to the regiment until 1 January. "I think, however, that the man was dropped as a deserter in order to make room for a live recruit. There was no proof, at the time, of his having been killed—or being a prisoner. I do not remember of course any man's case in particular. But in order to clear the

Muster Rolls of useless names—men who had not been heard from for a long period—'dropped as deserter'—was the easiest method and military necessity the excuse." Curiously, Thrasher seems to have been the only Twenty-ninth Infantry soldier killed or missing at the crater battle who was listed as a deserter under this policy.[62]

Although Thrasher's wife was pensioned, Tinsley's widow was excluded because of another complication. The soldier had been recruited in Louisiana, Missouri, in June, 1864, by future lieutenant Ferguson. Tinsley, a slave of Landon Tinsley of Prairieville, was taken to Quincy and mustered in a few days later. He was, as were most of Company F's men, credited to Milwaukee, in Wisconsin, a state he had never even visited. He met his first wife, Eliza, a slave of his owner's relative, Lafayette Tinsley, at Louisiana and was married in 1848 or 1850. Two widows claimed his pension. Eliza, mother of seven or eight children, filed in 1865. But, a pension examiner later wrote, "The soldier did forsake the claimant [Eliza] and marry one Matilda, about Dec 26, 1863, with whom he lived up to the date of his enlistment and thereby establishing a valid marriage." Eliza was found to have no case on a technicality, the result of slavery: prior to 11 January 1865 Missouri "recognized neither the marriage nor the record of marriages between slaves." Had the parties been white, the first wife would have been pensioned, but, an examiner wrote, Eliza was unfortunately excluded because "slaves had no legal rights which white men were bound to respect." Matilda, who was pensioned, died in 1882, and Eliza unsuccessfully filed several times up to 1900.[63]

Of Company F's men wounded at the crater, three of the most seriously injured were later discharged as disabled. Pvt. Henry Sink, born in bondage at Batesville, Arkansas, in 1837, was living in Green Bay, Wisconsin, when he enlisted. The story of how he arrived in the North is lost. He was treated for a wound in the left arm at Summit House Hospital in Philadelphia until his discharge in March 1865. He asked at once for a pension but did not receive one until 1890, being found one-quarter disabled and collecting five dollars monthly. He died at Fond du Lac in 1923. Pvt. Charles South, age forty-six, enlisted with his younger brother Collins, at Louisiana, Missouri, and both were counted as Wisconsin men. They had been slaves of a man named South at Olney, Pike County. Charles's right arm and left knee were severely damaged on 30 July, and he was treated at City Point. In October he was sent to Quincy on a twenty-five-day furlough. Admitted to the hospital there, he was discharged as totally disabled in early January; his later life was troubled. Collins South, perhaps inspired by his brother's pension, years after said he too had been injured at the crater, wounded by a bayonet that fractured some ribs. No army record substantiated this claim, even though former company commander Daggett deposed that the soldier had been wounded. It is likely that the captain had Charles South in mind, and the claim was not honored. The third soldier discharged as disabled was Sgt. Daniel B. Underhill, who was one of the rare Company F soldiers who actually enlisted in Wisconsin. He was released in June 1865.[64]

Company F Pvt. Martin Hammon probably should have been discharged as unfit for duty, but he served out the war. Hammon and his brother Rufus—who did not enlist—left their master in Lincoln County, Missouri, shortly before Martin's enlistment. Sent to City Point with a serious thigh wound, the soldier was soon moved to Alexandria, was furloughed for thirty days at the end of September, and rejoined his company. He was, however, sick for the rest of his service. Pvt. Phillip Smith, injured by shell fragments in the shoulder, stayed in the City Point hospital until at least the end of December, but he went back to the regiment and was promoted to sergeant. Other men were wounded, some seriously, but there were other losses. Cpl. Julius S. Rice had reported sick the night before the crater battle with, he said, "measeels and Chronic Diohrea." He remained in the hospital for colored troops at City Point and was forwarded to Summit House in Philadelphia. He went to Illinois on furlough in mid-October and was sent from Quincy hospital to the wife he married in 1863 and his mother at Clarksburg for home nursing. Summit House reported him a deserter in mid-January after he failed to return, and he never spent another day in the army. Starting in 1884, he was several times rejected for a pension because of his suspect status but finally was granted an allowance for age in 1916, the army finding, "The charge of desertion on Nov. 8, 64 arising from this man's failure to return to military control at the expiration of his furlo, and all subsequent charges of desertion against him have been removed and he has been discharged to date Nov. 8, 1864." Although this action was the result of an 1889 amnesty act, he no doubt saw it as a vindication of his long campaign to clear the record. Rice consistently claimed that his wife and mother often told an uncaring army that he was too sick to return. He died at Jacksonville, Illinois, in 1920, survived by his second wife.[65]

Discipline in Company F was particularly difficult to maintain after the 30 July fight. Well over two-thirds of the men were in uniform less than a month and had had little time to develop confidence in Captain Daggart, the only company officer, and the noncommissioned officers. Likewise, those leaders had no opportunity to evaluate the soldiers. Captain Daggart, who had been shot in the side, was not ready for duty, and 1st Sgt. James L. Williams deserted on 8 August. He was replaced by the orderly sergeant, Lloyd T. Bryon, a poor choice who was reduced to private, and then by John Walmslee, who, unlike Bryon, was illiterate. Sergeant Stark was dead, leaving just Sgt. Alfred Weaver of the original sergeants, and he was also later reduced to private. Of the seven corporals on the rolls on 30 July, two were killed in action, Julius S. Rice was ill, and Richard E. Johnson, the senior among them, deserted on 3 August. Finally, the only thing the company's enlisted men had in common were their past days in slavery, most of them in Missouri. They were not bound by loyalties to Illinois, where many of their noncommissioned officers had the advantage of living free when enlisted, and the majority of them were labeled Wisconsin citizens, when few had ever seen the state.[66]

The Twenty-ninth U.S. Colored Infantry lost thirty-eight men killed in action or died of wounds and thirty-two prisoners, of which eighteen died in Confederate hands. As for the regiment's wounded, only an estimate is possible, because poor records were kept on soldiers in the hospital and others who may have been treated by the regimental surgeon, but, based on Ferrero's count, seventy-five is a reasonable estimate. In all the Twenty-ninth Regiment's casualties were more than one hundred and forty, about 28 percent of its strength on the day of the battle. This rate of loss could not have been maintained, but the regiment had completed its single wartime major battle. Its future service would be arduous and sometimes hazardous, but casualties would be principally from illness caused by poor living conditions.[67]

The regiment had done its duty as well as had the other black regiments at the crater, all of which had suffered similar losses, but it was not allowed a rest for recuperation and to await replacements. It was ordered into the trenches with the rest of the depleted Ninth Army Corps. Illinois took little notice of the Twenty-ninth Regiment, apart from brief items in newspapers a day or two after the battle, and only a few mentioned the regimental commander's death. Bross's loss was commemorated mostly in the army, first by his division and brigade commanders, both of whom made special mention of him in their after-battle reports. Ferrero wrote what seems a perfunctory statement of the "great loss," but Thomas was more specific: "I desire . . . to pay a passing tribute to Lieutenant-Colonel

Bross, Twenty-ninth U.S. Colored Troops, who led the charge of this brigade. He was the first man to leap over the works, and bearing his colors in his own hands he fell never to rise again." Ferrero and some officers of the regiment wrote to Mrs. Bross, but only one enlisted man did; his letter reads: "Allow me to say, that although a colored man, a private in the 29th, I found in Colonel Bross a friend, on whom every member of the regiment placed the utmost confidence, for, and with whom, each one would help to defend the country to the end. . . . He was loved by every one, because he was a friend to every one. . . . Weep not for him who was one of God's chosen ones, who tried to deliver his people out of Egypt." Bross was remembered by the Army of the Potomac, as was the custom for high-ranking officer casualties, by its naming a fort on the Union secondary line near the crater after him, but the rest of the Twenty-ninth USCT's fallen were only statistics to the army.[68]

FIXING THE BLAME

Second-guessing began at once officially and in the press so as to assign blame for what Grant called the "stupendous failure" of the battle at the crater. This had two tracks, one to identify the officers who should be brought to account for actions, or lack of them, during the battle and the other to determine if the blacks had caused the defeat. Meade was determined to court-martial Burnside for insubordination and other offenses but settled for a court of inquiry, to which he appointed all members. Burnside's biographer believes that the deck was stacked against the corps commander but admits that the general was inactive at times he should have been active. Burnside testified early during the court's examination of witnesses and departed for his home in Rhode Island on 4 August, on a twenty-day leave from which he never returned, because Grant sided with Meade in the dispute. Grant wrote in his *Memoirs* that the failure at the crater was "all due to the inefficiency of the corps commander [Burnside] and incompetency of the division commander [Ledlie] who was to lead the assault." The court of inquiry's early September report did not severely criticize Burnside, merely finding him culpable for not seeing to clearing the parapets before the explosion and for failing to get Ledlie to move his troops beyond the crater. He was immediately replaced in command of the Ninth Army Corps by his chief of staff, Maj. Gen. John G. Parke. (Burnside was later governor of his state and died while serving in the U.S. Senate.) Meade was also corrected, albeit indirectly, the court suggesting that things might have gone better had one officer been given command of the assault. The severest criticism was properly reserved for Ledlie and Ferrero, the court finding that the first "was most of the time in a bomb-proof ten rods in rear of the main line of the Ninth Corps works, where it was impossible for him to see anything of the movement of troops that were going in" and that Ferrero was guilty of "being in a bomb-proof habitually, where he could not see the operation of his troops." Grant said of Ledlie that, "besides being otherwise inefficient, [he] proved to possess disqualifications less common among soldiers," and he too went on a leave, after which he was not given another assignment. His future did not suffer from his poor military performance. Ledlie returned to his engineering profession, working for the Union Pacific Railroad and in the Chicago harbor, becoming president of the railroad and chief engineer. Ferrero inexplicably escaped penalty for his behavior, which closely paralleled Ledlie's, and remained in command of the Fourth Division. He was promoted to brevet major general in December for service before Petersburg and Richmond.[69]

There was yet another crater inquiry, this time by a committee of Congress, but its investigation added little to the court of inquiry's findings. The committee's December 1864 report, however, cleared the nearly forgotten Burnside: "Your committee cannot, from all the testimony, avoid the conclusion that the first and great cause of this disaster was the change made on the afternoon preceding the attack, in the arrangement of General Burnside to place the division of colored troops in the advance." The committee, unlike the court of inquiry, commented on Meade's tactical change, which de-emphasized attack corridor protection, and censured Meade "who had evinced no faith in the successful prosecution of the work, and aided it by no countenance only when it was completed, and the time for reaping the advantage that might be derived from it." As for the blacks, the report continued, "The conduct of the colored troops, when they were put into action, would seem to fully justify the confidence General Burnside reposed in them." Grant, testifying for the first time, said that use of the black division to lead the attack "would have been a success," but he still supported Meade's decision. He was also the first to attribute part of the engagement's failure to the lack of division commanders on the battlefield. In the testimony by officers in both investigations the conduct of the black troops had generally been commended, although few were willing to second-guess Meade's decisions. Of course, Burnside did so, claiming, "I am forced to believe that the Fourth Division (the colored division) would have made a more impetuous and successful assault than the leading division," but Burnside may have been merely conducting his own defense rather than praising the black troops. He later qualified his praise, telling the congressional committee: "As far as I am concerned I do not say they are fully equal to our white soldiers, because they do not have the same intelligence; but they are easily disciplined, and, as far as my experience goes, they stand fire quite as well as any troops we ever had. And with the exception of the intelligence which prevails to a considerable extent among white soldiers, and which makes each man a pretty good judge of what he ought to do in a fight, I think the colored soldiers are as good soldiers as we have."[70] Thus, Burnside revealed prejudices that were probably shared by many senior army officers. The blacks were gallant enough, but not sufficiently intelligent as a race to match white troops. How these attitudes evolved and how white soldiers saw black troop performance in the crater battle were critical in determining how and for what purposes black soldiers would be employed by the army during the rest of the war.

Of course, not all officers and men in white regiments had been impressed by the black regiments on 30 July. Many thought the entire debacle should be attributed to them. Lt. George Barton, of the Fifty-seventh Massachusetts Volunteers, a white regiment, wrote home shortly after the attack, describing how the blacks "*broke & ran* like a *flock* of *sheep*, & black at that. . . . This war must be *fought out* by *white men* & we might as well make up our minds to do it first at last to say it," adding in another letter, "the entire failure of the undertaking is laid upon their [the blacks'] shoulders." A Fifth Corps private who observed the engagement wrote to his brother three days after the crater fight: "The slaughter of the Negroes was terrible, they gave way and were killed by the hundreds— there is no use talking about them, they will not stand the fire." He elaborated on this theme at the end of August: "From that performance [at the crater] I came to the conclusion that the only way to regulate the Negro, was to beat them as was done when they were slaves. I will say this for them, they march in much better order than whites, and do not fall out as much—this may be due to their great fear of being captured." A loftier observer, Col. Theodore Lyman on Meade's staff, was somewhat more objective: "Their officers behaved with distinguished courage, and the blacks seemed to have done as well as whites—which is faint praise." A Washington newspaper agreed with this analysis: "The report that the negro troops behaved especially bad is not corroborated by our latest information, which states that they behaved no worse, at least than others."

Lyman's opinion of blacks, however, was not high, and a few months later he remarked about how black troops should be handled: "If their intellects don't work, the officers occasionally refresh them by applying the flats of their swords to their skins."[71]

Perhaps more to the point were the comments about black troops appearing in battle reports just after the engagement at the crater. Nearly without exception, they say that black misconduct or simply the presence of black regiments on the field was responsible for the disaster. General Ledlie, who did not testify before the court of inquiry or the congressional committee, flatly claimed that the black regiments prevented formation of the First Division's line, and the commanders of the Second Brigade, Second Division; the Second Division; and the Second Brigade, First Division, agreed with him, all saying that the blacks packing into the crater and other shelters prevented organization of further advances and later resistance. Col. Stephen M. Weld, commanding the Fifty-sixth Massachusetts, also remarked on the crowding in the crater, although without criticizing the blacks for being part of it. It was impossible to use muskets, he said—"[I] literally could not raise my arms from my side." Thus, it can be concluded that blacks, and equally whites, who jammed into the available shelter caused the military situation to deteriorate, but that hardly was the reason for the operation's failure.[72]

Newspapers speculated about the causes of the defeat and the performance of blacks in the engagement. None of them spoke of the effects on the engagement of switching in the last hours from rested and trained black troops to worn-out and discouraged white regiments, probably because it was not widely known just after the battle. Some reported a fanciful tale that the assault had failed because the troops believed that the rebels had mined Cemetery Hill, but others found no easy excuses. A Hartford newspaper reported that the battle went well, "till the colored division was ordered to carry the hill." The blacks became "disordered and disorganized" and twice "recoiled before the destructive fire of the enemy." Another New England journal similarly singled out the performance of the black regiments, describing the "galling fire, which checked them, although quite a number kept on advancing. The greater portion seemed utterly demoralized, part taking refuge in the fort, and the balance running to the rear as fast as possible," all this without mentioning the equally confused skedaddle of the white regiments. The *New York Express*, however, may have expressed more clearly a popular opinion—a mix of pity, paternalism, condescension, and racial superiority:

How far the commander was right in sending negro troops to the post of greatest danger is proved by the result. Nothing could inspire the enemy to vengeance as their appearance in front, and nothing, as the telegraphic report shows, could have been more disastrous to the poor negroes themselves. It is impossible not to pity these victims to one of the most miserable delusions of the war, and that they can be relied on in positions of the greatest danger, and that it is not right to place them in such an attitude of exposure.[73]

In later years criticism of black regiment activities in the battle diminished, and participants' accounts of the action largely praise the performance of the U.S. Colored Troops, blaming their tardy arrival for the failure. One concluded, "I never saw men fight better than the colored division, but they came too late to avail us." Others agreed: "The colored troops fought well, but by then the Confederates had recovered"; and "They did some splendid fighting," although too late. Many speculated on what might have been. An officer who was at the crater flatly declared that the well-trained blacks would have seized Cemetery Hill "fifteen or twenty minutes from the time the debris from the explosion had settled," and another said the results might have been different if the white troops leading the attack had had the same training that the blacks had received.[74]

As for how the black soldiers evaluated their own performance in the battle, few accounts exist. None of these men had experience in military matters and so could not discuss the crater engagement in military terms. They certainly were aware that the attack on the Confederate lines was unsuccessful, but they were not likely to be sufficiently grounded in such matters so as to apportion blame. The battle had a deeper meaning for some of the soldiers because it was the opportunity for black soldiers to prove their worth. Blacks lately released from slavery saw sacrifice as necessary to persuade whites to accept the race. This was, in any event, the opinion of Sgt. Morgan W. Carter, a soldier from Madison, Indiana, serving in the Twenty-eighth U.S. Colored Infantry. He wrote that thinking of home caused him to "feale a little down hearted, but [I] soon Rally when i think in what Principal i am fighting which is for the benifit of my race." He explained:

[I] have bin in a good many veary close Places but by the lords Will i have Escaped with my life so far. i have bin wounded twice once by a piece of shell on the long to be Remember field of blood shed and Slaughter on the 30 of July. Thear many a poore fell[ow] lost theare life for thear country and theare people. but Poore fellows they died a noble death. and in this course if it is neaseary i Will give up my life most willingly to Benifit the Collored Race you who youre self [knows] that we have bin trampled under the white mans heal for years and now we have a chance to Elivate oure selfs and oure race and what litle i can do towards it i will do so most willingly if i should die before i Receive the benifit of it i will have to consolation of noing that generations to come will Recieve the blessing of it. and i think it the duty of all the men [of] oure Race to do what they can.[75]

Responsibility for failure is seldom fairly or evenly apportioned, and so it was in the Battle of the Crater. The battle's lessons about black troops were likewise ambiguous and unsettled. On the question of blame West Point naturally has fixed on commanders, who, in military doctrine, have the ultimate responsibility for success or failure. This theme was well expressed by a newspaper at the time which said the opportunity given by the mine "was converted by imbecility and cowardice" of Union corps and division commanders into a defeat costing five thousand men, and "every drummer-boy and mule-driver in the Army of the Potomac knew that a crowning disaster and a crowning disgrace had happened to it." With respect to improving the position of blacks in the army and in the esteem of their countrymen, as Sergeant Carter hoped, the crater did not change matters. It was already well known from earlier engagements that black troops would fight, but the unanswered question in mid-1864 was whether they were better used in major combat operations or on fatigue duties—hard labor on fortifications for white troops. Because blacks were, as General Ferrero put it, being accused of bad conduct and were subject to "many disparaging remarks which have been widely circulated," Army of the Potomac leaders were leaning toward the latter employment. Ferrero wanted to write a public letter to head this off, but he did not receive permission to do so. The battle had only one clear-cut result: the war in Virginia would now last six months more than it might have.[76]

Chapter 4

FURTHER WAR SERVICE

The six companies of the Twenty-ninth U.S. Colored Infantry which fought in the Battle of the Crater on 30 July were minimum size before that action, and the regiment itself was short four companies of infantry. Consequently, building up the regiment was the first priority in late summer. Some activities to obtain black recruits continued in Illinois, but there was no immediately effective effort in the state to find new candidates specifically for the Twenty-ninth USCT. Those who would soon be obtained in the regiment's home state would include drafted men or paid substitutes for draftees in addition to those tempted by bounties. Brokers made a business out of obtaining substitutes for drafted men, and, though the system was open to abuse, it was continued throughout the war. In early 1863 a white man could pay a black to be his substitute, but the practice was officially discontinued in midyear. Records of the Twenty-ninth Regiment indicate, however, that blacks continued to be enlisted in place of white draftees well into late 1864. By July 1864 when the Twenty-ninth Regiment's recruiting needs were heavy, the entire process of finding enlistees was better organized than it had been earlier. The call for a half-million new soldiers issued that month was accompanied by revised procedures pertaining to black troops. The army issued new regulations for loyal states recruiting in states in rebellion, allowing loyal states to count contrabands against their quotas. Recruiting officers would no longer be paid for recruits, and the men would be delivered to designated assembly points for assignment to regiments in the field. These administrative matters were accompanied by adjustments in pay and federal bounties correcting inequities, which had been a source of continuing unrest in black regiments.[1]

The July act that equalized pay for white and black troops—backdating the effective date to the first of the year—found approval in the Illinois press, where such action had been called for since the Twenty-ninth Regiment's recruiting began. The Springfield *State Journal,* praising the legislation, noted that "every colored soldier counts the same as a white man" and is subjected to a "greater peril to life in consequence of the disposition manifested by the rebels to deny them the rights of prisoners of war." Men enlisted prior to 1 January were paid the difference for that earlier service, provided that they had been free men before the war. This unequal treatment of free blacks as opposed to freed slaves continued for almost the entire war, but it had little impact on the Twenty-ninth USCT because few of its men had been signed up prior to 1864. It may, however, have been one reason why almost every recruit claimed to be a free man when he enlisted, but many could also have feared being found by their owners. Pensions were provided for widows and children of black soldiers killed or dead from disease contracted in the line of duty, and bounties for white and black troops were made a uniform three hundred dollars for a three-year enlistment, without distinction between slaves and free men. So black volunteers, substitutes, and draftees for the first time would receive federal as well as the state and local bounties that they had been collecting. By August the government allowed one- , two- , or three-year enlistments, paying bounties of one hundred dollars per year. The shortest period of enlistment was popular, but it made little difference in the Twenty-ninth unit because the regiment did not have much more than a year to serve anyway.[2]

Although the system of compensating black soldiers improved, it remained difficult to fill the regiment rapidly in the summer of 1864, perhaps because the pressure of conscription to meet the latest levy by Washington, D.C., was not immediately felt fully in the states. Company A received only one man from Illinois in August and two more Virginians from the replacement depot at Camp Casey. The first, a substitute for a drafted man (W. H. Bunker), Mississippi-born George Washington, age nineteen, enlisted in Chicago in mid-August. The other two, Pvts. William James and John Campbell, were enlisted in Virginia by agents of Northumberland County, Pennsylvania, and were credited to that state. James said he had been born about 1835 in Docksville, Virginia, and Campbell, age twenty-two, was a native of Culpeper in the same state. All three men served out the war, and James was promoted to corporal and sergeant, the only Company A recruit to wear the stripes of a noncommissioned officer. Obviously,

Captain Porter preferred his battle-tested veterans. September was a better recruiting month, with twenty-one new men reporting. All of them were enlisted at Camp Casey, and many were young natives of Virginia. The oldest new recruit was forty-three-year-old Pvt. Joseph Bhillet, who was not up to the task of soldiering and who died on Christmas eve. Pvt. Richard E. Crayon, age thirty-two, was born in Gallatin County, Tennessee, but the circumstances behind his arrival in Virginia are not known. Two other non-Virginians were also older than the average of this group, Pvts. Perry Gilworth from South Carolina and Benjamin Williams, who claimed a New York birthplace. Like Crayon, they did not describe for their records their lives before they enlisted. At least fourteen of these recruits were signed up by agents of six New York counties and several counties in New Hampshire which were filling some of their quotas with these contrabands. The recruiters had no connection to the regiment or to Illinois; their new soldiers were assigned to a pool at Camp Casey from which allocations were made to regiments in the field. Except for Williams, all of the September recruits were probably escaped or freed slaves, but, other than in two personnel files, that former status is not identified.[3]

Company B did better that August, with fifteen new soldiers, all but one Virginians or at least recruited in Virginia. Pvt. William Lumpkins came from the Old Northwest, although he had been born at Newport, Kentucky. Lumpkins, age twenty-four, had certainly been a slave before he made his way to Manomonie, Wisconsin. He was living there when he enlisted for one year on the last day of August. Although mustered in, he did not report to the state rendezvous camp at Madison until late September, and he did not arrive at the regiment in Virginia until the last days of November. The Camp Casey recruits were similar to those destined for Company A, mostly young men who were to be credited to other states. One man, Pvt. John H. Johnson, however, although a Virginia-born contraband, signed on at Camp Casey and was counted as an Illinois recruit. September's recruits fit the same pattern as did Company A's. They numbered fourteen, and eleven were recorded as having come from Illinois, but some of these were enlisted at Casey and credited to Illinois jurisdictions. A large number of the Illinois candidates took the new one-year enlistment option, unlike Company A's September recruits, who all signed up for three years or the duration of the war. Company B's roster was reduced in September by the desertion of Pvt. Joseph Hubbard, a twenty-two-year-old Virginian who had enlisted only a month earlier.[4]

Company C gained ten men from Camp Casey in August, all of them Virginians and all young men. Two of them, Pvts. Barney Gaines and Samuel Johnson, deserted before they had been in uniform a month, and a third man, Pvt. Charles Dorsey, deserted two months later. September's eleven recruits were largely from the Camp Casey pool (one was enlisted at White House Landing). These men were mostly former slaves born in Virginia or the District of Columbia, and the stories of their lives prior to army service are lost. One of them, Pvt. Alexander White, twenty-five, deserted thirteen days after he was mustered in, but the remaining Virginians, except for the medically disabled, remained with the regiment until it was broken up. September recruit Pvt. John Berlein, seventeen, was a freeborn Ohioan living with his sister at Newcomerstown, Oxford Township, in his home state when he was offered an opportunity to enlist. A white man, James Hamilton of Gurnsey County, Ohio, had been conscripted and, as he explained after the war: "I hired John Berlein as a substitute in the fall of 1864. I went with him to Uhrichsville O and he enlisted. . . . I paid him four hundred and eighty dollars." Mustered in at Camp Casey, Berlein, who could not read or write, did not notice that the enlisting officials put his name down as Berling, a matter that caused him much difficulty in future years when he sought to be pensioned.[5]

Company D enlisted seven men in August, two from Rockford, and one from Leroy, Illinois, but E and F, the remaining two companies, had only one new recruit between them that month. The emphasis was on organizing a new company, G, and its men were mustered into United States service in late August or early September, but not immediately into the Twenty-ninth Regiment. The Illinois regiment benefited from the recruiting success of the Twenty-eighth U.S. Colored Infantry, Indiana's single black regiment, which had exceeded its recruiting quota. About seventy new recruits for the Twenty-ninth Regiment were transferred from the Twenty-eighth in late October, and a scattering of men were recruited directly into the Twenty-ninth in Virginia and Maryland; only one was found in Illinois. The majority of the Twenty-eighth Regiment men sent to the Twenty-ninth were enlisted from among black slaves in Henderson County, Kentucky, and were found by agents from Evansville, Indiana, across the Ohio River, who were looking for substitutes for drafted men. A few were enlisted in the Washington, D.C., and Baltimore areas. Even the company's first sergeant, John Williams, a Norfolk-born former slave, working as a waiter at Leesburg, Virginia, enlisted originally in the Indiana regiment in August. Indeed, all the company's first noncommissioned officers were also former Twenty-eighth Regiment soldiers. One of them,

Sgt. William H. Rowens, a slave owned by William Thompson, Henderson County, later took the unlettered Williams's place as first sergeant. Rowens, like many other of the Kentucky soldiers, had been hired out to work in a tobacco factory, where Indiana's recruiters found him. Pvt. Harry Desha (later known as Nathan Bibb) was another tobacco worker. He knew little of his own background and thought he had been born in Fayette County, Kentucky, in 1846. He was sold in 1857 and then sold four times more. One of his owners, perhaps the first, was a Dr. Desha (or DeShea?) in Lexington. He was married—a "slave marriage," he called it—early in the war in Nebo, Hopkins County. His wife was owned by Edward Green, who had a tobacco factory at Nebo, and it is possible Desha was owned by the same man. Desha was taken to Evansville by an agent looking for substitutes. He was promised an enlistment bounty and the fee for substituting for M. A. Weir, a drafted man. The agent collected the bounty and fee, but Desha received only twenty dollars. Many soldiers were similarly cheated out of their payments. Pvt. Wesley Elam, for example, was recruited at Evansville as a substitute for J. D. Howard, but he said he was paid nothing at all. With thirty or forty others Elam was taken from his birthplace, Paris, Kentucky, to Tennessee early in the war to prevent the slaves from being freed by Union forces. His original owner, Thomas R. Ford, sold him in 1863 to John T. Hughes, who sold him to Bill Elam of Henderson. He had been married in 1860 but was separated when his wife was sold to a new owner in Tennessee in 1863; he never saw her again. After the war Elam assumed his father's surname and was known as Wesley Martin. A pension examiner wrote (in 1915) about the soldier's earlier name, "Slaves were enlisted under their masters['] names for the purpose of identifying them," and the practice made it easier for loyal slave owners to collect the bounty.[6]

Another soldier was confused about names. Pvt. Albert Stanley was born in Henderson County in late 1842 and was owned by Jonathan H. Stanley. He had been married in 1860 while still a slave. Known in Henderson as Albert Hart before his August enlistment at Evansville, "as many slaves did when they joined to army, He changed his name to Stanley to hide his identity," a pension examiner explained. He would not, of course, have thus concealed his enlistment from his owner, but he was not a clever man. Pvt. George Easton, on the other hand, did not seek to obscure his enlistment through a name change. Born in 1838 in Henderson County, he was a slave of George McClain. The latter's widow married

Robert Easton, who hired the slave out. From the age of fourteen he spent seven years working in Col. Jackson McLean's tobacco factory at Henderson. Easton married, slave fashion, during the war. Enlisting in the Twenty-eighth Regiment under his master's name and transferred to the Twenty-ninth, Easton served out the war and returned to Robert Easton's farm, where he was a farm laborer for some years before finding other employment. Pvt. James Williams did not use his master's name, Dixon, but he remained close to that man's family in later years. Married before the war, he and his wife settled after it in Henderson County, possibly working for his former owner and his family. The soldier was able to call on Robert Dixon's children in 1914 for affidavits supporting what was an unsuccessful claim for a pension based on advanced age.[7]

Pvt. Randall (John) Gregory was owned by Frances Gregory in Henderson, the sister of George Easton's mistress. He had been known as Jimmie Randall in bondage but took the name of his master when he enlisted. After the war he used his father's last name and was called George W. or Jimmie (sometimes James) Cheatam. Gregory went from Kentucky with Pvt. Richard Wilson to Evansville to enlist. Wilson, age twenty-five, possibly born in Louisville, was married before the war, but little else is known of him. There is no evidence that Easton, Dixon, Gregory, and Wilson were paid substitutes, but they likely were.[8]

Of the men transferred to the Twenty-ninth from the Twenty-eight U.S. Colored Infantry from the group recruited in Maryland, a few had long journeys to the army. Pvt. George (Arthur) Douglas was born in Somerset County, Maryland, in September 1848, a slave of George Robinson Dennis. Douglas changed owners when Dennis's widow married James Murray Rush, a Philadelphia lawyer, who owned Essex Farm near present-day Pokomoke City. Douglas said he "ran off from slavery" in October 1863 "in corn gathering time," seeking to enlist at Camp Stanton at Benedict, Maryland, across Chesapeake Bay and up the Patuxent River from his owner's farm. Arriving at the colored soldier recruit camp at Benedict, possibly helped to reach the place by recruiting agents, Douglas was rejected as too ill for the army. As he put it, "I was excepted from being a soldier at Benedict," and he went on to Baltimore. He was soon "working for the Government" at Alexandria, Virginia: "I was waiting on soldiers. I was at a place called Soldiers' Rest near where Cameron Station now is." In late July 1864, however, Douglas, again working in Baltimore, was lured into the army by the promised payment offered to substitutes for men seeking to avoid conscription. He enlisted at Baltimore in the Twenty-eight Regiment in late July and three weeks later was sent to Virginia. Issued a musket at Camp Casey, he was sent "right to the front without a day's drilling," a common practice at the time. He apparently was moved from place to place on the Petersburg front, an unassigned soldier, before reaching the Twenty-ninth USCT in October.[9]

Pvt. George H. Sherwood was born at the "Orphan's Home" in Auburn, New York, in May 1835. He enlisted in Company I, Twenty-second New York Cavalry, a white unit, in November 1863. He was accepted because he claimed to be a Seneca Indian, but army records show him consistently as "of African descent." Sherwood deserted from the Twenty-second Cavalry at the dismount camp in the District of Columbia in early July 1864. Concealing his military record, he enlisted on 15 August in Company E, Twenty-eighth U.S. Colored Infantry, at Baltimore, a substitute for Thomas M. Brown of that city, apparently for the payment. He signed the enlistment papers with a mark, although he could write his name when he first joined the army in New York. He also said that he was only nineteen and had been born in Frederick, Maryland. Sherwood's deception was not discovered after he was transferred to the Twenty-ninth Regiment, and his prior military experience did not earn him noncommissioned officer responsibilities. Sherwood's past would catch up with him long after the war, when he raised the issue of his service with the New York regiment.[10]

These new soldiers were far from ready to be sent to the front, the officer in charge at Camp Casey reporting to the regiment that the recruits had no equipment and needed much more drill. It appears, however, that they were forwarded anyway, because the Twenty-ninth Regiment was mainly assigned to support activities. Its duties in the month after the battle were relatively minor, the regimental history recording, "nothing of movement has occurred." At the end of August the black division was transferred from the trenches east of Petersburg to a position covering General Warren's corps on the left of the Army of the Potomac, near the Petersburg and Weldon Railroad, which had just been cut by Union forces with high losses. But the Twenty-ninth was not involved in the fighting. The regiment spent some time at Poplar Grove Church, which was to be the site of a national cemetery in which troops killed before Petersburg would be interred after the war, many of them Twenty-ninth Regiment men initially buried between the lines or in the crater. Of course, unknown soldiers greatly exceed the known, and not one Twenty-ninth USCT soldier is among the identified dead. Not even the name of Pvt. Robert Johnson, Company G, who died of disease there on 13 November 1864, was recorded, but today's cemetery was not organized until two years after the war. Other black troops were in battle, however, in another sector of the front, parts of two regiments were credited with beating back a Confederate attack on Tenth Corps, north of the James River. The corps commander said of them, "The colored troops behaved handsomely and are in fine spirits." At the end of September black troops participated in another series of attacks also north of the James before Richmond—two days of hard fighting in battles known as New Market Heights, Fort Harrison, and Fort Gilmer, or collectively as Chaffin's Farm. In all over 1,700 black troops and 1,550 whites were killed.[11]

The Chaffin's Farm battles resulted in many prisoners in Confederate hands, and General Lee asked Grant on 1 October for a "man for man" exchange. The Confederates stood to gain more by such a procedure because Lee's forces were stretched very thin and without hope of reinforcement, while Union armies continued to grow. Grant initially agreed to make an exchange but asked if Lee intended to deliver black soldiers on the same basis as whites. Lee answered that he would release soldiers "of whatever nation and color under my control" but excepted "deserters from our service and negroes belonging to our citizens." The same day Grant said he would go no further with exchanges because the Union "is bound to secure to all persons received into her armies the rights due soldiers," and this included blacks, without exceptions. A few days later Maj. Gen. Benjamin F. Butler, commanding the Army of the James, hearing that the rebels had put black prisoners to work on fortifications, told the Confederate commissioner of exchange that he would use an equal number of rebel officers and soldiers in Union hands on similar work. Lee told his secretary of war that it was a mistake to employ prisoners this way but wrote a long justification to Grant for using black former slaves— he said there were fifty-nine of them—on such military work. By the next day, however, Grant told Butler that Lee had discontinued the practice and directed Butler to do the same. As noted earlier, Lincoln had threatened to retaliate against rebel prisoners after reported atrocities against black soldiers at Milliken's Bend and other places in 1863, but there is no evidence that the president's order was a factor in Grant's and Butler's actions and decisions. More important might have been that the reported abuse incidents were an excuse to stop prisoner exchanges between Grant's forces and the extremely shorthanded Confederates. Certainly, the manpower motive would have been even more compelling in late 1864 than it had been a year earlier. The result of these last incidents was that no further exchanges were made between Lee's and Grant's armies until late in the war.[12]

Notwithstanding the fact that black troops were doing their duty, General Butler was showing some signs of discontent with them—not with his own black regiments, just Meade's. The day after his colored troops had done well in the Tenth Corps he wrote to Grant: "From all that I can hear the Colored troops belonging to the 9th Army Corps have been very much demoralized by loss of Officers, and by their repulse on the 30th [of July]." He recommended that Ferrero's division be broken up and the troops assigned to other corps. At the same time Major General Ord, Eighteenth Corps commander in Butler's Army of the James, wrote to Grant that "the rebels on Warren's front called out to our men that they were going to shell Burnside's Niggers and they (Warren's men) must not mind it. They have shelled every morning since." Meanwhile, Meade was also looking at Ferrero's division, and he ordered that the black soldiers be used "in the construction of Warren's redoubts, as they work much better than the white troops, and save the latter for fighting." This same view was expressed in the press, one newspaper putting a good face on some extremely hard work, cutting a canal across a bend in the James River at Dutch Gap so Union gunboats could get closer to Richmond while avoiding enemy fire. "That colored troops should be selected to perform such arduous duty, exposed as they are to the raking fire of the enemy from several batteries, is an evidence of their high standard in the estimation of their military chieftain," but, in fact, it was the opposite.[13]

The trend was certainly to put the Twenty-ninth USCT and its sister regiments back on fatigue duty and not to employ Ferrero's regiments in further active military operations on an equal basis with whites. Contributing to the belief that labor was the only useful place for the division was the fact that many of its regiments were badly short of officers and that discipline in them was so poor as to make them ineffective military organizations. Most of the companies in the Twenty-ninth Infantry were operating with borrowed lieutenants, and no regimental commander and staff were regularly assigned. Not a single new officer reported to the regiment in August, and the original officers were slow in returning from convalescent leave and hospitals.[14]

September and most of October were uneventful for the regiment; it continued to camp behind the front line and was "engaged principally in throwing up earthworks and fortifications," its companies working at several places along the Petersburg line.[15] As these now routine duties continued, new soldiers were arriving from several sources, many of them from consolidated recruiting operations at Camp Casey in Virginia and Ellicott Mills and other Maryland locations.

NEW RECRUITS

Company A gained only seven recruits in October, all but one signing up in Illinois. The exception, Pvt. William Clark, was a slave of Thomas McKie in his native St. Mary's County, Maryland, before enlisting at Baltimore. None of the remaining six were Illinois natives, but all of them were living in the state when they joined the army. It is possible that Pvt. Samuel Winston (sometimes Winsted) had been born in Illinois, but his records are incomplete. It is known, however, that he was not counted against Illinois's quota, which means he had been recruited by another state's agent. Pvt. Harvey Jones Frazier claimed on some documents that he had been born in 1830 in Springfield, Illinois, but it is certain that he had been a slave in Missouri most of his life. He had been married about 1854 in Palmyra, Missouri, "under the influence of my old Master (William Dudley)," meaning without clergy or official ceremony. The couple eventually had fourteen children, of which a number were alive when Frazier enlisted at Galesburg, Illinois. Pvt. George Mitchell, age nineteen, born in Mississippi, was mustered in at Alton, a substitute for Conrad Everbing, a drafted man, while Pvt. George Burke, Virginia born and the same age as Mitchell, was the only draftee among the company's October recruits. Although the October recruits were carried on the company rolls, some of them did not reach the regiment until November or later, delayed by processing at Camp Butler, Illinois's Springfield replacement center. There were only twelve more gains in the last two months of 1864, a mix of soldiers enlisted as substitutes credited to Illinois and a few recruited by other states. Pvt. Charles Foreman, a Pennsylvania-born sailor, was the only man mustered in outside Illinois. He was a substitute for John Sharp or Reuben E. Jackson, citizens of North Wilmington, Delaware, and had been processed at Camp Casey before joining the regiment prior to Petersburg. Two of the Illinois recruits recorded stories of their paths from slavery to the Twenty-ninth USCT. Pvt. Solomon Lee was eighteen and had been a slave in Cooper County, Missouri, and it is possible that he had been born in Virginia and had been carried west while a child and sold. He was owned by Fanny Tucker, a minor, and had belonged to her father since 1859. Shortly after the war Lee signed an affidavit certifying that he was the slave whom Tucker had named in a petition for the owner's bounty. That Lee had such good relations with his young owner might be inferred from Lee's unusual literacy, which could have been gained through Tucker's tutoring. Pvt. John Turner said that he had been born in bondage at Holly Springs, Mississippi, in 1845 and went to Memphis with his owner, Mr. Cockrill, early in the war. He ran away when federal troops occupied the city and worked on the river as a laborer. He arrived in Cairo, Illinois, and took a job in a sawmill. When work slowed in late November, he enlisted and was sent from Springfield to Camp Casey and to the regiment.[16]

Company B found only four replacements in October, all of which were credited to Illinois. Pvt. Lewis Ellsworth, eighteen, had been born in bondage to Charles Read in Hayward County, Tennessee. He escaped from his owner—or more likely from the Confederate army to which he was hired out—at Fort Pillow and made his way to Union lines. Ellsworth worked his way upriver to Cairo and was taken by rail to Mt. Henry County, Illinois, where he enlisted for one year. Ellsworth was to desert the regiment in May 1865 in Virginia after the war ended, and from there he went to St. Joseph, Missouri, where he worked as a barber. Despite his status as a deserter, he applied for a pension, had the charge withdrawn under an amnesty, received an honorable discharge, and was pensioned in 1897. The other three October enlistees, Cpl. Alexander Carter and Pvts. William Davenport and Thomas J. Shores, also took one-year enlistments, but very little else is known about them.[17]

Company C mustered sixteen soldiers in October, nearly all Virginia natives from the replacement pool of black soldiers at Camp Casey. Most of them were young Virginians, but a few had other backgrounds. Pvt. Charles W. Smith was born at Chatham, Kent County, Canada West, in 1838. He ran away from home when the war began and hired himself out as a servant to a Captain Lawson, of the Second Michigan Infantry. Lawson was cashiered for drunkenness and went to Washington, D.C., perhaps to contest his dismissal, bringing Smith with him. Smith had heard that his father was looking for him and wished to have him returned to Canada as a British subject. He also saw an uncle from Windsor, his hometown, in Washington, but he avoided him. Smith said later that he was easy to identify because he was nearly white in appearance. He decided to flee the capital, crossed the Long Bridge into Virginia, and enlisted at Camp Casey using the assumed name of William Young. He served under this name for the duration of the war. Smith was known for his neat appearance and so spent most of his active service detailed as an orderly at brigade head-quarters. He became sick or was wounded by "casual fire" before Richmond in February 1865 and was sent to the hospital at Portsmouth, Virginia, and did not return to the company. After the war he settled finally in Vicksburg, where he lived for thirty-two years with a woman whom he abandoned for another shortly before his death.[18]

A more typical Company C October enlistee was Aaron Washington. Born in Farquier County, Virginia, in 1835, probably in slavery, he married at Harrisonburg in 1854 and had one minor child when he enlisted at Camp Casey, a substitute for a draftee. Washington joined the regiment in late October, writing to his wife on arrival that he was well. He wrote again from Dutch Gap, where part of his company had been detailed, in early December. In answer to his wife's plea for money, Washington said: "I have none now I have spent it all and let it ___ iff you would have let me know when I was at Camp Casey[.] They would not let me out of Camp and you did not come and I stayed there Eight Days after you was iff you had come I could have let you have 80 dollars [probably part of the fee he received as a substitute]." Washington took sick in April and was sent to Point of Rocks hospital. He died there of pneumonia on the first of May. First Lt. John Aiken wrote of him, "Washington was a good and faithful soldier." His widow and child were pensioned until the widow remarried in 1870. Some years later another woman, Susan Norris, tricked Washington's widow out of her canceled pension certificate and fraudulently tried to reactivate payments to herself. She was unsuccessful.[19]

Company D gained fifteen new men in September, about evenly divided between recruits found in Illinois and those enlisted at Camp Casey; the latter were not credited to Illinois and may have been signed by agents from other states. In October the count was eleven soldiers, nine credited to Illinois. Few of these men left accounts of their earlier lives. One of them who did, Pvt. Dennis Hughes, was born a slave somewhere in northern Alabama in 1844. The war had allowed him to escape from bondage. A white veteran, J. M. Williams, of Company H, Eighth Wisconsin Infantry, explained in a 1909 affidavit how Hughes had come north. He said that the slave had appeared at a Union camp on the Memphis and Charleston Railroad seventeen miles east of Luscumbia, Alabama, with other contrabands in September 1862. Hughes was employed by a company officer as cook and servant. The officer resigned about July 1864 when the veterans of the Eighth Wisconsin went home. Hughes left the regiment at Chicago, planning to enlist in a black regiment. He was rejected as unfit but tried again at St. Louis, where an agent of the Twenty-ninth Regiment accepted him in October.[20]

The new men for these first four companies included only a few substitutes for drafted men, and most were volunteers, not draftees. The Illinois men were from all over the state, a few having enlisted for one year. It appears that most of the new Company A, B, C, and D men—save some Maryland and Virginia draftees—were induced to join the regiment by enlistment bounties and perhaps patriotism.[21]

Companies E, F, G, and a new company, H, mustered thirty-seven, twenty-one, twenty-two, and eighty-five new soldiers, respectively, in September and October. Nearly every one of these men was a draftee from Maryland, plus a few Maryland and Virginia substitutes and a handful of substitutes and volunteers from Illinois. Among the latter were four related men named Ashby who enlisted in Company G at Pekin on 21 September. These soldiers, Pvts. Marshall, Nathan, William J., and William H. Ashby seem to have been born in Illinois, in Peoria and Fulton Counties, and all were substitutes for draftees. Army records do not contain any further information about their lives before service, nor are details of their relationships explained. Their service was also undistinguished, except that William J. Ashby was absent from duty, ill with measles, lung disease, and rheumatism, for much of his military service. Despite his poor medical history, he lived to be eighty-five. Nothing distinguishes individual soldiers among the large number recruited in Maryland and the lesser number from Virginia. All appear to have been farm laborers, the majority of them slaves from around Baltimore and from some Eastern Shore counties.[22]

The new Company H, which was organized in October, initially was made up entirely of recent draftees and substitutes largely from Maryland, and not one was credited toward meeting Illinois's federal quota. None of the noncommissioned officers had more than a month's active service before appointment. William (Thomas) Demby, age thirty-three, was a native of Chestertown, Kent County, Maryland. He was drafted into the army for one year at Easton as a private in late September. Although illiterate, he was promoted to first sergeant, the company commander later recalling that he was "a very faithful Soldier." The literacy of the other noncommissioned officers cannot be verified, but it appears that none of them could write with ease. Sgt. John Costley (sometimes Cosley), age twenty-six, a barber before enlisting, and Sgt. Benjamin Wilson could probably write, but Sgt. William J. Polk, a Salisbury, Maryland, carpenter, and Sgt. John Ford, a twenty-five-year-old Virginian, certainly could not. Records do not make clear how well the company's eight corporals could assist in the company's paperwork, but they seem to have been less able to assist company officers in these matters than the four sergeants.[23]

Company H had a fair number of substitutes, all of whom were supposed to receive a payment at enlistment. Likely many of them were denied this money because of fraud or because they were unaware of and unable to insist on their entitlements. Pvt. Elija Tross, a twenty-year-old Virginian and probably an escaped or army-freed slave, was working in Baltimore as a waiter when he enlisted there in October, expecting to receive three hundred dollars as a substitute for a drafted man. He complained after the war that he never received the promised compensation. Pvt. John Dorsey was born to slaves of the Eiglehart family in Howard County, Maryland. He said that he was not himself a slave but "was bound out when I was 11 years old to serve until 21—was bound out to Charles Quinn who was a gardener close to the city [Baltimore]." Being twenty-one in 1864, Dorsey hired himself out to a Mr. Tyson at Carroll Manor near Ellicott City. He may have been temporarily at Rock Hall, Kent County, picking peaches when he was offered a hundred and fifty dollars to enlist. Hearing that a three-hundred-dollar bounty was being paid in Baltimore, he went to the city and enlisted at Camp Belger in late October. The soldier claimed that he was indeed given the promised bounty, but this assertion caused Dorsey a delay in receiving a pension in later years. He was thought to be an impostor because none of the other soldiers from Maryland polled by the pension examiner said they had been paid.[24]

Pvt. John Lindsey enlisted at Baltimore in October, a substitute for Charles H. Flexcomb, a drafted man. From a day or two before enlistment until he was sent to Company H in Virginia was the only connection the soldier had with Maryland. He had been born near Georgetown, Kentucky, but could not recall his age. "I was a boy, big enough to plow [fourteen to fifteen?], when the Mexican War was going on," he said. From 1850 to 1853 he lived in Scott County, as a slave owned by Wesley Rossell. In 1853 he was moved by his owner to a farm seven miles from Brackenridge (?), Caldwell (?) County, Mississippi, on the Hannibal and Jackson Railroad. In October 1863, no doubt because of the disruptions of war, Lindsey was freed or ran off. He joined the navy as a landsman, enlisting on the gunboat *Pequot* and serving for a year. He later claimed that his hearing had been damaged by concussion from an exploding gun in "a fight on the Gulf of Mexico." Lindsey was discharged at Fort Monroe, Virginia, on 22 October 1864 and went immediately to Baltimore, enlisting in the army two days later. The soldier got rheumatism in November and December standing guard duty before Petersburg, and he spent the rest of his service in the Fort Monroe hospital, being discharged there in March 1865.[25]

Perhaps so he could collect the bounty, Pvt. Jacob McCabe's master accompanied him to Wilmington when the slave was drafted in October 1864. McCabe was born Jake Mitchell in Anne Arundel County, Maryland, in 1846; when he was twelve to fourteen he was sold by his owner to Tom Dukes, possibly a slave trader, who sold him to McCabe. McCabe lived in Delaware on the state line with Maryland. The town, Sallyville, Bellingsville, or Showersville, was probably in New Castle County. At the enlistment office in Wilmington McCabe told officials that his slave was named Jacob McCabe and was twenty. The new soldier was sent to Baltimore the day following enlistment and four days later went by train to Washington, D.C., along with other recruits. Crossing the Long Bridge, he arrived at Camp Casey and a week later at the army replacement center at City Point. Presumably, his owner collected the bounty.[26]

Details of the early lives of Company H's other fall 1864 enlistees were not known to army—or later to pension bureau—officials, but some information survives. Like other companies, the unit accepted brothers, who almost always enlisted at the same time. Three related Ewings were mustered in at Greenville, Illinois. The oldest, Pvt. Archie Ewing, was thirty-four when he entered the service. He was born in Lafayette County, Missouri, and was possibly always a free man. He was working as a farm laborer and living in Greenville, Bond County, Illinois, not far from his place of birth, in 1853, the year of his first marriage. His wife died the same year, and he married again. Archie Ewing was to marry four more times, the last union in 1902, but he had only three children, all of whom he said were by his first wife, to whom he had been married less than a year. Pvt. George Ewing, Archie's half-brother, was ten years younger. Born and raised in Illinois at Hillsboro, Montgomery County, he was also living in Bond County when he enlisted. He too was married many times, three times with a ceremony. Pvt. James Ewing, twenty-four at enlistment, married only twice and was a widower when he died, long after the war. Much less is known about the Green brothers, both born as slaves in

Anne Arundel County, Maryland. Probably both, Pvt. John R. Green, twenty-two, and Adam Green, nineteen, were paid substitutes, recruited from their homes near Laural and enlisted at the Ellicott Mills, Maryland, replacement depot.[27]

September and October enlistments brought Company H up beyond minimum strength, and the company was mustered in during October. In November one more soldier joined, in December four, and the last enlistees, sixteen, were acquired in January. Company I was recruited mostly in December, but thirty-six new soldiers had been enlisted by October and a handful in November, when the emphasis was on filling up H. The tenth and final company, K, acquired only three men by the end of October, the main flow of its recruits still to come in December. Company K was to be mustered in at the end of December, placing the regiment at full strength, less ten or twenty spaces per company available for replacements, by the first days of 1865.[28]

In addition to those soldiers assigned to companies, another eighty-seven replacements, many of them substitutes, were enlisted and mustered in at various Illinois towns and cities from August through October 1864. These unassigned recruits were counted as members of the regiment and were part of Illinois's quotas, but none of them joined the regiment in the field; with the regiment's enlistments from Maryland and Virginia rapidly filling vacancies, by the time these Illinois recruits were assembled at Springfield for forwarding to Virginia, they were largely surplus. Few Maryland and Virginia recruits were credited against Illinois's quota. Draftees were all designated as from Maryland, and the substitutes were claimed by a wide variety of states. The unassigned recruits from Illinois partially balanced the men found in the East who did not fill Illinois's Washington-imposed troop levies. During the next three months another one hundred and fifty surplus volunteers were signed into the regiment, and another three hundred black men, all of them credited to Illinois, were enlisted in Illinois for twenty-seven U. S. Colored Troops infantry, cavalry, and artillery units raised in other states. Over those same months, November through February, the Twenty-ninth Regiment received some Illinois-enlisted and Illinois-credited men, twenty to thirty per company, but until January the regiment depended heavily on the continuing supply of fresh troops from Maryland and Virginia replacement depots.[29]

The regiment lost only nine men in the period from the crater battle through October, about half from disease. Company F's Pvt. Jackson Mackay had died of crater wounds at City Point in August, and, unknown to the regiment at the time, Pvt. Lewis Williams of Cook County died a prisoner of war in Petersburg in the same month. Company C's Pvt. Adolph Cofield, an eighteen-year-old former slave from Kentucky, was accidentally shot and killed on the march on 5 October, and Pvt. Wesley Robinson, a soldier wounded at the crater, deserted from Company F five days later. Of course, there were also a number of serious injuries. In September Company D's Pvt. Archibald Hopson lost part of his right index and middle fingers from an accidental discharge of a rifle while on picket duty near the Weldon railroad south of Petersburg. Hopson, treated at Summit House Hospital in Philadelphia, was discharged as disabled the following May. Company C's Pvt. John Bird may have been similarly injured by his own carelessness, but, when seeking a pension six years after the war, he had one of his comrades certify that on 4 October both men had been: "in one of the rifle pits, loading and firing at the enemy, and while John Bird was in said Riffle pitt he was shot by a ball in the right hand, that this was in the middle of the night, and that after said Bird was shot, . . . [I] went with him to the hospital. Known as the flying hospital, in the rear of the regiment." The soldier said that before daylight Dr. Mackay or another doctor cut off Bird's right hand middle finger at the joint and two weeks later Bird was sent to the hospital in Alexandria. Bird was in Alexandria until mid-December, was given leave to his home at Shawneetown, Illinois, and finally returned to duty in late April, after hostilities were over. After the war Bird was pensioned at three dollars a month for the loss of his finger.[30]

Firearm accidents appear to have been common, understandable given the minimum training recruits received before being placed on full duty—as well as the former slaves' unfamiliarity with firearms. Company A's Pvt. William Burke, a nineteen-year-old born in Farquier County, Virginia, one of the soldiers enlisted in mid-September by agents of Westchester County, New York, could not have been with the regiment at the front for more than a few days when, on 5 October, while on picket duty, he accidentally shot himself. He was taken to Alexandria, where doctors amputated his left forearm. He was eventually returned to City Point hospital and was discharged. Burke was single, and hospital records show his nearest relative as Emmeline Burke, Columbus, Ohio (his mother?). Although clearly qualified for a disability pension, Burke never applied. Another Company A man, Mississippi-born Pvt. George Mitchell, may also have been a casualty of a firearm accident. He died just two months later of the effects of a gunshot wound and disease at the Point of Rocks, Virginia, army hospital within days after his arrival in Virginia. Had his wounds been caused by enemy action, the army would have so noted them on his record, so he was apparently a casualty of his own or a comrade's carelessness.[31]

No doubt a number of soldiers were found to be unsuited for army life because of misconduct, but records about these men are incomplete. Pvt. Willis A. Bogart, the literate soldier from England, was released from the service in October as unfit for continued duty because of an injury inflicted on him by an unnamed officer of the regiment. The officer shot him, in the words of Bogart's disability certificate, "on account of disrespectful and mutinous language to Superior officer while under arrest, which has rendered the arm powerless ever since." From Chicago shortly after the war Bogart may have hoped his record was incomplete, because he applied for a pension for, among other things, a "Gunshot wound in left arm/above the Elbow." He also claimed that he had been injured on the way from Spotsylvania Court House to Petersburg in June 1864, having "Reced Hernia by Mule falling thro the Bridge & throwing him on the Pomel of the Saddle." Even though he supplied affidavits supporting the claim from comrades Sgt. Charles Greenwell and Cpl. James Smith and Company C musician Logan Davis, his unsatisfactory service was better documented than he thought. The records showed that Bogart had the hernia at enlistment and that his wounded arm was a result of his misconduct. He was never pensioned, and he narrowly escaped prosecution for attempted pension fraud.[32]

Other soldiers made postwar claims for injuries that they admitted were the result of army punishment. Company E's Pvt. Moses Alexander, for example, tried to justify a pension for disabilities he said were received when "'Little Joe' Arbuckle & I were tied back to back and made to stand on a barral[sic] [for two hours] for fighting at Petersburg, Va." Alexander's argument may have been the same as that Pvt. William R. Baynard used equally unsuccessfully in trying to convince the pension bureau that he was entitled to payments. Baynard, a substitute from Caroline County, Maryland, said that he had received an "Ingiry" "while in the service while being inhumanely punished by being tied by the wrists for over 15 hours at which time I recived[sic] the Ingiry to my arms and wrists." His offense was "stealing a pocket book in front of a Lieutenant's tent" in August 1865, well after the war. That Baynard thought the punishment excessively severe did not influence the pension examiners. Pvt. John Ender, a Louisville, Kentucky, native who enlisted in Company B at Chicago at the beginning of 1864, was tried and convicted of deserting his company while on a reconnaissance at the front in late October 1864. For punishment "he was ordered by Robert Porter, Capt. Commanding Regt to carry a knapsack weighing 60 lbs. for eight hours each day for five days in front of Hd. Qrs. . . . And to be drummed through the camp labeled 'Shirk.'" Unlike the other two soldiers, Ender did not claim pensionable injuries from the disciplinary action; he was paid, however, for more common rheumatism and diarrhea complaints.[33]

Disease claimed a steady number of the regiment's soldiers, and several died or were disabled during the fall of 1864. Pvt. Charles Murry, born five miles from Hannibal, Missouri, in 1846, and his family had been slaves of Francis Brown. They fled from bondage in 1863 and lived at Galesburg, Illinois, where Charles worked in a lumber yard. The soldier, who survived the crater fight, became ill with typhoid fever in August, and he died at the "Hospital for colored troops" at City Point on 2 September. Since Murry had contributed to his family's support in Illinois before entering the army, his mother and later his father were pensioned. Another victim of typhoid, a month later, was Company F's Pvt. John Douglas, at forty-five one of the oldest soldiers in the regiment; like others whose enlistment age was shown as the maximum permitted, he may have been older. Born in Albemarle County, Virginia, he was married there with the consent of his "Master & Mistress." Years later his widow had trouble proving the marriage because of, she said, "the laws of Virginia not permitting legal marriages of slaves." A soldier whose records show to have been forty-six when mustered in was another casualty of old age and disease, although he did not die in the army. Pvt. Alexander H. Howard, a carpenter who lived five years at Alton, Illinois, before joining Company E in February 1864, was apparently too ill for active service beginning with the march from White House Landing to Petersburg in June 1864, the regiment's first strenuous activity. He was made a nurse in the divisional field hospital and was later assigned to "attend the amputation Table" at the City Point hospital for black troops. He developed "diliopatic Ersipelas," a malady that caused his legs to swell and burst, and he was discharged as disabled. Company B Pvt. James Stewart, the free Chicagoan whose brother Jordan was killed at the crater action, was hospitalized in September and was sent north two months later. His records show that he was under arrest at the Philadelphia hospital for unknown reasons. Transferred to Fort Monroe hospital, he remained there until discharged. It cannot be determined whether Stewart had been prevented from returning to his regiment for disciplinary or health reasons.[34]

MORE REORGANIZATION AND SUPPORT DUTY

While the Twenty-ninth Regiment was being brought up to strength and reconstituted, the Ninth Army Corps was reorganized, its three white divisions combined into two and Ferrero's command renumbered the Third Division. The corps was also moved from its positions near Fort Davis where the Union siege line crossed the Jerusalem Plank Road south of Petersburg southwest to Fort Howard, less than a mile from the Weldon Railroad. Ferrero's Third Division was, by 30 September, spread rather thinly from Weldon Railroad to the Jerusalem Plank Road, a distance of over three miles, but this was a quiet sector, more than a mile from Confederate positions. By 5 October, however, the division moved once again to Poplar Grove Church and was assigned responsibility for about a mile of rear-line fortifications between Forts Cummings and Duschane. All this maneuvering was part of Grant's continuing effort to run around Lee's supply lines south of Petersburg and force the Confederates to abandon their capital. The lieutenant general looked to cut off the vital railroads running from North Carolina to Petersburg-Richmond by moving along the southern edge of the Confederate defensive positions. The Twenty-ninth U.S. Colored Infantry was called on to participate with the rest of the Second Brigade, now commanded by Colonel Russell (soon to be promoted to brevet brigadier general) of the Twenty-eighth USCT, in the next round of this continuing contest, an action six miles west of the Weldon Railroad, where the Boydton Plank Road crossed Hatcher's Run. The regiment saw very little action in the two-day battle in late October and reported but one man wounded.[35]

Discipline in the regiment was improving because many new officers reported for duty. First Lieutenant Samuel A. Johnston, formerly a soldier in the 140th Pennsylvania Infantry Regiment who fought at Chancellorsville, Gettysburg, and all of the Army of the Potomac's battles through Cold Harbor, was assigned to Company A, as was 2d Lt. James Morvan Smith, of Pittsburgh, Pennsylvania, commissioned from civilian life without any recorded prior military service. John Aiken, a Free Military School graduate who had been sergeant major of the 126th Ohio Volunteers and had seen action in West Virginia, replaced the resigned Robert Gale as first lieutenant of Company B (Aiken later went to Company K). Second Lieutenant Michael J. Hassler, who had participated in the crater battle before his commissioning, likewise joined Company B. The company's new commander, replacing Hector H. Aiken, who had been killed at Petersburg, was Capt. Wellington V. Heusted, age twenty-four, a native of Genesee County, New York, but living in Michigan when the war began. As a sergeant in the Third Michigan Cavalry, he fought in several western engagements before he was given a thirty-day leave to attend the Free Military School in Philadelphia. After being examined by a Washington Casey board, he was recommended for captain. Returning to the Third Michigan Cavalry, then in Arkansas, to wait for his commission, Heusted was wounded when the riverboat on which he was traveling was fired on by bushwhackers. Consequently, he was delayed joining the Twenty-ninth USCT and did not reach the regiment until late December. First Lieutenant Thomas A. Palmer, from Maine, a former quartermaster sergeant in the First (West) Virginia Cavalry, was assigned to Company D, and Company C gained 2d Lt. George G. Smith, a bond clerk drafted as a private soldier in Pennsylvania in 1863. Second Lieutenant Thomas J. Eddowes, from Philadelphia and formerly a private in the 118th Pennsylvania Volunteers, reported to Company D (and later went to Company I) after completing the Free Military School course and being approved by a Washington, D.C., Casey board. Second Lieutenant Jacob Sanders, an enlisted man in the 142d Pennsylvania Volunteers, was assigned to Company E. Company F gained 2d Lt. Frederick W. Brownell, age nineteen, a former private in the Forty-seventh Massachusetts Volunteer Infantry, who completed the course at the Free Military School and who would soon be promoted to first lieutenant of the company.[36]

The new Company G received its three officers in October, Capt. William A. Southwell, 1st Lt. David D. Fickes, and 2d Lt. Albert L. Granger. Southwell, a Pennsylvania farmer, had been a corporal in the 143d Pennsylvania Volunteers and had been wounded at Gettysburg and again in the Wilderness battle. He was a graduate of the Free Military School and had been approved for a commission by a Casey board in October. Fickes was also a former private in a Pennsylvania regiment and a Free Military School graduate and had been a signal corps soldier in the West and at Fredericksburg and Chancellorsville; Granger had been a private in the Eighth Illinois Cavalry, in which he enlisted in February 1864. Company H, also newly formed, was assigned its three officers by November. The commanding officer was Capt. Francis E. Newton, who had been first sergeant in the Seventh Kansas Cavalry, with which he had served in Kentucky, Tennessee, Alabama, and Mississippi. He was found qualified by the St. Louis Casey board in September 1864. First Lieutenant Nimrod Ferguson, the Missourian who had fought at the crater before being commissioned or mustered in, also reported to Company H, as did 2d Lt.

Abiel L. Wentz, a Free Military School alumnus who had fought at Vicksburg and other western battles and, as late as July 1864, at Atlanta with the Twenty-fifth Iowa Volunteers.[37]

By early November 1864 the Twenty-ninth Regiment counted 20 officers mustered in and 713 enlisted men. By late that month it had all its company officers but, because it was still shy two companies, had not yet been authorized a colonel, regimental adjutant, quartermaster officer, chaplain, or surgeons. Major Brown was back as acting commanding officer, and Surgeon Mackay, although not filling an authorized position, remained with the regiment. As before, company officers were used to make up administrative shortages, but, since recruiting had reached full stride with threats of the draft and new quota calls, the army had regimental staff officers in the pipeline. Lieutenant Chapman of Company B, who had been acting as regimental adjutant, was made assistant adjutant and inspector general in November, not an authorized position in a regiment. Chapman complained that officers junior to him were being promoted, and he sent in his resignation. The position he occupied, possibly at brigade level, was apparently just temporary, and it appears he was induced to stay on by the promise that he would be appointed the captain commanding new Company I when it was ready for mustering in. Chapman was replaced by Conant, earlier promoted to first lieutenant and reassigned to Company E, in the acting adjutant's position, but Conant returned to company service in December, being replaced in turn in January 1865 by 1st Lt. Henry F. W. Little, an officer who may have been forced on the regiment by General Butler. Little had been an enlisted man in a New Hampshire regiment stationed at Bermuda Hundred with Butler's Army of the James, and he said later that he was at the time severely disabled by swollen feet, the result of too much marching in earlier campaigns in South Carolina and Florida. Assigned for a few days to Company H and then B, he welcomed the staff assignment as adjutant because he was allowed a horse. The regimental Descriptive Book says of him: "App'l'd to the reg't by Benj. F. Butler, Maj Gen'l U.S. Vols. Actg Adjutant from Jan. 24th 1865 until March 8th 1865, at which date he left the reg't on leave of absence. He never reported back for duty & was dismissed [from] the service per Special Orders 254, . . . War Department A.G.O. Washington, D.C., May 26th 1865. Dropped as a deserter April 3rd 1865." Little's dismissal order was revoked by the War Department in 1868, but his record does not say if the action was taken at his request or if his absence was excused in one of a number of postwar amnesties.[38]

Assistant Surgeon Clarence Ewen, of Middletown, New York, reported in early November and Chaplain George S. Barnes, age thirty-five, a Methodist Episcopal minister from Greenland, New Hampshire, later in the month. Ewen had experience with the Fifty-sixth and 182d New York Regiments, but Barnes had no prior military service. Chaplains, who had rank and pay equivalent to captains, were elected by a regiment's officers and had to show credentials and recommendations from a religious denomination. They had many administrative duties, such as postmasters and organizers of schools to teach soldiers basic reading and writing skills. In addition to providing religious services, chaplains were responsible for setting up a library and securing, Barnes said, "the means of improvement and amusement of the troops." (Over half the black officers commissioned in the war—excluding Louisiana Native Guards, who were decommissioned early—were chaplains elected by white officers in black regiments.) Acting Quartermaster Gosper and Chaplain Barnes were the regiment's last officer casualties. Gosper lost a leg, the result of an enemy shell hitting his quarters on 4 December 1864, and Barnes was slightly wounded by the same explosion. Lieutenant Palmer, Company G, took over the quartermaster job temporarily, the position finally being filled in February 1865 by 1st Lt. Jason M. Case, a former private in the Eighth Connecticut Volunteers who was from Middletown, Connecticut.[39]

November and December acquisitions of recruits for Companies A through H who had been enlisted earlier were few, the new companies being emphasized instead. Fifteen men were mustered in for Company A, half of them substitutes born in Mississippi, Canada, Kentucky, and Missouri, and most enlisted in Illinois, but these men did not report in Virginia for duty until one or two months after enlistment, usually arriving in large groups from Camp Butler at Springfield. Company B received only four men, three from Camp Casey, and one, Pvt. Allen Gunnell, who enlisted in Chicago but was in fact a displaced Virginian. Ten soldiers, four from Illinois and the rest from Maryland and Delaware, were Company C's new men, and Company D found just three. Companies E, F, G, and H signed one, twelve, seventeen, and five recruits, respectively, in November and December, most of them from Maryland sources. The additions, however, were insufficient to meet even the relatively few losses from disease and misadventure in the regiment. For example, Company A's Pvt. Nelson Geter, who was forty-five, was not up to the rigors of campaigning, and he was discharged, suffering from an unspecified lung disease, a condition thought by army doctors to have existed prior to his enlistment. Pvt. Francis Day, Company B, lost an eye from an accidental bayonet or gunshot wound, and Pvt. Richard Carroll, of Company D, who may have been wounded at the crater, was treated and discharged for epilepsy. Carroll thought that his illness was a result of a fit caused by the excitement of battle and from drinking water contaminated with blood, but the doctors found he had a preexisting condition. Within a month of his disability discharge Carroll enlisted at Chicago in the Thirteenth U.S. Colored HeavyArtillery, a unit raised in Kentucky, and he served out the war in that organization, apparently without further epileptic attacks. Many soldiers became sick from exposure in late 1864 and were hospitalized from time to time, particularly in December, which was a cold, wet month.[40]

Company I was mustered in during December and Company K on the first of January. Both companies were initially made up almost entirely of substitutes and draftees from Maryland and Delaware, with a few scattered Illinoisans, and each had about a hundred enlisted men. Company I's first enlistments were made in September, twenty-nine men, but these did not appear at the regiment in the field for at least a month. Twenty of these men were slaves or former slaves conscripted in Kent County and were mustered in at Easton, Maryland, and with few exceptions further details of their lives before army service are not noted in their records. Pvt. Henry Miller, once a slave near Chestertown, had been freed by his master, George Westcott, in about 1861. He was living at Still Pond when drafted. Being forty years old at the time, he was married and had eight children. Probably because of his age and possible infirmities, he spent most of his service assigned as an ambulance driver. Pvt. George Senia told recruiters that he had been free and working for wages at Worton when he was conscripted. The soldier was able to read, indicating that he may have been free for many years, but his wife, whom he married in 1856, was certainly a slave. Pvt. James Ringold was not a slave because his mother was a free woman, but he had been apprenticed to a Thomas Bowells (or Bowles) until he was twenty-one, a form of bondage. Bowells hired Ringold out as a house servant and coachman to a Nathan Vorshel at Easton. Ringold was freed from this work three years before he was conscripted, but he appears to have remained a laborer.[41]

Two soldiers, Pvts. Thomas Morgan and Isaac Scott, were drafted together from Elmwood Farm at Still Pond, where they were the property of Dr. Thomas Kinnard. Each soldier had had seven children, but not all of them were living. The men had another common distinction: both were rather along in years and were to die in the army of disease. Morgan succumbed to pneumonia in February 1865, but where and by what cause Scott died cannot be determined. Scott's widow received a letter from him dated 8 March 1865, in which he reported Morgan's death. The letter (one of the few from a black soldier to survive) on U.S. Sanitary Commission stationery, certainly dictated but not written by Scott, read:

> My dear Wife
> I wrote you sometime since, but not hearing from you I concluded it was not received. So, I write again hoping to get a reply. I am quite well & have been so since I came out. We are lying on the front about six miles from Richmond. Our labor is not hard, yet we find enough to do. How glad I would be to see you & the children, but this cannot be at present. The boys we heard were killed are all living. I have seen them—see them frequently. We are expecting to be paid off soon & I will send you some money if you wish me to do so. Give my love to all our friends & reserve a large share for yourself & the children.
> Fresby Brown [likely Pvt. Perry Brown Jr.] is well and sends his love to his sister Ellen & his wife & wishes them to write him how they get along. Thomas Morgan died about the first of February [22 February]. Send word to his wife.
> Tell sister Hennetta to write how she & her family all are. Berry, too[;] how is he & all the rest of them.

Mrs. Scott received this letter but heard nothing more from or about her husband for the rest of the war. Six months after the end of hostilities she encountered a returning soldier, Pvt. George Rasin, of Company H, in Maryland and asked him "what became of Isaac and he said he was dead." It seems the army had lost track of the soldier, who apparently had died in an army hospital. No record of his admission or death was recorded. Failure to notify wives of their husbands' deaths seem to have been common, and the wife of Pvt. Edward Hogan had an experience similar to Mrs. Scott's. Hogan, age forty, a native of Cecil County, Maryland, was living with his family at Odessa, Delaware. Married in Maryland in 1851, he had three children. Hogan was hospitalized in early 1865, and he died in early April at the army hospital in Portsmouth, Virginia, of chronic diarrhea. That same month the widow had a letter written to the chief surgeon at Portsmouth requesting official notification of her husband's death, which she said she had heard of "through a friend." She applied for a pension but had the usual difficulty documenting her marriage because, her deposition said, "the State of Maryland at that time did not make any Record of the marriage of Colored People." Despite this obstacle, she was eventually pensioned.[42]

Only two substitutes were signed on for Company I in September, one soldier from Maryland and another from Virginia, the last man recruited by an agent from New York. Finally, three men enlisted in Wisconsin, two in Illinois, and one in Delaware. In the following month only three recruits were found, a draftee from Maryland and substitutes from Delaware and Illinois. The last, Pvt. Thomas Scott, was born in Dixon, Illinois, in 1835. He began his war service in July 1863, enlisting as a landsman on the USS *Clara Dolson* of the navy's Mississippi Squadron. Having completed his one-year enlistment, Scott was discharged from the USS *Benton* at Natchez. Three months later, after working his way to Illinois, he enlisted as a substitute at Dixon, Lee County, probably attracted by the bounty payments.[43]

In November the company acquired nineteen new men, only two of whom were enlisted in Wisconsin or Illinois. The Wisconsin man was Pvt. Richard Tilford, a native of Jefferson County, Kentucky. Tilford, who was forty-three at enlistment, was in poor health. He was hospitalized at Portsmouth a few months after arriving in Virginia and was finally discharged for "general debility old age" without returning to his company. Pvt. Jefferson Berbo (sometimes Bobo), age eighteen, was South Carolina born. He enlisted at Alton, as a substitute for a William Lutz, but how he came to be in that Illinois town is not in his records. The remaining sixteen soldiers were a mix of Maryland and Delaware draftees and substitutes. Two of them, John A. Benson and John Wallace, quickly earned sergeant's stripes. Benson was born in 1848 near Toronto, Canada, and was working as a teamster in New York when he was apparently attracted by bounties or substitute payments offered at Wilmington, Delaware. Wallace, born in Madison County, Maryland, was a substitute for D. B. Laughlin, a drafted man.[44]

December 1864 was a successful recruiting month for Company I; forty-four new soldiers enlisted, a sufficient number to allow the company to be mustered in. Just three recruits were found in Illinois; two, and perhaps all three, of them were substitutes. The rest were mainly untraveled men from Maryland and Delaware, although a few substitutes came from outside those states. Pvt. Peter Hawkins was born in Jamaica in 1841; his occupation as a sailor brought him to the United States. In October 1863 he enlisted aboard the USS *North Carolina,* served on the *Penobscot,* and was discharged at Philadelphia from the depot ship *Princeton* in April 1864. Pvt. William Smith, a Delaware native, was another of the company's navy veterans. Also enlisting on the USS *North Carolina,* but a month before Hawkins, he was assigned to the *Supply* and later the *Dandelion* at New York and was released from the navy in Philadelphia. A few soldiers gathered up from their homes to be employed as laborers and servants for the army found themselves finally in Company I, Twenty-ninth U.S. Colored Infantry. Pvt. Edward Mabree (Maber) was born at Hick's Ford, Greenville County, Virginia; he had been a slave owned by Bill Lucas. Liberated by the Union army, he was taken to City Point. With a large number of other contrabands, Mabree was put to work under guard at the supply center. After several months the blacks were transported by boat to Baltimore. Moved to Maryland's Eastern Shore, they were given the opportunity to enlist in the army and may have been told they would be drafted if they did not volunteer. Mabree, however, took the volunteer option, signing up for three years to get the maximum bounty. Born in slavery at Conway, South Carolina, in 1835, Pvt. Daniel Newton was hired out by his owner to work in a Florida turpentine factory. Captured by Union forces at Jacksonville, Newton was made an officer's servant but was eventually taken by government ship to Philadelphia. He probably worked his passage as a sailor, which was the occupation he claimed when he enrolled in the regiment at Wilmington, Delaware. Pvt. Clarence Miller was another South Carolinian. He was enlisted as a substitute for John R. Morris at Wilmington, brought to that place by his employment as a sailor, probably on a merchant vessel. Miller was likely literate, and he was promoted to corporal and later to sergeant in Company I.[45]

Seven men who were born free were among Company I's December recruits, two of them foreigners. Pvt. William H. Jackson, twenty-five, a cook living in Baltimore, claimed he was a native of London, England. He was a paid substitute for Oliver Natkins. Pvt. Jacob Yugnando, twenty-eight, born in Cuba, was probably a substitute when he enlisted at Easton. Both soldiers were ill for most of their time in uniform, and neither explained when or how he arrived in Maryland. The five other free men were all natives of Pennsylvania, drawn to Delaware and Maryland by payments being made for substitutes. The two Delaware enlistees were Pvts. George Brown and Noah Jefferson. Brown, a mature twenty-nine-year-old butcher, was soon promoted to corporal, and he completed his service in that grade. Jefferson, born at Graydon in 1845, earned no stripes and spent most of his time in the regiment ill with pleurisy. Richard Wright, age twenty-six, was the most successful of the Pennsylvanians enlisted in December. Having previously been a Philadelphia barber, he was made a corporal almost at once and sergeant a few weeks later. Very little is known about Pvts. James H. Washington or William Limehouse, except that their birthplaces were someplace in Pennsylvania. Limehouse, when enlisted, was working in a stone quarry in Washington, D.C.[46]

One December recruit, Pvt. John H. Davis, a Virginian enlisted as a substitute for Samuel F. Zegler at Frederick, Maryland, was in Company I less than one month and may never have joined the company in the field. He deserted the service on 10 January. A second early deserter, Pvt. Tobias Watkins, twenty-one, was born a slave in Appomack County on Virginia's Eastern Shore. He enlisted at Easton, Maryland, as a substitute for B. F. Langford. He was probably with Company I for slightly more than a month before deserting, in late February, while on detached service at Point of Rocks. Neither soldier was heard from again.[47]

Frederick A. Chapman, who had fought with Company B at the crater as its first lieutenant and had since been acting regimental adjutant, was appointed Company I's commanding officer and was promoted to captain in February. He did not occupy that position, however, because he was assigned as an assistant adjutant general on General Russell's Third Brigade staff. Jacob Sanders was transferred from Company E and promoted to first lieutenant, but he resigned in a few months. The third officer was twenty-one-year-old 2d Lt. Richard J. Hipwell, Crystal Lake, Illinois, a veteran of the Seventeenth Illinois Cavalry and a Free Military School graduate, who was mustered in on 30 December 1864 and who was the only officer serving with Company I for most of the regiment's remaining service.[48]

Company K, the tenth and final addition to the regiment, was organized on 1 January 1865, primarily with conscripts from several Maryland recruiting depots; ninety-six men were mustered in during December. These men had much the same backgrounds as other former Maryland slaves; most of them were untraveled farmworkers. First Sergeant William Lee, age twenty-two, may have been living as a free man in Baltimore when he was recruited, in mid-December. He had some education and could read and write, no doubt the reason he was made a noncommissioned officer at enlistment. More is known about Pvt. Lewis Bell's early life. He was uncertain of his place and date of birth but remembered that he had been owned by Jim Burley, of St. Landry Parish, Louisiana, and that he was about thirty-one when he was freed by or escaped to the Union army. He was hired in 1862 to be a servant of a Captain Freemain of a cavalry regiment assigned to Maj. Gen. Nathanial Banks's command and accompanied his employer to Alexandria, Natchitoses, and Pleasant Hill during the unsuccessful Red River campaign. The command retreated to New Orleans, where Captain Freemain resigned. Bell accompanied another officer, Lieutenant Snyder, to Baltimore. After two weeks there Bell was sent to Hancock, Maryland, and enlisted at nearby Cumberland, as a substitute for a drafted man.[49]

An unusually large number of Company K's Maryland men concealed their true names at enlistment or were confused about their lineage. William Curtis, from Sandy Bottom, St. Mary's County, said his father, Anthony Chesley, had been "a slave man before the war" and "my mother was a free woman and I was free." Drafted at age twenty-one, Curtis was made a corporal when he enlisted at Camp Stanton, Benedict, Maryland. The soldier used his mother's last name in the army but his father's after discharge. William H. Cutchimber also enlisted at Benedict as a corporal. He used the name William Henry, but it is not known how he came to chose either name. He was a slave of Thomas Gardner and had been married while a slave. His master's daughter recalled in 1902 how, as a young girl, she had made a wedding cake for the couple. Pvt. Joseph H. Downes explained that the last name Brown, which he used when he enlisted at Baltimore, was his stepfather's name and that he had used it to conceal his true identity. He did not say why, but it must have had something to do with his status as a slave. Pvt. Alexander Morgan called himself George A. Barnes in the army, perhaps for reasons similar to Downes's. When asked about the matter, Morgan claimed he had been a free man, which, if it were true, meant he would not have been trying to avoid his master. Finally, a third soldier, Pvt. Joseph Murray, on likewise unspecified grounds, called himself John (sometimes George T.) in army records.[50]

Company K's new commander was 1st Lt. J. Mason Dunn, soon to be promoted to captain. Dunn had a varied military career, enlisting for three-month service in 1861, enlisting again as a private, and working up to captain in the Fifteenth Ohio Volunteers. He resigned because of poor health, later reenlisting as a private in an Ohio cavalry unit, from which he was sent to the Philadelphia Free Military School and was approved for a commission by the Washington, D.C., Casey board. His first lieutenant was John Aiken, transferred from Company B, but Aiken was transferred again (to Company C) within a month. Second Lieutenant John C. Rollman, born in Berlin, Prussia, and formerly with the Sixteenth New York Heavy Artillery, was mustered in with the company in early February, effective 1 January 1865.[51]

COMPLETING THE REGIMENT

From 1 January 1865 the Twenty-ninth U.S. Colored Infantry was organized, but it still had room for more enlistees to fill it to the authorized capacity of eighty-three privates and eleven noncommissioned officers per company. No longer were draftees and substitutes from Maryland, Delaware, and Virginia being sent in large numbers to the regiment. These men were now being directed to black units being formed by states other than Illinois. Now, however, recruiting in Illinois had reached full efficiency and was soon producing recruits in numbers too large for the Twenty-ninth USCT's now small requirements. Company A acquired twenty-one new soldiers in January and eight in February, the final recruits in the company. All were recruited in Illinois, but only a few were native to the state. Most were former slaves, and some left narratives of their lives before army service.

Pvt. William Buckner, age twenty, was born in Ste. Genevieve, Missouri, where he had been owned by Mary Valle. His father's name was Toussaint Gilford, or Gilbord, apparently a Creole, and it is said that Buckner spoke with an accent. Valle married Charles Rosier, and before the war, as was the practice, Buckner used the man's last name. A brother, with whom Buckner escaped from slavery and who called himself John Johnson, said the two had followed their escape with "steamboating on the Mississippi River and other rivers." At some point the future soldier changed his name to Buckner—possibly after yet another owner. He enlisted under that name in late January and was sent to Camp Butler, where he was put to work in the corral. He was not assigned to a company until February, probably because of the large number of recruits on hand and the shortage of vacant regimental positions for them. Consequently, Buckner did not reach the regiment in Virginia until after war's end. Pvt. William Freeman was also Missouri born, and he was freed or freed himself early in the war, being put to work as a contraband laborer by Union forces in late 1861. He was a servant in the mess of the First Illinois Infantry and later worked for individual officers. When work dried up in January 1865, he enlisted at Springfield. Pvt. Samuel Mumford also was employed by the Union military before hard times caused him to join the army. Born a slave of John Hubbard of Hopkinsville, Kentucky, he was sold to Billy Mumford, in Clarksville, who freed him in 1864. Mumford went to work as a fireman aboard a steamboat of the army's commissary department on the Mississippi. He worked at this and at carpentry for a year and a half before enlisting.[52]

Companies B and C gained twenty-four and twenty-two final enlistees in January and February, and only seven of them from Camp Casey reached the Twenty-ninth USCT before the war was over in Virginia. Pvt. William Patterson, one of Company D's nineteen enlistees in this period, was among the few about whom details are recorded. He was born in early 1826 in Louisiana, Kentucky, and was sold in childhood to William King, who brought him to Shelby, Mississippi. Patterson was then known as Major King. As he said later, "My master would not let his slaves go by any other name than King." He ran away from King at Woodville, Mississippi, in 1863 and fled to Helena, Arkansas. Patterson explained why he left his master: "My back is marked all over by the lash of the Cruel Slave owner and the scars are as . . . the bars on 'our Flag.'" At Helena he enlisted as a landsman in the navy and served aboard the *General Bragg*. His duties were as a cook for the officers and "shell passer" for a thirty-two-pound Parrott gun. Patterson, still using the name King, was discharged after one year, and he went to Cairo, probably working his way there on the steamer *Gray Eagle*. He was employed as a hotel cook and then decided to join the army under the name Major King.[53]

Company E enrolled twenty-four soldiers in January and February and Company F twenty-five, eleven from Camp Casey and recruit depots in Maryland. Pvt. Anthony Brandyman, probably an Illinois native, may not have reached his regiment or was only on duty a few days. He was found to have "Tertiary Syphilis," a condition that led to his hospitalization for the rest of his military service. A venereal disease was considered evidence of misconduct and called for discharge. Companies G and H had a similar number of recruits, twenty-three and seventeen, to round out their ranks, and Company G had one of the last men to join the regiment, Pvt. James Crevis, enlisted in Maryland on 1 March.[54]

The last companies organized, I and K, had a share of January and February recruits, twenty and thirteen, respectively. Twenty-year-old Cpl. Samuel Arbuckle, of Company I, one of the several related Arbuckles in the regiment, enlisted on 7 March. Pvt. William Robinson, of the same company, was known by several names: Dobson, derived from his father's; Roberson for no specified reason; and Robinson, after one of his owners. Born in Owensboro, Kentucky, in 1849, he was owned by Alexander Moreland. Robinson was sold for one thousand dollars when he was fourteen to William Blair, of Gallatin, Tennessee, and again to Nathan Bedford Forrest, soon to be a noted Confederate general, in Memphis. He was sold by Forrest in a few months to Harrison Beard, in Coahoma County, Mississippi. He escaped from Beard after two years but was recaptured and sold to Abe Bass, a slave trader from Lake Providence, Louisiana. In 1863 George Robinson, another trader, bought him and hired him out to the government. He worked on breastworks for the Confederate Army at Fort Pillow and was sent to Milliken's Bend. He escaped from that place "before the Yankees got there," going over to Union territory. First employed by the army on the quartermaster vessel *Fairchild*, Robinson went to Helena, Arkansas, to work as a servant for a Union officer. He was found by a recruiting party and was taken to St. Louis and finally Cairo, where he enlisted as a substitute (for a white man, he said) and was paid four hundred dollars. After two weeks at Camp Butler at Springfield, according to Robinson, he and several hundred other recruits for the Twenty-ninth (and other regiments?) were sent to Alexandria, Virginia, by train, arriving in early March. Pvt. Alexander Settles (sometimes Alex Saddler) was mustered in on the same day as Robinson. Freed when the Union army occupied the area near his home at Corinth, Mississippi, he was put to work caring for horses at the contrabands' wage of ten dollars a month, plus food and clothing. He was moved by the quartermaster to Columbus, Kentucky, and he went to Cairo to enlist when there was no more work with the army. A third Company I man, with a known background, Pvt. Reuben Watson, has confused records because the army for some reason believed he was Cal Royce, though the soldier swore he had never used that name. Born a slave in Louisville forty years before enlisting, he was brought in bondage from Kentucky to Missouri but was freed before his 1854 marriage. Watson lived in Sparta, Illinois, before his army service, supporting eight children as a farmworker. Because of his advanced age, for much of his service he was assigned as company cook.[55]

So successful had recruiting finally become that the regiment had too many enlisted men and was ordered in February to designate seventy-three for reassignment to the Eighth U.S. Colored Infantry. The regiment tried to meet this quota by transferring soldiers in the hospital and those detailed as teamsters to the division and corps, men already lost to the regiment, but the ploy was not allowed. The War Department told the regiment to direct new recruits from Camp Casey to the Eighth Regiment. Meanwhile, back in Illinois, state recruiting chief Colonel Oakes ordered that no further enlistments be accepted for the Twenty-ninth, but enlistments for other regiments outside the state and for recruits subject to assignment were to continue.[56]

Now that the regiment had ten companies mustered in, it was authorized a colonel and lieutenant colonel, rounding out its complement of officers. Both of these were assigned effective on 1 January 1865. Col. Clark E. Royce, of New Lebanon, New York, was twenty-seven years old when he was appointed. He had enlisted as a private soldier in the Forty-fourth New York Volunteers at the beginning of the war and within a year was a captain commanding a company. His regiment had seen hard fighting, beginning at Yorktown in April 1862 and continuing through the battles of Hanover Court House, Second Bull Run, Antietam, Shephardstown, Fredericksburg, Chancellorsville, Gettysburg, and several later engagements. He applied to Casey's board for an appointment in a black regiment and was commissioned lieutenant colonel of the Sixth U.S. Colored Infantry, with which he had served through hard fighting at Petersburg and before Richmond. Royce had earned his colonelcy, and he headed the Twenty-ninth Regiment until its mustering out. How well he did so is not on the record, but he court-martialed two officers, and he constantly sought to keep the troops under strict discipline.[57]

Royce's lieutenant colonel was not sometime acting regimental commander Brown, as might be expected, because Major Brown was still ill. He resigned because of disability in February, Dr. Mackay certifying that he had "Chronic Anaemia and *Coup de Soliel.*" Brown had had problems earlier in the war, quarreling with his commanding officer and resigning his commission. Perhaps a similar situation in the Twenty-ninth USCT, rather than health, prompted his resignation. The regiment's junior officers—but none of the more senior ones—wrote that they thought he deserved to command the regiment, "to wear its crowning glory," as they put it, but instead he departed for home. The new second-in-command was Lt. Col. Fred E. Camp, of Middletown, Connecticut, who began the war as a enlisted man in the Twenty-fourth Connecticut Volunteers. He was soon a lieutenant and fought at Port Hudson—where he was wounded—and Franklin. His regiment completed its enlistment, was mustered out, and Camp applied for a commission with black troops. He was appointed a captain in the Twenty-ninth Connecticut Volunteers (Colored) and was promoted to major. After the war he joined the regular army. Camp's biography in the officers' register lists service with the Connecticut regiment but does not mention that this was a black unit and fails to list the Twenty-ninth U.S. Colored Infantry at all. Brown's replacement was Maj. H. J. Hindekoper, of Meadsville, Pennsylvania, who was mustered in on 24 March 1865. Hindekoper was a soldier for three months early in the war, and he was selected by a Casey board to be a captain in the Seventy-ninth U.S. Colored Infantry, from which he was transferred to the Twenty-ninth Regiment and promoted.[58]

The regiment was also permitted to recognize officially a few soldiers for headquarters functions. First Sergeant McCoslin was confirmed as regimental sergeant major, and Sgt. Joseph N. Scott, the Pennsylvania-born barber who had probably been performing the duties of the office for some time, was appointed regimental quartermaster sergeant. Company C's Orderly Sgt. James H. Brown was named regimental commissary sergeant, and Cpl. Lewis T. Wood and Pvt. Richard Blue were appointed principal musicians. Wood had been assigned to headquarters in June, but his appointment as a principal musician was not made until February 1865. Blue, who enlisted in Company A that same month, was appointed to the staff with Wood. He was born in Dayton, Ohio, in 1844 and had been employed as a farm laborer by Judge James Raybern near Bloomington, Illinois, when he enlisted. Blue might have been given musician duties because he was somewhat disabled by a foot injury he had received chopping wood in 1857, eight years before he entered the army. Hospital Steward George A. Francis, who enlisted in August 1864, completed the headquarters' roster of enlisted men.[59]

In mid-November General Grant decided to move Ferrero's Third Division out of its Poplar Grove Church positions to the other end of the battle line thirty-five miles away, north of the Appomattox River. The Twenty-ninth and Thirty-first Regiments were ordered to Point of Rocks on that river and the rest of the division to the Bermuda Hundred a few miles east on a bend in the James River. The entire division was now assigned to General Butler's Army of the James and was without a corps assignment, being named temporarily Ferrero's Division, Defense of Bermuda Hundred. The move of Ferrero's division may have had an important military reason, but more likely it was the result of a belief among Grant and his senior generals that mixing of white and black units was disruptive and not fully effective. At the same time, the integrated Tenth and

Eighteenth Army Corps were abolished and the white troops in them re-constituted as the Twenty-fourth Corps. Effective 3 December 1864, a new all-black army corps, the Twenty-fifth, was created and assigned to the Army of the James. The Twenty-ninth Regiment was placed in General Russell's Third Brigade, Second Division. The corps commander, recently promoted Maj. Gen. Godfrey Weitzel, was an 1855 West Point graduate who had been Butler's chief engineer. A newspaper reporter wrote about the "long projected scheme of organizing all the negro troops into a separate corps. . . . The rebels seemed to know just when it went into effect. Day before yesterday the necessary movements towards carrying out the project began, and early yesterday morning the enemy's pickets wanted to know when the 'smoked Yankees' were to confront them."[60]

In early December the Twenty-ninth Regiment was again preparing to move eight or nine miles to new positions north of the James River. On 8 December Third Division commander Brig. Gen. William Birney ordered drill to be suspended and baggage to be reduced in preparation for a march. The soldiers were not told their destination but only to carry rations for four days. The march appears to have been without incident, although several soldiers later recalled that the weather had been cold and wet. Captain Porter wrote:

> The roads were knee deep in mud from continuous rains during the day and every man was drenched to the skin[;] when night set in it became freezing Cold Sleeting and later Snowing with a piercing wind the whole night. At midnight we were halted in from Fort Harrison—the waggons failed to reach us till next-day and officers had to Stand or lie down in the Snow and no fire was allowed. It is impossible for [one] to exagerate the suffering we experienced from the cold and exposure of that night.[61]

Not a few soldiers would claim injury from frostbite and exposure, occasionally finding themselves without shelter during the regiment's moves. Company H Pvt. Levin Williams, for example, claimed his feet had been "frosted" on Christmas Eve, and he was later pensioned for the resulting damage. Captain Heusted, who joined Company B in mid-December, froze his right hand in the snowstorm described by Porter, but, unlike Porter, he was not able to secure a pension later. Pvt. Thomas Lilly, Company G, claimed two injuries during the moves. He said he had been burned by gunpowder in a skirmish on 30 November, but it seems more likely that he was a victim of an accident. He also claimed that he "fell into a sink hole about twelve feet deep" during a night march just before Christmas, straining his right hip and foot. The damage was sufficient to get him hospitalized at Point of Rocks for a month.[62]

A few soldiers appear to have been wounded by enemy action during December, but evidence supporting this is weak, based as it is mainly on postwar requests for compensation which are frequently fanciful. Cpl. Henry Clay's proof was sufficient for him to gain payments for a buckshot wound in the elbow received on 18 December, but Cpl. Martin Campbell's gunshot wound to the arm two days later could not be verified. He unsuccessfully tried to improve on his claim by alleging that his legs had been severely scalded by boiling coffee shortly afterward. Following the war Company G's Cpl. Richard Wilson asked for compensation for a wound he said he had received in late 1864. Doctors verified that he had a small bullet lodged below the skin on his forehead, and he was to carry it there for the rest of his life. Although he was pensioned for the injury in 1883, army records do not clearly represent it as service related. The only certain serious wound that month was Lieutenant Gosper's loss of his leg to the explosion of a random artillery round, the same incident in which Chaplain Barnes was slightly injured.[63]

By the first day of 1865 the regiment was relocated in the Chaffin's Farm area, by then a quiet sector. Settled into winter quarters, the Twenty-ninth USCT saw no action for almost three months, allowing time for training as well as work on fortifications. The regiment helped build up Fort Burnham and trenches covering artillery positions and was for some of the time in the front line a mile south of Fort Harrison. The unit was not, however, up to army standards, probably because of so many inexperienced new soldiers; daily demands by brigade, division, and corps for large work parties; lack of training time; and winter weather. The army's inspector general reported the regiment to be "in poor condition, proper care and energy has not been exercised by its officers to keep the men clean and build comfortable quarters." Inspection also revealed an "indifferent" military appearance, inefficient officers, and "bad" sanitary conditions in quarters.[64]

The record of the regiment's activities is otherwise thin for the period, and the new army corps and its commander were adjusting. General Weitzel attempted to bring the black corps some pride with his heroic order creating a badge, a square with a smaller square set diagonally on it:

In view of the circumstances under which this Corps was raised and filled, the peculiar claims of its individual members upon the justice and fair dealing of the prejudiced and the regularity of the conduct of the troops which deserve those Equal rights that have hitherto been denied the minority, the Commanding General has been induced to adopt the *Square* as the distinctive badge of the Twenty-Fifth Army Corps.

Wherever danger has been found and glory to be won, the heroes who have fought for immortality have been distinguished by some emblem to which every victory added a new luster. They looked upon their badge with pride, for to it they had given its fame. In the home of smiling peace it recalled the days of courageous endurance and the hours of deadly strife—and it solaced the moment of Death, for it was the Symbol of heroism and self-denial. The Poets Still Sing of the ["]Templar's Cross," the Crescent of the Turks, the "Chalice" of the hunted Christians, and the White Plume of Murat, that crested the wave of valor sweeping relentlessly to victory.

Soldiers! to you is given a chance, in this Spring Campaign, of making this badge immortal. Let History record that on the banks of the James thirty thousand free men not only gained their own liberty, but shattered the prejudice of the world, and gave to the land of their birth Peace Union and Liberty.[65]

Two Twenty-ninth Regiment companies, C and K, and detachments of others, spent time at the nearby Dutch Gap canal excavations, but whether they were on work parties or providing infantry cover is not recorded. The two companies were returned on 19 March, the regiment was moved out of the line four days afterward, and on 26 March it joined a parade of twenty-five thousand Twenty-Fifth Corps soldiers in honor of President Lincoln, who was visiting the troops, the review perhaps thought of as another morale builder.[66]

The Twenty-ninth U.S. Colored Infantry was about to end its relatively dormant period in winter quarters and to participate in a long march that saw the surrender of General Lee and his Army of Northern Virginia. Winter quarters service had been relatively easy on the men, although they were frequently on work details behind the front line. Casualties were not from enemy action, of which there was little. A small number of what were by now routine illnesses and injuries lightly depleted the ranks. Among the officers, Company D's Captain Knapp's discharge for incontinence, effective in March, required some adjustments. Knapp was not replaced with another captain, nor was one of the regiment's lieutenants promoted. First Lieutenant Fickes was transferred from Company G, and First Lieutenant Palmer, acting regimental quartermaster after Gosper was wounded, until 3 February, was ordered from Company C to Company G. This shift of officers made Fickes the acting Company D commander, a position he held for the rest of the regiment's service. At the same time, 2d Lt. George G. Smith was promoted and took Lieutenant Little's place as regimental adjutant when the latter went on leave on 8 March. Since Little did not return from this leave, Smith remained adjutant. That Smith was chosen for this important job seems strange, because his health had not been good. He was suffering from an unexplained fever from early 1865 but did not report to the hospital. Instead, he continued to perform his Company C duties, relying on Lieutenant Dunn, then the company's acting commanding officer, and Chaplain Barnes, advised by Surgeon Mackay, for his care. Perhaps it was this devotion to duty, along with his seminary education, which inspired Colonel Royce to choose him. His selection, however, and the moving of other officers left 1st Lt. John Aiken Company C's only officer.[67]

Private John Brown (also known as John Shorter), a Company E substitute enlisted at Baltimore in October, died of disease at the Point of Rocks hospital in late March, leaving behind a wife and child. A second John Brown, of Company I, was sent to the same hospital a few days before the first Brown died. He had been born in Virginia and had enlisted at Baltimore in January, as a substitute for William T. Humpfries. Brown never rejoined the regiment and was mustered out at Point of Rocks. Another Company I soldier, Pvt. William E. Young, also became ill just after arriving at the regiment's winter camp at Chaffin's Farm and did not return to duty. Young, born in Surrey County, Virginia, in 1846, had been a slave of John H. Hankins. He enlisted at Baltimore, giving his residence as Williamsport, Maryland, and indicating that he had been freed and brought north by the Union Army. His maladies were several: pneumonia, frostbite, sunstroke, and a slight gunshot wound. Sent to Fort Monroe hospital, he was discharged from there some months later. Company I soldiers with fatal diseases were Pvts. Isaac Demby, George Reed, and William White. Demby, age thirty-three, a draftee from Kent County, Maryland, was sent to Point of Rocks and then to the Portsmouth hospital, suffering from chronic diarrhea (probably dysentery), from which he died in early April. He may have been the brother of Company H's First

Sergeant William Thomas Demby; both men were mustered in on the same day in September 1864. Born in Accomack County, Virginia, Reed, age twenty-four, enlisted at Ellicott Mills as a substitute for Fred Sypes. He was sent to Point of Rocks when he reached the regiment and died of consumption on 11 March. White, also twenty-four and a draftee from Kent County, had the same short service, dying of an unspecified illness at City Point in mid-February.[68]

Three weeks of hard field service were about to replace the routine of camp at Chaffin's Farm, bringing further casualties to the regiment.

Pvt. William Buchner, Company A, on the right, with an unidentified soldier. Tintype dated 1872. Courtesy of the National Archives.

Pvt. David Curtis, Company A. Photograph taken about 1883. Courtesy of the National Archives.

Pvt. James Harris, Company H. This 1893 photograph was taken in Baltimore. Courtesy of the National Archives.

Pvt. John Dorsey, Company H. Photograph taken in 1892. Courtesy of the National Archives.

Grave of Pvt. Reuben Wilson, Company E, who died of crater battle wounds, 30 August 1864. Alexandria, Virginia, National Cemetery. Photo by the author.

Recruits at Charleston, 1865. *Harper's Illustrated.*

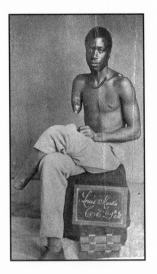

Pvt. Lewis Martin, Company E. Medical Department photograph, 1865. Courtesy of the National Archives.

Pvt. Jefferson Michie, Company A. Photograph taken in 1908. Courtesy of the National Archives.

Swearing in the First South Carolina Regiment (Colored), later Thirty-third USCT. *Frank Leslie's Illustrated Newspaper.*

A typical black soldier. *Harper's Illustrated,* 2 July 1864.

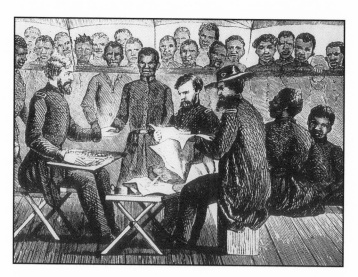

Payday. *Frank Leslie's Illustrated Newspaper.*

A soldier's rest in Alexandria, Virginia. Courtesy of the Library of Congress.

Kitchen at the soldier's rest in Alexandria, Virginia. Courtesy of the Library of Congress.

Wartime camp at Quincy, Illinois. Courtesy of the National Archives.

Black soldiers in action. *Frank Leslie's Illustrated Newspaper.*

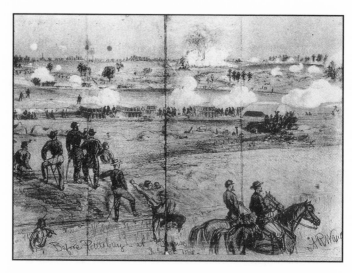

Before Petersburg, 30 July 1864. Drawing by Alfred R. Waud. Courtesy of the Library of Congress.

Explosion of mine at Petersburg, 30 July 1864. *Harper's Illustrated*, 20 August 1864.

Charge after mine explosion at the crater, 30 July 1864. Drawing by Alfred R. Waud. Courtesy of the Library of Congress.

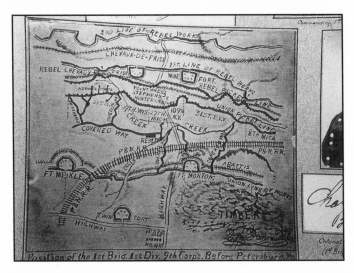

Map drawn by a participant, showing Ledlie's division and lines at the crater.
Courtesy of the U.S. Military History Institute, Carlisle Barracks, Pennsylvania.

Black troops of Ferrero's Fourth Division on the front at Petersburg, 9 August 1864.
Courtesy of the U.S. Military History Institute, Carlisle Barracks, Pennsylvania.

Camp of the chief ambulance officer, the Ninth Army Corps, Petersburg, August 1864. Courtesy of the Library of Congress.

Maj. Gen. George Meade, commanding the Army of the Potomac, 1864. Courtesy of the Library of Congress.

Maj. Gen. Ambrose Burnside, commanding the Ninth Army Corps, summer 1864. Courtesy of the Library of Congress.

A drawing of Gen. Burnside by a soldier of the Ninth Army Corps, 1864. Notice the artist's comments in the upper left corner. Charles Wellington Reed Papers. Courtesy of the Library of Congress.

Brig. Gen. Edward Ferrero, commanding the Fourth Division, Ninth Army Corps, and staff, June or July 1864. Courtesy of the Library of Congress.

Brig. Gen. James H. Ledlie, commanding the First Division, Ninth Army Corps, and staff, June or July 1864. Courtesy of the Library of Congress.

Maj. Gen. Benjamin F. Butler, commanding the Army of the James, probably late 1864. Courtesy of the Library of Congress.

Brig. Gen. Henry G. Thomas, commanding the Second Brigade, Fourth Division, Ninth Army Corps, at crater. Postwar photograph. Courtesy of the Library of Congress.

Lt. Col. John Armstrong Bross, commanding the Twenty-ninth U.S. Colored
Infantry at the crater. Drawing shows rank of colonel and full beard, neither of
which he had on 30 July 1864. Photograph taken from *Memorial of Colonel
Bross*, Chicago, 1864.

Brig. Gen. Godfrey Weitzel, commanding (as major general) the Twenty-fifth Army
Corps, late 1864. Courtesy of the Library of Congress.

Illinois governor Richard Yates. Courtesy of the Library of Congress.

General Weitzel's Texas expedition: The fleet at Hampton Roads, June 1865. *Harper's Illustrated.*

Chapter 5

WAR'S END AND
FINAL SERVICE

Although the weather was not much improved early that spring, Grant prepared to renew his pressure on Lee, once again seeking to cut more of the Confederate supply lines south and west of Petersburg. He hoped to deceive Lee about his intentions, moving most of General Ord's Army of the James south of the James and Appomattox Rivers to cover vacated positions of the attacking force, the Army of the Potomac. The Third Division, now commanded by Maj. Gen. David B. Birney, was the only Twenty-fifth Corps division joining the Sixth and Twenty-fourth Corps. General Russell, the Third Brigade's commander, was appointed City Point commanding officer in mid-March, so his replacement, Col. William W. Woodward, would lead the Twenty-ninth Regiment's brigade in the coming operation.

The Twenty-ninth Regiment continued to accumulate casualties from disease while it waited for orders to join the planned movements, and a few new officers and men reported for duty. Company G's second lieutenant, Illinois-born Albert L. Granger, was promoted and transferred to Company B to help make up an officer shortage in that unit. Because Lieutenant Conant resigned for personal reasons and was discharged on 14 March, another officer, 2d Lt. John Parker Jr., was commissioned on 9 March and named to assist the only remaining Company E officer, Lieutenant Ferguson. Parker, a native of Quincy, Massachusetts, was working as a carpenter when he enlisted as a private in the Fourth Massachusetts Cavalry. He served with that regiment at Petersburg, where he was wounded. At that time he was assigned with a detachment of the Fourth as one of the orderlies of Brig. Gen. Robert S. Foster, who commanded the First Division, Twenty-fourth Army Corps. That position surely helped Parker obtain the commission. It may have been, however, that Parker's wound, a gunshot over his heart, was sufficiently grave so as to prevent his immediate muster into the regiment. He was not mustered until July, but the delay may have been simply because his discharge from enlisted status was slow in arriving. Second Lieutenant Charles H. Wickham, a former private in the 142d New York Infantry from Schroon Lake, New York, was commissioned on 18 March but, like Parker, was not mustered into Company F before July, also because his discharge from his old regiment was tardy. Both Parker and Wickham were put to work by Colonel Royce on arrival, and they acted as officers for several months, without the appropriate pay, however, and without official authority as officers. Company G's 2d Lt. John Broderick, commissioned in March, was mustered into the regiment on the same day, his former regiment, the Ninety-eighth New York Infantry, being more efficient in providing newly commissioned men with discharges from enlisted service. Being a farmer, born at Moira, New York, in 1838, he had been a corporal in the New York regiment.[1]

The Twenty-ninth departed its winter quarters after dark on 27 March 1865, crossing the James River to join the Army of the Potomac and moving south toward the left flank of the Union army, the men expecting to be in a battle. The first casualty on the march may have been Company D Cpl. James H. Patton, who sought a pension later for injuries, a strained leg and ankle that he said were the result of falling into a ditch near the regiment's winter camp. There is some doubt, however, about whether Patton was indeed hurt, because his story of the incident is confused. He thought that it had occurred the day General Lee surrendered, but it was not unusual for veterans to have poor recollections of dates and places in later years. Patton was not disabled at the time by his injuries, but at forty-four years old his health was generally poor. The soldier was hospitalized later and remained sick after the regiment was broken up. He reached his family at Eldorado, Illinois, in February 1866, well after his comrades were discharged, and he died at home two years afterward, leaving behind a widow and five minor children.[2]

After a two-day march the regiment reached the left of the Army of the Potomac astride Hatcher's Run about a mile and a half east of the Boydton Plank Road, where it began constructing breastworks on 30 March. As usual when the troops were put to heavy work on fortifications, a number of them were hurt. Pvt. Dennis Hughes, a twenty-year-old who had been born in Alabama and enrolled in Company D at Chicago, for example, later claimed that he was ruptured from "the sharp point of an Abbatis in front of the breastworks" about the first of April. The regimental chief musician (bugler) Lewis L. Wood also claimed an accidental injury, a leg hurt when he caught it between the logs of a corduroy road near Hatcher's Run, but he was not hospitalized nor later pensioned for the damage.[3]

The division and its regiments had but a small role in the first operations against the rebels, the largest part of the engagement taking place to the west. On 31 March the Third Brigade, of which the Twenty-ninth was a part, beat off a small counterattack, and Company A's Captain Porter with the regiment's sharpshooters, men chosen from among all the companies, spent the remaining hours of the day sniping at the enemy. The black brigade was withdrawn that night and ordered forward again the afternoon of 1 April. Following a heavy bombardment of the lines by Union artillery, the federal forces advanced all along the line on 2 April, and Lee evacuated Richmond and Petersburg that night. Grant was concerned that Lee might get away to join Gen. Joseph E. Johnston's forces in North Carolina, thereby prolonging the war and drawing Union forces away from their base before Petersburg and Richmond, so the fall of those cities did not mean the immediate end of the fighting.[4]

The Twenty-ninth USCT was preparing to attack a fortification on its front, but orders to advance were delayed until 3 A.M. on 3 April, "when we marched into, and passed through Petersburg without opposition," entering the city at 6 A.M. "At 8 + o'clock same day moved out on the Lynchburg road in pursuit of Lee's Army." The hard march continued to the village of Blacks and Whites on the fifth, the high bridge beyond Burkesville on the sixth, and two nights later the regiment reached Appomattox Court House. On 9 April the black brigade was advancing on the extreme left of the Union line moving due west to engage Lee "when news came of Lee's readiness to capitulate." The Twenty-ninth unit's troops "joined in the triumphant shouts and salutes that signalized Lee's surrender."[5]

The regimental history says of the first action that the Twenty-ninth Regiment "participated in the operation of the 30t of March & of the 1t and 2n of April & lost in action three men killed & two wounded." Two of the men killed were Company D Pvts. Baptist Beeson (sometimes John B. Bisson) and Thomas Shipman, both on 30 March. The first, who was enlisted at Praire Du Rocher, Illinois, was reported missing in action for the rest of the war, but he was finally declared dead. Shipman was twenty-three and a native of Pekin, Illinois. Neither was a crater battle veteran. Pvt. Joseph Robinson, age nineteen, was killed on 2 April; he had been born in Missouri but was also an Illinoisan, having enlisted at Alton. Robinson had fought at the crater with Company E. It is difficult to identify the two men whom the regiment listed as wounded in the small engagement because after the war a large number of soldiers swore that they had received injuries in this period. One of the casualties who can definitely be identified was Company E Pvt. Robert Cassels, a Maryland draftee. He was wounded by a cannonball on 2 April. Enlisted in his native Baltimore, it is not known if he had been a free man all his life. Cassel was taken to Fort Monroe for treatment, and his right leg was amputated at the hip. The recovering soldier was furloughed in early December 1865, reported a month later to Hicks General Hospital in Baltimore, and was discharged on 11 January. He filed for a pension at once because the amputation was such that he could not be fitted with an artificial limb, but he was not pensioned until twenty-four years later.[6]

Two Company A soldiers, Pvts. Henry Vantrece and Lewis Harris, filed for pensions after the war, both certifying that they had been wounded in early April 1865, but they were not specific about dates. Vantrece had joined the army in December 1864, declaring that he was born in Tennessee and also claiming a Georgetown, Illinois, home. He described two wounds, gunshots in the arm and leg, and said he had been hospitalized for two weeks before rejoining the company. The army, however, had no record of the injuries nor of the hospital stay, and Vantrece was unable to secure a pension because of these wounds. He was finally pensioned for infirmities of old age many years after the war. Harris was born at Paris, Tennessee, a slave of John Harris. His master hired him out to work "in [a] Cole yard" for two years, and he was a bartender in Harris's store until he ran away, ending up in Palestine, Illinois, where he enlisted in January 1865. He claimed to have been wounded at Hatcher's Run in the jaw by a bayonet and in the hand by a gunshot, but his military records do not show these injuries. Harris changed his name after the war to his father's and was known as Peter Coleman until his death. He fathered eleven children, supporting them by working on steamboats and as a common laborer. He was not pensioned, however, until 1912 and then not for service-connected causes. Company C Pvt. John J. L. Cole was nineteen when he enlisted in his native Baltimore in January 1895. His claim of a wound in the left knee was verified by army records, but it was judged superficial, and there is no evidence that he was hospitalized for it. Cole said the injury was suffered at "Fort Hell," the nickname given Fort Steadman, where a battle was fought on 24 and 25 March—but not by units of the Twenty-ninth Colored Infantry. Probably, an imaginative pension agent embellished the account of the illiterate soldier, but without success, as Cole had to wait until old age qualified him. Company F's Pvt. Solomon Williams (later known as Solomon William Gray) damaged his eye at Hatcher's Run, the cause variously described by him as a shell burst or by being hit by a twig while he was running through the woods. William had been born in Hardy County, Virginia, about 1841 but, he said, had been "sold South" to an unnamed place nine years before the war. Having been freed or having escaped from slavery, he was recruited as a substitute in December 1864 at Camp Casey. He was pensioned at eight dollars a month for eye loss almost twenty years following his service; he was the father of twelve children and died in 1906. Finally, Pvt. Major King (William Patterson), the navy veteran in Company D, unsuccessfully asked for compensation for an unspecified wound received at Hatcher's Run. Other than these largely suspicious wound claimants, additional Hatcher's Run casualties cannot be identified.[7]

Dead and wounded were not the only regimental losses now that the Twenty-ninth USCT had returned to active service, after its less dangerous if not more restful time in winter quarters. At least four men deserted between 27 March and 2 April. Pvt. David Cole, a former Maryland slave, who enlisted in December as a substitute for George C. Deakins at Baltimore, deserted "while on march" in late March, but he was to return to the regiment in October 1865, about a month before mustering out. He may have been apprehended by the provost marshal, or he turned himself in. He appears not to have been punished. Another deserter from the same company, Virginia-born Sgt. Richard Martin, was twenty-two years old when he enlisted at Baltimore in late November, a paid substitute for Frederick Marle. He "deserted April 1, 1865 near Petersburg Va. while in presence of the Enemy" and was not heard from again. Pvt. Jesse Wilson, another Maryland enlistee, deserted Company H a day later and, like Martin, disappeared.[8]

At least Company H seems to have been at the scene on 9 April when General Lee surrendered the Army of Northern Virginia to General Grant at Appomattox Court House after it was clear that the Confederates had been defeated and had no other option. Pvt. James Harris, a Baltimore draftee, recalled of Lee, "I saw him ride down on his gray horse." Harris, born to a slave father and a free mother, was, therefore, a free man. Before his service he made his living brick making and shucking oysters, the work he would return to after the war. Pvt. Levin Williams, another Marylander, who enlisted at Wilmington, Delaware, and who was probably a substitute, had no more to say about the historic occasion he witnessed than "I saw General Lee surrender with his staff." Sgt. John Costley, of the same company, claimed that he had been wounded the next day by "some unknown Missell to me, Gun Shot wounds in the line of my duty." Because so many others were sick from the hardships of the march, he had not reported to the medical staff for treatment, even though postwar examination verified he indeed had gunshot wounds in his left arm, hand, and thigh. It is possible that Costly was confused about the date and that he had been wounded a few days earlier. Company A Pvt. William Freeman likewise sought to be pensioned for an unspecified wound he received the very day of Lee's surrender. He said it had been caused by a "lick from bull [ball?] of a musket in the hands of the enemy near Appomattox Court house," but he too must have been uncertain about dates. Like Costly, Freeman received a pension for this and other disabilities twenty years later.[9]

While Costly and Freeman may have been the last two soldiers of the regiment to be wounded by rebel action, another man, Company I Pvt. John Collins, said he had been injured in what seems to have been an accident at the end of the war in Virginia. He said his injury was "eyes burned in Battle of Clear Hill Lee's surrender by explosive of powder." Collins, once a slave, had been drafted in Maryland, but nothing more is known about his early life. Despite the injury, he served out his enlistment in the regiment. Collins eventually lost his sight, however, but not until thirty years after the war, when already pensioned for other infirmities.[10]

POSTWAR EVENTS

With the war over some soldiers must have seen little reason to remain in uniform, and the first of a number of desertions followed Lee's capitulation. Sgt. Josephus Turpin, an elderly forty-four-year-old, failed to return to the regiment after a furlough to his home at Quincy, Illinois, and was immediately dropped from the rolls as a deserter. No action appears to have been taken to return him to duty or to punish him, and he applied for a pension—which he did not receive—about 1890. Pvts. Charles Fisher and William Curtis, among the few Company K men enlisted in Illinois, deserted on 10 and 13 April, respectively, and Company F Pvt. Simon Holland, a Maryland draftee, left his unit on 18 April. Only Curtis was heard from again, when he unsuccessfully sought a pension seventeen years later.[11]

On 11 April the regiment moved from Appomattox Court House to Petersburg. Arriving on the evening of 17 April, the Twenty-ninth USCT went into camp for the rest of the month. The troops should have been pleased with their accomplishments and endurance, even though their role in the fighting was minor, having covered two hundred and fifty miles since leaving the Richmond front on 27 March. The regiment was on the move every day but one on that long march. Captain Brockway, commanding Company C, wrote of the three weeks: "Discipline of the company good throughout. Never saw troops march better. No stragglers."[12]

Black troops had once again behaved well, but their performance in a secondary role during the final campaign against Lee did not inspire praise within the armies before Richmond and Petersburg. The Third Division's officers were pleased with the service of the Twenty-ninth Regiment and the other black units supporting the assault forces that brought about the surrender at Appomattox. The Twenty-ninth's brigade commander, Colonel Woodward, wrote in his report ten days following his arrival at Petersburg after the surrender, "The long and fatiguing march was borne with patience and fortitude creditable to old soldiers, and should forever put an end to any doubt as to whether colored troops can stand a campaign, no matter how severe it may be." Within two weeks, however, Maj. Gen. Henry W. Halleck, commanding the new Military Division of the James at Richmond, wrote to Secretary of War Stanton, "The Twenty-fifth (colored) Corps is reported to me as being poorly officered and in bad discipline, and altogether unfitted for the military occupation of Virginia. Would it not be well to send this corps to the Rio Grande, in Texas, to cut off Jefferson Davis' retreat into Texas?"[13]

It may be that the quality of officers in the Twenty-fifth Army Corps, rather than prejudice, inspired Halleck. A black newspaper correspondent with the army in Virginia, noting this, wrote that "many officers who heretofore manifested nothing but contempt for negro discipline and valor, and especially for those who commanded them, have signified their willingness to accept positions in the sable military establishment." He thought these officers, who, now that fighting was almost over and white units would soon be discharged, were seeking to stay on in the army, "should not . . . be permitted to compromise their prejudices." Colonel Royce was aware of the declining state of the Twenty-ninth Regiment's discipline while in camp at Petersburg. He told his soldiers that he expected them to take better care of themselves and the bivouac area: "All soldiers who have any respect for themselves, and do not wish to have their camp used as a privy, should endeavor to detect criminals in the act, that an example may be made of them, and the regiment be rid of men who are only fit to live with pigs."[14]

There were other signs that discipline was breaking down, but the army had a way to deal with such matters: the court-martial. At about this time Company A Cpl. George M. Washington, possibly then a sergeant, was sentenced to be reduced to the ranks by a "field court martial" and was fined sixteen dollars for an unknown offense. The record is more complete regarding two other soldiers in the same company. South Carolina–born Pvt. Perry Gilworth, who was mustered into the army at Camp Casey in early September 1864, was convicted in May by a "field officer court," consisting of Major Hindekoper, of stealing fifty dollars from Cpl. Charles Gossberry (sometimes Gasbery or other variations). His sentence was confinement on bread and water for thirty days. A few days later Pvt. George Green, a January 1865 Chicago enlistee, was convicted by the same officer of taking Pvt. Robert Barber's rifle without permission, but the sentence was only ten days on bread and water.[15]

MISSION TO TEXAS

There was more to Halleck's suggestion than the prospect that Confederate President Jefferson Davis, a fugitive until 10 May, was seeking refuge with Gen. E. Kirby Smith's surviving rebel forces in Texas, although that possibility was there. The other motivation for a Texas expedition was the French presence in Mexico supporting the Austrian Archduke Maximilian, who had been installed as emperor in April 1864. Grant proposed to send Maj. Gen. Philip H. Sheridan to the border with a substantial force to break up or destroy Smith's command and to "aid [Benito] Juarez in expelling the French from Mexico." The troops selected were twelve thousand men from Arkansas, twenty-five thousand from west Mississippi, the Fourth and Twenty-fifth Army Corps, and other units, totaling eighty thousand troops, of which fifty-two thousand were directed to Texas. When Sheridan assumed command on 29 May, Smith had surrendered, although some of his soldiers in Texas crossed into Mexico. In light of the decreased threat Sheridan was to muster out much of the Texas force in short order, but not before most of it proceeded to the state. As Grant said, "Those troops got off before they could be stopped."[16]

The Twenty-fifth Corps' orders came to the camp outside Petersburg on 1 May, sending the corps and all its detached regiments and companies to City Point—actually to Camp Lincoln, two miles below the supply center on the James River, an installation that had just been constructed by the Seventh U.S. Colored Infantry and other troops. The corps began its movement, passing through Petersburg on 5 May, but the troops had not yet been told their Texas destination. Certainly, rumors of the corps' impending movement to the border with Mexico circulated, but they were not accepted enthusiastically by the men. An officer wrote that "strange stories got around among the colored troops": "The story was that the Government was going to send them south to work on the cotton plantations to pay the national debt, and many went to their officers to ask if it was true, and, being assured there was no truth in it, would declare themselves satisfied; but a marked change came over them, and they became sullen and dissatisfied."[17]

In addition to such unfounded threats, other, real ones existed for some of the enlisted men. The troops were supposed to be paid monthly, but this was often neglected, soldiers not seeing their salary for six to nine months. Many soldiers in all Twenty-fifth Corps regiments had been drafted or otherwise enlisted in Virginia and Maryland, and some of them were followed by their refugee families. Were they to go to Texas, their wives, children, and other relatives would face difficult times. What they did not know was that, just before the troops sailed for the Southwest, the army would discontinue providing rations to soldier families, causing, when word reached them, some mutinous conduct among the troops. Some others may have been discontent knowing that white volunteer organizations—most of them with more service than black regiments— were being mustered out and sent home in large numbers, but no Twenty-fifth Corps regiments were included in the demobilization. By mid-May "that the negro corps . . . has received marching orders is well known throughout their camps," a black newspaperman wrote, "and they are putting on their war-paint with the impression that they are going to Texas.

They look forward to the embarkation with a great deal of satisfaction."
The army kept the soldiers busy with regular drill and dress parade every
evening, a routine that may have become tedious, but unrest and even
mutinous conduct were not regularly demonstrated. The colonel commanding the Thirtieth U.S. Colored Infantry, as had Colonel Royce, found
some of his soldiers slovenly, and he ordered them "put under arrest with
logs on their shoulders," a common field punishment. Private Williams,
the Company H soldier who witnessed Lee's surrender, recalled that the
punishment "kicked up a big row and there were threats to shoot the
officers and for a while it looked bad." Williams said that the Thirtieth
Infantry's officers did not give in, kept the offenders under arrest, and, he
claimed, court-martialed and shot them when the regiment reached Texas.
They were not executed, however, although they might have been sentenced to prison terms.[18]

General Weitzel alerted his command for the move on 18 May: "The
Regiments and Batteries of this Corps are hereby ordered to be prepared
for embarkation at City Point at an hour's notice." General Halleck reported to Grant on the same day that Weitzel was ready to load his corps
provided with forty days' rations but was running into problems with
some white artillery units attached to the Twenty-fifth Corps. These batteries were, he said, "very unwilling to go" with the blacks to Texas. Grant
was sympathetic and the same day told Halleck that "white men with
batteries may be detached and sent here [to Washington] for muster out."
Weitzel would have to make do with about twenty guns as well as a smaller
than authorized number of horses.[19]

The corps was ordered from Camp Lincoln to City Point to board
steamers to take the black regiments down the James River to Hampton
Roads. Since the corps and attached units numbered almost twenty-two
thousand men, its movement was a major logistical operation for the quartermaster. Even though it would leave behind most of its cavalry, artillery,
and team horses, 2,139 horses and mules were to be transported to Texas.
The quartermaster reported that transporting the corps, its animals, and
"its guns, ambulances, wagons and harness, subsistence and ammunition"
required fifty-seven ocean steamers for a planned twelve-day voyage. The
Twenty-ninth U.S. Colored Infantry was assigned to the steamers
Wilmington, capacity 450 men, and *William Kennedy*, capacity 473 men,
which left City Point on 25 May, with other transports carrying the rest of
the Third Brigade. Colonel Royce was senior officer aboard the
Wilmington, and brigade commander Colonel Woodward was with his

staff on the *Kennedy*. The first ship departed Hampton Roads for Texas at 1 P.M. on 29 May and the second at 10 A.M. on 31 May. Among the last of the corps' troops, Russell's brigade boarded its transports and left City Point in early June. Russell was told to allow half his officers to disembark from the transports at Fort Monroe and go to Norfolk for their pay. No similar arrangements were made for more than a few of the enlisted men, and some if not most of the few were unsuccessful. A soldier from the Twenty-third U.S. Colored Infantry, Hospital Steward Albert W. Brown, recorded in his diary on 1 June, "Went to Norfolk and failed to get my pay."[20]

While lack of pay and those cases in which soldiers' families were left to their fates caused distress among the troops, other problems arose. The First U.S. Colored Cavalry mutinied on the way down river aboard the transport *Meteor* and refused to obey its officers. At the direction of Maj. Gen. Nelson B. Miles, who was commanding at Fort Monroe, the regiment was disarmed by other troops, and order was restored. A sergeant of the Twenty-ninth Connecticut (Colored) regiment described his unit as in bad discipline on the trip down the James because "it was whispered about that the officers had covenanted together to take the soldiers on board, to Cuba, and sell them as slaves," and literate black enlisted men serving as clerks were likewise thought part of the plot. He described the voyage to Fort Monroe:

> I was astonished at the behavior of the soldiers. They gave themselves over to all kinds of sports and jestings, which disgusted me most thoroughly. Many were unruly, even threatening the lives of those who favored going to Texas whither we had been ordered for garrison duty. Some of the gang were arrested for insubordination. My heart was made to shudder at the degrading and shameful life which was manifested on board the ship. Their swearing, drinking, gambling, dancing, etc., was heartsickening. It was indeed a revelation and shows what men will do when not under the eye of authority.[21]

The Twenty-ninth U.S. Colored Infantry leaving for Texas was, unlike when it fought at the crater, a large regiment, having benefited from the government's July 1864 call for men and the final call in December. Each company had close to or more than its maximum authorized strength, over one hundred noncommissioned officers and men, by late February, so orders halting black enlistments did not affect the regiment. Some late enlistees from Illinois continued to arrive from Camp Butler, but all of them were signed up prior to the cutoff and had been delayed by processing and transportation. These late arrivals had lives and experiences similar to their comrades. For example, Pvt. James Henry (later James Daniels) was born in 1843 or 1844, a slave in Nashville, Tennessee. He ran away from Dyer County in the western part of the state, went first to St. Joseph, Missouri, and eventually arrived in Chicago. When he reached the regiment at Camp Lincoln, he was suffering from rheumatism and scurvy, but he was well enough to join the move to Texas. Pvt. John Ridley, a Company E soldier, was born in 1844 at or near Jackson, Mississippi, a slave of John Ridley. His owner's son took him to Nashville, and he ran away from there in 1861. He went to Chicago and worked in the city as an expressman until his enlistment in February 1865. He too suffered from scurvy—but he said it was a result of the trip to Texas, not of conditions in Virginia. There were no further significant officer losses; only one, Company I Lieutenant Sanders, decided not to go to Texas. He resigned effective 19 May and presumably returned to his home at Crystal Lake, Illinois, taking up studies for the ministry and retiring many years later in Washington, D.C. Another assistant surgeon, David J. Evans, of Morgantown, Pennsylvania, who had prior service with the 131st Infantry from his state, joined in June, just before the movement to Texas. His addition to the medical staff would be useful because the regiment was going to a place where health conditions were even worse than they had been in Virginia.[22]

For all of 1865 prior to embarking for Texas, thirteen men deserted the regiment, and about thirty died, most of them of disease, at Point of Rocks, Fort Monroe, Portsmouth, City Point, or Dutch Gap. Of the desertions about half occurred when word of the move to Texas was likely to have been circulating; the rate does not indicate that Twenty-ninth USCT soldiers shared the unhappiness of troops in other regiments. A few prisoners of war were found and released, and some rejoined the regiment.[23]

The ships carrying the Twenty-ninth Regiment and its brigade took on water and some provisions at Fort Monroe and, with orders for Fort Morgan near Mobile, sailed on 27 May. The *Kennedy* reached Mobile Bay on 7 June, landing four companies at Navy Cove. Conditions ashore were poor— intense heat and swarms of stinging insects— so when the *Wilmington* arrived two days later with the rest of the regiment no one was put ashore, and the *Kennedy*'s complement was anxious to go to sea again. Sailing on 9 and 10 June the flotilla took four days to reach Brazos de Santiago, Texas, but was unable to disembark the troops because of rough weather. Steaming to Corpus Christi, where a landing was not attempted because of high waves, and then to Galveston, the vessels took on coal and water, and at least some troops were allowed to go ashore on 20 June. Here Captain Dagget, commanding Company F, was brought up on charges that he fraternized with enlisted men; specifically, he swam with them off the Galveston pier, was drunk at the time, and asked enlisted men to procure more alcohol for him. The question was not resolved at Galveston because the regiment reembarked, set sail for the south, and was finally landed at Brazos on 22 June.[24]

It had been a long trip, and not much is known about conditions onboard the transports. A physician who investigated the rate of disease in the Twenty-fifth Corps in Texas wrote that the spaces between decks were "dark and illy ventilated," and half to three quarters of each regiment landing at Brazos de Santiago was ill, with possibly fifty to one hundred men sick enough to be hospitalized. It cannot be determined how many Twenty-ninth U.S. Colored Infantry soldiers arrived too sick for duty, but three died at sea on the voyage from Virginia. Pvt. Anthony Sepp, age twenty-two, from Kentucky, who enlisted in Company B at Marengo, Illinois, in the fall of 1864, died on 9 June and Company K Pvts. John Clemens and Washington Marks on 2 and 12 June, respectively. All three of them were aboard the *Wilmington*. Another soldier, Company G Pvt. Jordan D. Morse, died of disease, made worse by the voyage, when the ship was at Galveston. Probably some other soldiers were injured aboard ship, but only Company C First Sergeant Easley's incident is known. He said he fell down an open hatch on the *Kennedy*, injuring his back, possibly enough to disable him temporarily.[25]

Chaplain Barnes reported much "recklessness and profanity" aboard the *Kennedy;* he attributed it to crowded conditions and idleness of the men. He did not, however, immediately comment on the men's health. Whatever reports Surgeon Mackay and his two assistants wrote at the time have not survived, but some later comments by Mackay have. Writing to support a pension claim of the regimental adjutant, Lieutenant Smith, whom he had been treating for a fever since early 1865, he said that the officer, and by inference the rest of the regiment, were "subjected to an ordeal that resulted fatally to many on a crowded steamer, transporting [the] regiment to Brazos Santiago, furnished with bad water and worse food—under a sweltering atmosphere during the months of May and June." For another soldier's application based on the effects of scurvy, he recalled, "The transport was over-crowded and filthy, ventilation wretched, soldiers were fed on rancid pork and mouldy 'hard-tack,' with bad water under a tropical sun for at least a month." Not all agreed that the soldiers suffered aboard ship. The Twenty-ninth Connecticut's quartermaster sergeant wrote that the six hundred to seven hundred aboard his transport, the *Blackstone*, fifteen days at sea, "had a most pleasant trip and enjoyed the ocean waves and breezes." The officers could fish to introduce variety into their menu, but the men who could not were restricted to the usual army ration of salt pork, hard tack, and coffee—little wonder that scurvy was a common ailment in Texas. The sergeant, however, said the sick on his ship suffered primarily from "yellow jaundice, malaria, chills and fever."[26]

Because the eighty-bed hospital at Brazos de Santiago was the only one in south Texas and could not provide for the five hundred patients it was handling per week, two hundred to three hundred sick were sent to New Orleans for treatment at the Corps d'Afrique General Hospital for black soldiers. Twenty-two Twenty-ninth Regiment soldiers died in that city from July through September of typhoid, dysentery, or respiratory diseases, and an unknown but significantly larger number were being treated throughout the period. The men who died were representative of the regiment and included a few veterans enlisted when the unit was formed; later draftees, substitutes, and voluntary enlistees from Illinois; and, the largest number, soldiers mustered in late in the war at Maryland recruiting stations and at Camp Casey. Two veterans from Company D were Missouri born and had fought at the crater battle. They were Pvt. George Robinson, age twenty-nine, and Pvt. Albert J. Wilson, age twenty, enrolled at Chicago and Quincy, respectively. More common late arrivals in the ranks were Company A's Pvt. David White and Pvts. Peter Shaw (Company H), Isaac Anderson, and Payton Colwell (both Company I). White, twenty-one, was born at City Point, Virginia; recruited by an agent from New York, he was mustered in at Camp Casey in the fall of 1864. He fell ill on arrival in Texas and was sent to New Orleans, where he died of typhoid in early September. He had no known family. Forty-five-year-old Shaw was drafted at Baltimore. Married in 1856, he had three daughters, born in 1856, 1860, and 1863. Assistant Surgeon Ewan and Captain Newton certified that the soldier died of complications from scurvy, the result of conditions on the trip from Virginia, sufficient proof to allow Anderson's wife and dependent children to be pensioned from the date of his death. Mustered in at Danville, Illinois, Colwell, a native of Tennessee, did not join the Twenty-ninth Regiment until March 1865. Being about age thirty, he was ill on arrival in Texas and was sent at once to New Orleans suffering from the unidentified lung disorder that caused his death. He had no dependents. A soldier who did was Company G Pvt. William Buchanan. Entering the army from Baltimore, he was mustered in at Ellicott Mills in late 1864. His home was at West River, Anne Arundel County, where he may have been a slave. Buchanan had fathered ten children before the war; it is not clear whether he was drafted or joined the army to receive the one-hundred-dollar bounty for a one-year enlistment. Because of his age, he was signed on as a musician, yet he served as an infantryman. He was landed at Brazos de Santiago but was already ill with what seems to have been dysentery, so was sent to New Orleans, dying there on 11 July. His widow successfully applied in 1866 for a pension on her own behalf and for five children under sixteen; the other five had died earlier. Pvt. William Ash of Company I was one of the last to die in New Orleans. He too was sick on arrival in Texas and went at once to the Louisiana hospital. Born in Caroline County, Maryland, in 1836, Ash had likely been a slave. Drafted in December 1864, he enlisted at Easton, was sent to Camp Bradford in Baltimore for processing, and arrived at the regiment before Richmond for the hard winter. He died of chronic diarrhea on 28 September and had no known survivors.[27]

Only one soldier in the regiment, Company B's literate Private Griffin, wrote about his Corps d'Afrique Hospital experience. His comments, however, were restricted to the weather. He had been in Texas for only two weeks when he was disabled by scurvy, arriving at New Orleans about mid-July. In a letter home he said: "It has been vary warm here this summer but it has turned a great deal cooler than what it was[.] I always heard that New Orleans was a hot climent and I found it to be so for I have seen days here since I have been here hot enough it seems to roast an egg." Three other soldiers went together to New Orleans, possibly with Griffin and probably aboard the same ship. Unlike Griffin, who rejoined his company, Company A's First Sergeant Heithman remained in the New Orleans hospital for the rest of his time in service and may have been demoted to private because of his inability to serve in the company. With him were Pvts. John E. Barker, a Virginian enlisted at Alton in early February 1865, and William Ross, a former slave from Fulton County, Missouri, but living in Anderson, Illinois, who was mustered in as a substitute and joined the regiment after the war at Camp Lincoln outside City Point. Barker and Ross did no more company service and, with Heithman, only rejoined the regiment while its discharge paperwork was being processed. Many other Twenty-ninth Infantry soldiers were at the New Orleans hospital the entire time that the regiment was in Texas. For example, Company K Cpl. William Curtis (later Chesley) and Pvt. James T. Locks, both Maryland former slaves and draftees, were sent to New Orleans shortly after their arrival in Texas. Curtis sought a pension well after the war, but it was denied because his records were confused with those of another William Curtis, who had deserted from the company only thirty-two days after his February 1865 enlistment. The matter was straightened out because the second Curtis was forty-four when he joined, and the corporal was but twenty-one. Locks was so ill that his time at Corps d'Afrique Hospital went beyond the regiment's stay in Texas, and he was not discharged from the army until two months after his comrades. Born in Frederickstown, Maryland, he was inducted (as James Socks) in December 1864. His owner was probably James Wilkerson or could have been a man named Rawlings. He had been working on Benjamin H. Bowen's farm, to which he returned after the war. He applied immediately for a pension, but one was not awarded until 1904. All these men were suffering from scurvy, a disease, then as now, which is readily preventable. Dr. Mackay's remedy was, he wrote twenty years later, "rations of the juice of the aqua Americanus plant of the neighborhood—[which] were issued—to be used by all—3 times daily." Prevalence of the disease among the troops showed that medical and military authorities failed in their duty.[28]

The troops were being distributed along the whole coast of Texas, with the largest concentration near the Mexican border following the purpose of the expedition outlined by General Grant in late May: "it is the intent to prosecute a vigorous campaign in that country, until the whole of Texas is re-occupied by people acknowledging allegiance to the United States." He further directed the Twenty-fifth Corps to secure "a strong foothold on the Rio Grande," the corps to proceed up the river "to the extent of supplies." Grant cautioned his commanders to "observe a strict neutrality towards Mexico, in the French and English sense of the word." The latter may be interpreted as license to support Juárez's Mexican troops against Maximilian, the sort of neutrality Britain and France had practiced in their relations with the Union in the Civil War and which

France was applying in Mexico. Sheridan, however, who believed that the Maximilian matter was a direct extension of his war against the rebels, did not violate a stricter form of neutrality. Since Maximilian's area of influence in Mexico was on the wane, Union troops in Texas had more civil than military duties. These were largely routine matters, such as "paroling prisoners, administering the oath of allegiance, and, . . . in the absence of any regularly constituted civil authority, to act as a magistrate in all cases of dispute."[29]

Because the large number of troops sent to Texas was far more than was needed for this work, much of the force was redirected home soon after arrival. Nonetheless, the Twenty-fifth Corps was excepted from this reverse movement and was deployed as originally planned. The Twenty-ninth U.S. Colored Infantry spent only a few days at Brazos de Santiago, and the troops had to have been relieved to move on, because the camp lacked sufficient fresh water and was infested with "fleas, mosquitoes and sand burrs." Not all the black troops were so fortunate, one soldier writing that the routine at Brazos was half-rations and only one cup of water daily. Medical attention was described as poor, as it would be elsewhere when new hospitals were opened, and the troops had not been paid for nine months. Three soldiers, too sick to march or be carried in wagons and who were left at Brazos, died of disease. Company B's Pvt. Lewis Ringold was a Virginia-born crater veteran who enlisted at Chicago in January 1864. The other two men, Caesar Polland and Henry Butler, were Maryland recruits with short service. Other soldiers not fatally ill also remained at Brazos. Cpl. Matthew Johnson was a possibly free Virginian who, before his September 1864 enlistment at Camp Casey, had been working in Alexandria, Virginia, a laborer in the army's quartermaster department bakery on Gibbons Street. Assigned to the brigade wagon train, he was hospitalized at Brazos for sunstroke and was afterward assigned to tend horses, "light duty with the Post Qr M."; he did not rejoin the regiment for some time.[30]

The Twenty-ninth Regiment left Brazos on 24 June and marched to White's Ranch, about ten miles to the south and four miles from the mouth of the Rio Grande, where it remained encamped until 12 July. Colonel Royce reported 729 men present at White's and 447 absent on details, sick, and so on. He was no doubt unhappy to read the recent report of an inspection of the regiment which noted "Discipline lax," "Officers indifferent," and such other deficiencies as long hair, poor paperwork, and inadequate policing of the camp. Not much is known about the regiment's activities at White's, but while there Colonel Royce ordered Captain Daggett to be placed under arrest and returned to Brazos to await trial by general court-martial. Before long the charges went beyond the original offenses; Daggett was later accused of fighting with enlisted men, striking an enlisted man, and being drunk in uniform in public at Brazos and, while serving as defense counsel in another's court-martial, was charged with being insolent to the court. Daggett's first lieutenant, Frederick W. Brownell, had also, on 22 May, been ordered under arrest by Royce. He was charged with being drunk on duty while officer of the day at City Point on 17 May and for breach of arrest. Royce wrote in the specification of the latter offense that the day after being placed in close arrest Brownell "did send to said regimental Commander an application for one Canteen of whiskey." Daggett was tried, convicted, and sentenced to be dismissed from the service, but the disposition of Brownell's case is unknown. Neither man, however, was immediately punished; both returned to Company F before 12 July to await review of the courts-martial proceedings. Daggett, although dismissed, stayed with the regiment through muster out and accompanied it to Springfield. Daggett's name (and Brownell's) appears on a roster of officers mustered out with the regiment and signed by Colonel Royce, but he was clearly dismissed on 10 October before the Twenty-ninth USCT left Texas.[31]

Cpl. Booker Punch likewise encountered army justice. He was called before a general court-martial for a serious offense. The charge brought by Company A commanding officer Captain Porter was "conduct to the prejudice of good order and military discipline." According to the specification, Punch was ordered by 1st Sgt. George Templeton to go to his quarters. He refused, cursing, "Go to hell *God damn* you. I will not go for you or any *god damn* Man, *Jesus Christ* or the Colonel, or words to that effect." Since several heard this, including Lieutenant Johnston and Sergeant Hazell, the court swiftly found him guilty and sentenced the soldier to be reduced to private, serve three months at hard labor, and pay a thirty-dollar fine. He appears to have been confined until the regiment left Texas. Company G's 1st Sgt. Henry F. Cotton was punished by a field court-martial on 1 October 1865 for a less serious offense than that committed by Punch, though the exact charge is unknown. Born in Massachusetts, Cotton enlisted as a private in late October 1864, a substitute for a Maryland draftee, William Tilman. He had an exemplary record, being promoted to corporal in January 1865, to sergeant in April, and to first sergeant in July. His sentence ended his military accomplishments; he was reduced to private and fined a month's pay. Cotton remained a private until he was mustered out with the regiment.[32]

On 12 July "the Reg't marched from Whites Ranche Texas, and on the 13th of July reached Brownsville, At three (3) A.M. on the 16 took up march from Brownsville. Continued the route, with the rest of the 3rd Brig. 2d Div. 25 A.C. marching according to the following method. Reveille at 2 A.M. March commenced at 3 A.M. Halt from about 10 A.M. until 4+ P.M. March then until about 7 P.M. Reached Ringgold Barracks, Texas, on Saturday July 22, 1865. The Regt is encamped in a pleasant position three fourths of a mile below the Barracks, close to the Rio Grande."[33] Ringgold was at Rio Grande City, a village about one hundred miles upriver, halfway to Laredo, a grueling march over bad roads in midsummer.

Because of heat and no rain to settle the dust, conditions on the road were not good, and many soldiers became disabled or ill as a result. Sgt. Peter Cooper, a freeman who enlisted in Company G in September 1864, was incapacitated by swollen legs and circulatory complications, but he completed the march, perhaps going some of the way in an ambulance. His records show that he was not hospitalized beyond a few days but was, according to an affidavit from Captain Southwell, unfit for duty until his discharge in September, when his one-year enlistment period was up. Company H Pvt. Jacob Cole, an eighteen-year-old Maryland former slave mustered in at Ellicott Mills, claimed similar leg injuries from the march which he attributed to "carrying a heavy nap sack &c." Cole said he was left behind on the road and was taken later to Ringgold Barracks by boat. Another man left in the wake of the march was Pvt. John P. Arbuckle, who said he was disabled by sunstroke that left him with partial deafness, impaired vision, and fits. He admitted in an 1888 pension claim that he had never been hospitalized for these ailments in the army, but he excused that weakness in his story by asserting that he had been so sick that his comrades had left him unattended on the road. He was taken care of by "an old white Man and a lot of Mexican fisherman for about a month," when he flagged down a passing supply boat on the Rio Grande to take him to Ringgold. Arbuckle's imaginative compensation request was unsuccessful, but he was finally entered because of advanced age in 1905, after making many applications, including requests for assistance which he sent to President Theodore Roosevelt and to his senators and congressman. Pvt. James Ewing, one of three brothers in Company H, recalled that he had been ill with "black scurvy" and remained at

Brownsville while the regiment went on to Rio Grande City. He said that his brothers Archie and George had stayed with him, and the three had caught up with the company two weeks later. James sought a pension from 1886 on and was awarded one for throat and mouth diseases. For twenty years he sought increases, at one point asking for more compensation because, "I use to be a good singer but I cannot sing at all now." Tennessee-born Pvt. Henry Cruthers, who joined Company F in November 1864 at Galeburg, Illinois, had another original justification for a pension. He said he had been "poisoned with prickly Pears" and had foot problems caused by drilling at Brazos and marching to Ringgold Barracks without shoes. He somewhat compromised his argument because he said the most damage was done on a fifty-mile march from City Point to Fort Monroe, a trip the regiment made by ship. Although the army had no record of in-service injuries, Cruthers was entered on the pension rolls because he had toes and later both feet amputated and so was unable to perform manual labor.[34]

The soldiers of the Twenty-ninth Regiment must have felt abandoned at remote Rio Grande City; Chaplain Barnes called it "this desolate and thorny region." He thought that the regiment's soldiers were reasonably cheerful under the circumstances, considering that the troops were camped out of doors without their tents and other baggage that had not kept up with the movement to Ringgold Barracks. Not only were living conditions primitive; the natives were also not thought well of. A Twenty-ninth Connecticut Regiment soldier wrote of Brownsville, a larger town than Rio Grande City: "The houses were little huts; the people dressed in their shirts and drawers; the women dressed in a long shirt with their breasts exposed, seemingly caring nothing for decency or modesty." Another soldier did not record the same impression but said of the Mexicans he had encountered in Brownsville, "We find them a very nice class of people as long as one keeps on the sunny side, but treacherous when you get in the shade." In general life for the black troops on the border was difficult, food shortages common, and medical care inadequate. The latter was supplied at the post hospital at Brownsville, a long journey from Ringgold for the Twenty-ninth Regiment's soldiers. Seven hundred patients were kept at Brownsville, but they were "treated as if they had been brutes, doctors and nurses being without feeling," and troops died there at the rate of ten a day. Ten Twenty-ninth Regiment soldiers died at Brownsville from the last of July to mid-September, some of them men hospitalized when the regiment was in the town and others who were sent from Ringgold Barracks, probably by wagon and steamer. Half were Maryland draftees, half substitutes and draftees from Illinois, and none were crater battle veterans.[35]

Given the poor state of morale, one would expect many desertions, but there were few places for a disgruntled black soldier to go. Consequently, only seven Twenty-ninth Regiment soldiers deserted from June to October, and some of them may have been in hospitals at the time in New Orleans or elsewhere. Pvt. Sandy Johnson, a soldier seriously wounded at the crater battle, went absent without leave in late October and was not heard from until he applied for a pension in 1892. Another battle survivor, Musician William A. Harris, a free man from Kankakee, Illinois, deserted Company C in September 1865. He spent the next five and a half years in Mexico and then moved to San Antonio. Despite his lack of an honorable discharge, Harris applied for a pension about 1900. In 1902 he was given the discharge under a March 1889 law that granted amnesty to certain Civil War veterans, opening the way for a pension. Harris also applied for a travel allowance (which was refused) and an unpaid bounty (which was paid). Company I Pvt. William Price enlisted as a substitute (for John R. Dick) at Baltimore in December 1864. He left the regiment at White's Ranch and was thought to have gone to Mexico.[36]

Deaths from late July through September were seven at Ringgold, and one man, Pvt. John Parker, Company G, a draftee enrolled at Ellicott Mills in August 1864, was drowned swimming in the Rio Grande on 20 July, probably while cooling off during the march to Ringgold. Company A Pvt. Daniel Yates was the last soldier to die at Rio Grande City. He had enlisted at Springfield, Illinois, in January 1865. He was born in St. Louis, Missouri, in about 1837, probably in slavery. After his death from an unknown disease his widow and three young children were pensioned. She remarried in 1867, causing her pension to be discontinued (payments to the minors continued). Mrs. Yates's new husband was "shot and killed by a colored man name of Taylor" in Springfield, and she married for a third time. That husband was also "shot and killed" in the same city when he went "to collect a bill." The three-time widow thereupon successfully applied for a resumption of Yates's pension.[37]

The Twenty-ninth USCT reported 31 officers and 1,055 enlisted men on the rolls as of the end of August, of which 3 officers and 309 men were absent, most of the latter sick in army hospitals. Of course, losses among soldiers who had been left behind at Fort Monroe, Portsmouth, and Alexandria, Virginia, continued, but they were few. These deaths were largely from lingering illnesses such as tuberculosis and heart trouble and diseases like typhoid fever and pneumonia. The largest reduction in the regiment's strength was in late September when 50 men completed one-year enlistments and were discharged and sent home.[38]

HEADING HOME

As for one reason the troops were on the border, the situation in Mexico, it did not have any impact on the troops, because Juárez's forces had essentially confined Maximilian's French troops to the Valley of Mexico. France had earlier requested that the United States withdraw Sheridan's troops and offered to negotiate withdrawal of its own, but nothing came of these maneuvers. France did not remove its troops from Mexico until the spring of 1867, following considerable diplomatic pressure from the United States and more than a year and a half after Sheridan's force was sent home. Perhaps the favorable tide in Mexico had been foreseen by Grant, but, more likely, the return of troops was ordered to reduce expenses of the military establishment after a costly war. Sheridan was authorized on 1 August "to cause all volunteer white troops . . . serving in the Department of Texas, that you think you can dispense with, to be mustered out of the service." Five weeks later he was directed to do the same with "all organizations of *colored troops* in your department, *which were enlisted in northern states.*" It could not be said that the Twenty-ninth Regiment was entirely enlisted in northern states, and probably half of the soldiers serving when the order was received had been recruited in Maryland and Virginia. The procedure was, however, that regiments be discharged en masse, so the Twenty-ninth Regiment companies that had only a handful of men enlisted in the North were not considered separately.[39]

Two points were designated for each regiment's processing, one for mustering out and the second for payment. The Twenty-ninth Regiment was to go to Brownsville for the first and to Camp Butler at Springfield, Illinois, for the second, and it departed the camp near Ringgold Barracks at 3 P.M. on 11 October. The regiment marched over several days to Edinburg, about forty miles east. From there it was transported by steamer to Brownsville, arriving at 8 A.M. on 17 October. Morning report entries stop on 25 October, the date the officers completed the muster-out rolls, which were basically pay documents, recording issue of equipment, charges against enlisted men, bounty installments unpaid, date of last payment received, and so on, and discharge papers were to be prepared for each of the 31 officers and 978 enlisted men, not all of whom were present, on the rolls. The directive outlining these procedures cautioned that "regimental officers will be held to strict accountability in order to insure accurate and complete records of the enlisted men, and the better to establish the just claims of the non-commissioned officers and privates who have been wounded, or of the representatives of those who have died from disease or wounds, or been killed in battle." Paperwork completed, the regiment, "having been mustered out of the service in accordance with instructions from the War Department . . . is hereby ordered to Springfield Ills. for final discharge."[40]

A further casualty resulted from the march to Brownsville; Company D Pvt. Andrew Cowan, about twenty-five, died of disease at Edinburg on 14 October, just after the regiment's arrival there. Cowan was born in Tennessee and had enlisted at Rockford, Illinois, in August 1864; little more is known about him. Company I Pvt. Samuel Henderson, who had been in the Brownsville post hospital since shortly after the Twenty-ninth Regiment landed at Brazos de Santiago, died on 30 October of what was recorded as chronic dysentery. Born in Franklin County, Tennessee, in 1836, the soldier was mustered in at Danville, Illinois, in December 1864, a substitute for William Mickelbury. Pvt. Sidney Jones, from the same company, was also sent early to New Orleans; he died there of "remittent fever" on 21 October. Born in Georgia, he was just over twenty and had enlisted at Alton, Illinois, in December 1865. None of these men had recorded dependents.[41]

The actual mustering out was not a ceremony but simply the date when the rolls and other paperwork were complete, had been reviewed by brigade and division officers, and the regiment was ready to depart for the state rendezvous. The Twenty-ninth USCT's official mustering-out day was 6 November, and the regiment then sailed for New Orleans by steamer. The regiment changed there to the riverboat *W. H. Osborn*, departing at 5 P.M. on 8 November 1865, for Cairo, Illinois, the next leg on the trip home. A Springfield newspaper reported: "The 29th Regiment of United States Colored Infantry, consisting of twenty-eight officers and eight hundred and ten men, was mustered out at New Orleans, La., . . . and placed *en route* for this city, for muster out and payment." Units headed for the state rendezvous were still under the command of their officers and retained their arms, colors, and some equipment but, at the muster-out camp, turned over to the quartermaster everything not required for the trip to the home state. Soldiers could purchase their muskets (at six dollars and fifty cents each), and they were allowed to keep knapsacks and canteens without charge. An officer of the regiment—the regulation specified "a discreet and responsible" one—was to be put in charge of the boxed records until he could turn them over to an official at the state camp. The Twenty-ninth USCT's responsible officer was the regimental adjutant, 2d Lt. George G. Smith.[42]

In addition to 28 officers and 810 men sent north for final processing, the Twenty-ninth USCT had on its rolls about another 160 sick men who did not accompany the regiment to Camp Butler. Men in the hospital and not present for duty with the regiment were paid only to the mustering-out date, a source of complaint by the Illinois adjutant general. Others were paid up to the date of final processing at the camp of rendezvous at Springfield. Many sick soldiers later reported to Springfield for their final payment and discharge papers, over seventy appearing in the week after the regiment had broken up. Officers and men of black regiments were permitted to request payment and discharge certificates where they had been mustered out, as were white troops, and about a dozen soldiers of the Twenty-ninth USCT were released at Brownsville and New Orleans, among them Surgeon Mackay, who was to take a job with the War Department's Freedmen's Bureau and was later city physician in the latter city. Company G Pvt. Isaiah Wells, one of the soldiers transferred from the Twenty-eighth U.S. Colored Infantry, had been a sergeant but was reduced to the ranks in June for what might have been theft; he chose a New Orleans discharge. He stayed there and at Buler and Vicksburg, Mississippi, for three years following his army service. He was, as a pension examiner noted, "somewhat of a wanderer," moving to Arkansas; spending eighteen years at Mt. Carmel, Illinois; living in Nashville, Texarkana, and Topeka; and arriving in Kansas City in 1897; even then Wells's wandering was not yet over. Pvt. Jacob McCabe, the Company H soldier whose master had accompanied him to the recruiters at Wilmington, Delaware, took the New Orleans option when his one-year term of service was over in September 1865. He, and several hundred other black former soldiers (McCabe and one other unidentified man were the only Twenty-ninth Regiment veterans), accepted a job in Washington County, Mississippi. He worked on a plantation for Bvt. Maj. Gen. George Leonard Andrews, a West Point graduate from Massachusetts with black soldier command experience, who tried his hand at being a planter. Andrews gave up the venture in 1867 and returned east, but McCabe, known by then as Jake Mitchell, stayed on and worked on plantations until his death of senile debility in 1923.[43]

The New Orleans provost marshal reported that Pvt. James Williams, of Company K, had been detained in that city under a murder charge. No soldier of that name was in the company, however, so Williams must have been confused with a soldier from the Twenty-ninth Connecticut or another regiment. The Twenty-ninth USCT reached Cairo by steamship about 15 November, arriving by rail at Camp Butler at Springfield on Saturday, 17 November. Here an army paymaster, Maj. Edward D. Redington, prepared to complete the regiment's final processing. The state had responsibilities, however, because it ran the rendezvous camp, and Illinois Gov. Richard J. Oglesby was earlier asked by the army to expedite discharge procedures and was offered federal help if needed. By the time the Twenty-ninth reached Camp Butler the machinery was well oiled.[44]

While the troops waited for final payment, local citizens took notice of the unusual unit, a newspaper reporting, "The colored people of this city will give a public dinner to the 29th Illinois colored regiment and all other colored troops in this city, on Wednesday afternoon [November 22]." Ceremonies were held "on the Common, north of Old Cottage Garden," the regiment beginning the events by parading around the square and to the governor's mansion from where Oglesby, a prewar abolitionist and a former major general with a solid military record, reviewed the troops. The dinner for the soldiers, " a barbacue," followed, served on tables set with white paper tablecloths. After the meal the soldiers were assembled around a speakers' stand, and the governor was introduced. Noting that a reception like this one would have been impossible a few years earlier, he spoke to the soldiers gathered there "of their having been a downtrodden and enslaved race, with the whole white race prejudiced against them, and he wished he could say it was all gone." The governor also made the customary mentions of great Union generals and Lincoln and said that he was sure blacks had made a contribution to the war, although he was unaware what it was. Finally, he remarked that he was pleased about what the regiment's officers said of the men and "on their fidelity, discipline and good behavior on all occasions," and he told the soldiers they should learn to read and write.[45]

That or the following evening a soldier wrote, "We had a big carousin['] in camp, fiddlin' and dancin'." The next morning the regiment had its last formation, and the officers and men received their pay and prepared to leave Springfield for their homes. Company G Pvt. George Douglas said he went to the railroad depot with Cpl. Charles Dix to get his tickets back to Baltimore but found a large crowd there and decided to wait. Douglas fell asleep, "tired out from the carousin' in camp": "When I woke up

Dicks [*sic*] was gone and so was my money and everything. . . . I had no money to get back to Maryland and that is the reason I stayed in Springfield." Another Maryland soldier, Company H Pvt. John Dorsey, joined a group of the about three hundred Maryland veterans in the regiment, each of whom received twenty dollars in travel money. He explained that "Lt. Layton [not a Twenty-ninth Infantry officer] took charge of about 47 of us that were coming east," and they arrived at Baltimore without incident. The last official act on behalf of the regiment was on 24 November, when Colonel Royce turned in the regimental records and colors. The Twenty-ninth United States Colored Infantry had completed its military service.[46]

The last regimental casualty may have been Pvt. Alexander Hill, age thirty-one, a draftee from Howard County, Maryland. He apparently was taken ill on the trip up the Mississippi from New Orleans, and he died at Camp Butler of "inflamation of the bowells" on 21 November, just before the regiment had been paid. Probably more soldiers died in government hospitals in Virginia, New Orleans, and other places, and some of them were no doubt forgotten by the army. Others may have been overlooked had they not sought to straighten out their status and secure a discharge certificate. Pvt. Thomas Nelson, enlisted in Company C at Coswell, Virginia, was mustered in at Camp Casey in the last days of 1864. He took sick and was sent to Fort Monroe Hospital in April, where he was discharged some months later, apparently without receiving a certificate. He said that he went to Washington, D.C., and stayed at a soldiers' rest there over the winter of 1865–66. Later on his status was questioned, and Nelson found that the army had reported him "dead and berried" at the hospital. He finally got proper papers in 1866. Company A Pvt. John Oscar Hawkins from Port Tobacco, Maryland, was likewise lost, but it appears to have been through his own mistakes. He was at the Corps d'Afrique hospital in New Orleans but was too ill, with an unidentified malady, to join the regiment's move to Springfield. In February 1866 he wrote to General Oakes at Camp Butler, asking for a discharge and explaining why he had never appeared at Butler to claim one. He said the hospital had sent him north and told him to report to Camp Butler. He had made it to Cairo by ship and then took a train that left him at Centralia, Illinois. Then, he said, "I was brought to Burlington Iowa by Mr. Tallant with whom I am now staying." He did not explain the circumstances further, but he was sent a discharge in a few days.[47]

How much had these blacks contributed to Illinois's war effort? It is certain that few in the state took much notice of the regiment's record. Most citizens were like their governor; they did not give the matter much thought, and the same was true nearly everywhere in the nation. It was not a question of numbers of black soldiers, because the total nationwide (179,000 in 149 regiments and batteries) was substantially less than Illinois's manpower contribution to the Union alone (255,000). The state received credit for 1,811 black enlistments, but the number is deceptive, because three or four hundred of the men found in Maryland and Virginia had never before seen the state; on the other hand, most early Illinois enlistees in other states' black regiments were not credited to Illinois. To further cloud the picture, a large percentage of recruits counted for the quota were recent fugitives from slave states who had never resided in Illinois. And, finally, the army listed two thousand officers and enlisted men in the Twenty-ninth USCT, a number that includes Company F, of which most soldiers were counted by Wisconsin, and the unassigned recruits who never served with the regiment but does not include several hundred blacks counted for Illinois and recruited in that state for other states' USCT regiments. Actually, serving in the regiment in the field were just short of fourteen hundred men enlisted in Illinois, Wisconsin, Maryland, Delaware, and Virginia.[48]

Three officers and about sixty-two noncommissioned officers and privates were killed in battle or died of wounds or poor treatment in Confederate prison camps; the total includes soldiers missing in battle but never found. Almost sixty men deserted, and about one hundred and twenty-five can be identified as having died of disease or accident, but the latter number is probably low, because some of the soldiers left in the hospital on mustering-out day died later. The rate for battle deaths of U.S. Colored Troops regiments was 16.11 per 1,000, compared with white volunteer regiments' 35.10; the Twenty-ninth USCT's was about 45. These rates may not be entirely comparable because the army's postwar numbers do not include those who died of wounds, and they are not adjusted for length of service, but they do show that by this measure the Twenty-ninth Regiment did its part.[49] Casualties are, however, as often indicators of bad luck, unfortunate circumstances, or poor leadership as of valorous conduct.

A better measure of a Civil War military organization's worth may be its rate of death from natural causes, because a low rate showed that officers and noncommissioned officers took care of their men and that the men obeyed. The Twenty-ninth Regiment's rate of about 91 per 1,000 was substantially less than the USCT average of 141, not as good as the white volunteers' 59, and was much worse than the Army of the Potomac's 38 per 1,000. The army's adjutant general concluded that the high sickness rate of blacks was the result of their being "less able than the white to endure the exposures and annoyances of military service." He did not, however, put this down to physical inferiority but thought "the greater susceptibility of the colored man to disease arose from lack of heart, hope, and mental activity, and that a higher moral and intellectual culture would diminish the defect." Another office wrote that the black was "very susceptible to disease which comes from exposure and [was] without skill to take care of himself. . . . So, under ordinary privations, he was apt to become disabled, give up in homesickness and quickly sink to the grave." Most black soldiers dying of disease during the war were stricken with respiratory illness (2,434 of them), usually described as "inflammation of lungs." Scurvy, acute diarrhea (dysentery?), and smallpox took 388, 706, and 806 lives, respectively.[50]

Another way to judge unit efficiency is rate of desertion. With almost 60 deserters, 42 per 1,000, the Twenty-ninth U.S. Colored Infantry appears better than all black regiments (67) and white volunteers (62), but once again the rates do not reflect all circumstances, such as incidence of hard fighting, opportunities to reach home, living conditions, and duties. The adjutant general found desertion to be "a crime of foreign rather than native birth." Europeans ran off, he said, not Americans. When the Twenty-ninth U.S. Colored Infantry is compared to another black regiment from a similar state which filled four companies with Virginia and Maryland blacks and with the same military campaigns and assignments, the Twenty-eighth U.S. Colored Infantry from Indiana, the regiments have much the same record.[51] It appears, therefore, that numbers do not distinguish the Twenty-ninth Regiment from other regiments, black or white, but its record was honorable, and its men should have been proud of their military service.

What they expected as a result of wearing the Union uniform was not recorded, and the state itself seems to have made little note of this unusual military unit and its veterans. The soldiers' departure day from Springfield for their homes in Illinois and other states was the last time the unit met; it did not organize a veterans' association, and the regiment's accomplishments were largely forgotten. These accomplishments were probably most important for slightly improving the position of blacks in the state, although equality was far from achieved. Prejudice still dominated how white Americans saw their black fellow citizens.[52] The war changed that very little, and postwar politics in the North and government policies in the South allowed the suppression of blacks to be restored in most of the nation. The struggle for equality, having been so little assisted in Illinois by the war, went on.

Chapter 6

THE LATER YEARS

About 60 percent of the officers and men of the Twenty-ninth U.S. Colored Infantry or their survivors filed applications for government pensions. Relatively few of the applications were submitted just after the war by widows, children, and dependent parents of men who had been killed or died in service and few by soldiers disabled by wounds or service-connected injuries. The law in force was the "general law pension system," which was approved by President Lincoln on 14 July 1862. A pensionable injury had to be a direct consequence of military duty, and widows, children, and other dependent relatives could be pensioned, providing the death of the soldier was traced to injuries or disease contracted in military service. Payments were eight dollars to thirty dollars monthly, depending on rank, for total disability from manual labor, and widows received twelve dollars monthly plus two dollars for each child under the age of sixteen.[1]

Twenty-five years after the end of hostilities it was no longer necessary to demonstrate that a disabling condition was the result of military service. The Disability Pension Act of 1890 provided pensions to veterans who had attained a certain age or if it could be determined that the former soldiers were sufficiently infirm so as "incapacitate them from the performance of manual labor to such a degree as to render them unable to earn a support." The amount of payment depended on percentage of disability: need was not a factor. Widows and children were pensionable regardless of the cause of the soldiers' deaths. The widows' rate provided in the 1890 law was eight dollars monthly, plus two dollars for each child under sixteen years. Under the 1862 "general law," providing pensions for soldiers with service-connected disabilities and their survivors, the rate was twelve dollars. A widow was first allowed ninety-three dollars yearly income; this was raised to two hundred and fifty dollars in 1900, and in 1908 widows were pensioned regardless of income. The general law remained in effect and sometimes provided a higher pension than did the 1890 law, so applicants (or their dependents) after 1890 often claimed that disabilities (or death) were caused by in-service injuries or diseases. The 1890 act, subsequently further liberalized, caused a flood of pension applications from Union veterans.[2]

It is difficult to draw conclusions from pension files, because each applicant sought to maximize his disabling conditions and, consequently, at times provided unreliable information on his medical and other personal circumstances. Standard government forms sought some biographical data: places of residence since the war, family status, and sometimes occupation. Of course, the files are thick with physician and examiner reports, but they also include affidavits from comrades describing their recollections of events in which a soldier might have been disabled and from neighbors testifying about the degree of disability. Naturally, most of them read much the same and are often the obvious result of coaching by the claims agent preparing the petition. To their credit the examiners of the Bureau of Pensions were thorough, demanded substantial proof, and often detected fraud. Collectively, therefore, the files allow conclusions to be drawn about soldiers' lives, which is particularly useful regarding veterans of black regiments composed mainly of illiterate men who left few other records.[3]

Most of the Twenty-ninth U.S. Colored Infantry Regiment's veterans returned to the places where they were living immediately before they joined the army. For the most part that is where they stayed, almost all of them in menial occupations, for the rest of their lives, sometimes in touch with former comrades but most often not. The former slaves primarily from Kentucky, Tennessee, and overwhelmingly Missouri, who were enlisted in Illinois, Indiana, and Wisconsin, remained in Midwest states, some returned to the border states where they had been in bondage, and a small number started new lives elsewhere. Of the several hundred soldiers enlisted in Virginia, Maryland, and Delaware, most of them former slaves, the choice of remaining in Illinois, the state that they first saw only days before the regiment's discharge at Springfield, was not as attractive as returning to friends and family in their home states. Not many of them relocated even later in life. Free black Illinoisans were not much different from those who were recently in bondage, and most of them died at or near the places where they had enlisted in the Twenty-ninth U.S. Colored Infantry.

One can only speculate why the black veterans of the Twenty-ninth USCT did not scatter to new places and situations after the war, but these largely unlettered men appear to have given little thought, except in terms of their freedom, to lives other than those they had always known and places their families had often been for generations. Furthermore, they did not have the means nor the skills to relocate, and in postwar America opportunities for black men were limited. So the veterans, primarily farmers and laborers, returned to their former activities, some of them acquiring property and security but most remaining as they had always been, poor and dependent on day labor and without the means to sustain themselves in their later years.

Regimental officers had a different world to return to, but, aside from literacy, many of them had the same low skill levels as did their men, and only a few of them were able to lead comfortable lives. On the other hand, former officers were decidedly mobile and scattered all over the nation, many of them to the West, where, it was said, there were new opportunities.

CRIMES, FRAUDS, AND CONFUSION

Regimental commander Clark E. K. Royce first tried his hand at the law in Scranton, Pennsylvania, moving to the West in 1876 with his wife and son and establishing his practice in San Francisco. He seems to have lived in comfortable circumstances for about fifteen years, when he was accused of embezzling twenty thousand dollars "by falsifying his returns to the Secretary of the Association" of the Veterans' Home of which he was treasurer. Sentenced to seven years in the penitentiary, his conviction was reversed by the California Supreme Court on the technical ground that the home had never asked Royce to return the money he had stolen. Nonetheless, his reputation and legal practice were ruined, and his financial situation deteriorated. In 1893 he tried unsuccessfully to kill himself in a San Francisco hotel. In late 1897, however, he returned to his native New York to visit relatives; staying at a hotel on Forty-seventh Street and Park Avenue in New York City, he committed suicide by breathing illuminating gas. A newspaper said of him: "Colonel Royce's tragic death is the last act of a self-wasted, a self-ruined life. It is the letting down of the curtain on a dreary drama where one elected to steep his honorable name in dishonor, blot his soldierly record with crime, prove recreant to the trust of his loyal friends and betray the cause of his old battle comrades."

Although her son was an Oakland attorney, Harriet Royce was left without means, and she petitioned the government for a widow's pension, not mentioning at first that her husband had died by his own hand. Once having revealed the matter, however, she was qualified on the ground that her income was less than two hundred and fifty dollars annually. She died in Oakland in 1918.[4]

While Royce's crime was the only serious one revealed regarding the Twenty-ninth USCT's officers, among enlisted men attempted pension fraud, intentional and not, was relatively common. But there were also more serious offenses. Pvt. Robert Smith, at enlistment a blacksmith from Quincy, had been serving a life sentence for murder in the state penitentiary at Joliet for five or six years when he applied under the new law for a pension, claiming he was incapacitated for manual labor partly from a wound he said he suffered at the crater battle. Following the war Smith in succession ran a laundry in Springfield, supervised a boardinghouse, ran a barber shop, traded in poultry, and was a dealer in rags and scrap. He was awarded twelve dollars monthly in 1890 but died in 1894 of "fatty degeneration of the heart." His widow thereupon sought a survivor payment, but it was denied on grounds that she ran a disorderly house and was in adulterous relationships with two men. Pvt. Isaac Gaskins, the soldier who had been a prisoner at Petersburg and was now residing in Springfield, gave evidence on the wife's behalf, but the pension bureau's decision stood.[5]

Daniel Rogers, another Company A private, was confined under sentences for theft in the Joliet penitentiary beginning in 1890 and again in 1896 and was paroled in 1907. If a veteran engaged in criminal or illegal activities, he was not denied a pension (nor was an existing one discontinued) unless the alleged acts caused or aggravated the claimed disability. Rogers was always poor, working as a common laborer in Springfield whenever he was not in prison, and, consequently, a pension was attractive to him. He sought certification for various maladies, the most serious of which were injuries received in an 1882 sawmill accident. In years to come he improved on his claim, certifying that he had been burned in the crater attack and also that he had been trampled in the stampede back to Union lines. The pension bureau refused the wound claim, even though Rogers was supported by depositions from comrades William Freeman and David Curtis, also Springfield laborers; he was later suspected of falsifying his age to qualify for increased payment. The bureau decided not to prosecute, and Rogers spent his last days in the Southwest Branch, National Home for Disabled Wounded Soldiers at Milwaukee; he died in 1912. He had divorced his first wife and abandoned the second, so none of his survivors was pensioned.[6]

Isaiah Wells, the soldier labeled as "somewhat of a wanderer," reached Kansas City in 1897. His wandering ended there when he was convicted of grand larceny—a burglary—and was sentenced to three years in the Kansas State Penitentiary at Lansing. After his jail term he continued his roving, going to Leavenworth and to Carroll County, Missouri. In 1901 he entered the Illinois soldiers' home at Danville and later transferred to the Quincy facility. In 1907 he was dismissed from the home for mail fraud. A report reads that Wells, "late an inmate of the Soldiers' and Sailors' Home at Quincy, . . . is under arrest charged with having forged the endorsement of Isaac Webb, an inmate of said home." Wells left with the money and was apprehended in Iowa. He was not sentenced for forgery, as he might have been, because the judge thought him an ignorant man and gave him only thirty days in the Sangamon County jail. Wells went to Wisconsin next and moved later to veterans' homes in Indiana and, finally, Ohio in 1916. His wife, whom he had married in Texarkana in 1887, and all their six children were dead by 1915. Wells died of heart disease in 1921 at the Ohio home, previously pensioned only for advanced age.[7]

One soldier's possibly disqualifying military past caught up with him in the pension process, but the man was certified in 1888, nevertheless, because of war wounds and general disability. The veteran was Company F commander Capt. Willard E. Daggett, who failed to mention to the pension bureau that he had been dismissed from the army in Texas by sentence of a general court-martial for public drunkenness and conduct unbecoming of an officer. Daggett, a bookkeeper who lived after the war with his wife and children in Chicago, Boston, and finally Brookline, Massachusetts, had been accused of desertion while an enlisted man but was apparently not punished for the offense before his muster in the Twenty-ninth USCT. Support from fellow officers may have been a factor in calming the suspicions of examining bureau physicians in 1888, who were considering disqualifying Daggett for alcoholism: "This claimant was reportedly drunk while acting as Captain of Colored troops and it may be that intemperance had something to do with his 'broken down' condition." In any event Daggett's constructive descriptions of his military background were not considered serious fraud, nor was drinking seen as the cause of his disability. He remained pensioned until his death, in 1899, of chronic enteritis at Battleboro, Massachusetts.[8]

Pvt. Walter Kelly returned to his native state after the war, working as a laborer in Alexandria, Virginia, for a man named Maj. George Johnson. Kelly was tried for voting twice in an election but, on his employer's advice, fled to the District of Columbia in 1868 before sentencing. There he took his employer's name, was married, and worked under the assumed name for almost ten years. Kelly had often been ill during his military service, was hospitalized at Fort Monroe from January 1865, and was not with the regiment in Texas nor at its disbandment at Springfield. He applied for a pension in 1885 based on service-connected rheumatism, related heart disease, and a bayonet wound, but the process was complicated by his dual identity, which raised questions about whether the claimant really was the former soldier Kelly. Then residing in Youngstown, Ohio, and later Harrisburg, Pennsylvania, the couple remarried under the Kelly name in 1894 as part of the process that eventually resulted in a pension. Walter Kelly died of bronchial asthma in Boston in 1908 while visiting a daughter, and his widow, not without difficulties caused by double marriages and names, was later also pensioned.[9]

While Kelly's claim seems to have been justified, another pension was erroneously granted to an individual claiming to be Company A's Pvt. John Coleman. Coleman was a Virginian, but the claimant to his pension appeared in Gowanda, New York, under the name Joseph Deemis. He was married under this name in 1876, and his wife and neighbors apparently were not aware of his Coleman identity until after the 1890 pension bill was enacted. Then Deemis told his acquaintances that Deemis had been his name in slavery, and he had assumed it after the war. His pension application—he claimed disability from chronic diarrhea, lung disease, and other infirmities—was accepted in 1892, the year of his death from heart disease. His widow, then residing in the Erie County poorhouse with some of the children, applied for her pension, prompting a reexamination of Coleman's original file. In it were six affidavits found to be fraudulent, and the 1876 marriage could not be satisfactorily proved. Probably, had Coleman/Deemis outlived his wife, and thus not had his status reexamined, he would have remained pensioned.[10]

The Coleman/Deemis example seems to have been a clear case of intentional fraud, but other pensions were improperly awarded because of confusion by the examiners and the illiteracy of the recipients. Pvt. John

Turner returned to Cairo, Illinois, where he had enlisted. He worked there, at Memphis, returned to Cairo, and once more relocated at Memphis, working as a farmhand and day laborer. He did not get around to applying for a pension until 1908, citing rheumatism and a hernia. While the claim seemed entirely legitimate, Turner was denied because another individual, alias Ben Turner, had been pensioned for eighteen years. Further complicating the matter was yet another John Turner who had enlisted in the Twenty-ninth USCT at Baltimore in October 1864. The Maryland Turner was found at the time to be a minor, and he was discharged in mid-January 1865, not having served the ninety days required for veteran benefits.

Ben Turner was interviewed by pension officials, and they found him "densely ignorant" and incapable of planning such a successful fraud. Born in Glascow, Virginia, he apparently had been a civilian teamster on a wagon train from City Point to Washington, D.C., and from there, he said, to Springfield, Illinois. Ben was living in Taylorsville, Illinois, when he applied for a pension in 1890, claiming under examination that his real name was John but that he was called Ben. The examiners were confused about the apparent error in the name and the existence of the Maryland Turner but accepted Ben as the Illinois John, even though much of the story of his birth, background, and other details did not check out. The error was not discovered until the real John Turner decided to apply in 1908. Ben's pension was stopped and John finally pensioned but not until the pension bureau went to extraordinary lengths to verify his identity. A Taylorsville newspaper writer thought Ben was unlikely to have "impersonated a colored brother" intentionally and, furthermore, that it would be difficult to prosecute him for it. He continued: "Even twenty years ago Turner's memory was poor and no one credited him with sagacity enough to impersonate another. He was then, as now, an old, decrepit, ignorant colored man." The pensioned John Turner died in Memphis in 1924.[11]

Sometimes pension examiner vigilance prompted questioning of a veteran's pension status and suspicion that he should be prosecuted for pension fraud. Pvt. George Douglas, the Maryland soldier who had remained in Springfield because his money was stolen by Cpl. Charles Dix, worked in a coal mine and at odd jobs in the Springfield area after discharge. He traveled to Oklahoma Territory, Indiana, and other places in search of work, and he made several trips to Maryland to visit relatives. In 1913, on his last visit home to Rehobeth, Maryland, he applied for a pension increase, the request nearly resulting in

Douglas being dropped from the rolls and being prosecuted as an impostor. The reason for this was that another George Douglas had asked to enter the Indiana veterans' home in 1912, and he was considered a legitimate applicant. After a year's investigation the new Douglas, like the first, was found to have enlisted in the Twenty-eighth Regiment and been sent, as excess, to another. The second man, however, had gone to the Twenty-third U.S. Colored Infantry at the same time the first had been sent to the Twenty-ninth. Consequently, both men retained their pensions, and the first died at Willow Grove, Pennsylvania, in 1917.[12]

Confusion over identity was common, and much of the time it was due to mistakes and misreading of army records. Pvt. John Dorsey was pensioned in 1891, but the award was challenged eight years later on the grounds that Dorsey had not previously proven his identity satisfactorily. A Hannibal, Missouri, woman had filed for a pension as the widow of John Dorsey, but the pensioned soldier was alive in Maryland and had never been married. The issue was settled in 1900, the pension bureau concluding that the widow's husband had been a soldier in Company C who had enlisted at Quincy and had died in the soldiers' home there in 1897. Yet Company C rolls do not list a John Dorsey.

Not all mistakes were due to records and duplications. Pvt. William Limehouse's pension was held up because he incorrectly identified his regiment. Being a freeman from Pennsylvania, he had enlisted as a substitute at Washington, D.C. After discharge he lived at various places in his home state and spent some time in the Bucks County Poor House. His 1896 pension claim was rejected because he said he had been a soldier in the Twenty-ninth Pennsylvania Infantry, a white regiment on whose rolls his name did not appear. Limehouse was entered about 1905 for blindness, his proper regiment having been identified. He died in a soldiers' home in Kearney, New Jersey, in 1907. Pvt. Charles W. Lewis's case was somewhat similar. Returning from the war to Illinois, he settled after several moves at Bloomington. His 1890 pension request was delayed two years because he could not recall his regiment's number and was uncertain about whether he had been in a volunteer or regular army organization. He was then married to a second wife, the first having divorced him for "extreme and repeated cruelty," for which she was awarded alimony, custody of the children, and a residential property. Lewis, all his life a laborer, died at Bloomington of "Appoplexey" in 1918.[13]

Pvt. John Steward, once a slave in Anne Arundel County, Maryland, lived after the war in Washington, D.C., and never had regular work. He was often in the city workhouse and jail for criminal offenses and was sent twice to the penitentiary, once for "cutting a man" and another time for stealing chickens. He was pensioned in 1892 for rheumatism. Steward's wife tried to claim half his pension as the law allowed for deserted spouses, but he said she drove him from home in 1887. The wife countered with an accusation that Steward was a heavy drinker, which, if proven, might have led to a loss of pension for "vicious habits," also as the law allowed. The matter was not then resolved, and Steward died in the Alms House Hospital in Washington in 1907. His widow began a new attempt to be pensioned, but, when it became known that she had an undivorced, living husband when she married Steward, her request was rejected.[14]

A veteran more obviously a victim of a woman's deception was Pvt. John J. L. Cole. Before the war Cole was a tanner in Baltimore and may have returned to that work after discharge. He first tried to be pensioned in 1878; later he was accepted based on his advanced age. Cole, then seventy-two, was on his deathbed when he married Marie William, age twenty-three, but the circumstances were suspicious. The attending doctor said Cole was unconscious when the ceremony was performed by an elderly minister. The new widow applied for a pension but was instead indicted for fraud along with a coconspirator. Two trials failed to convict her, but Marie was never pensioned.[15]

Company G 1st Sgt. John Williams was jailed in Washington for pension fraud in lieu of payment of three hundred dollars bail, but he was finally pensioned for a rupture he said was caused while the regiment was constructing breastworks on the Richmond front in 1865. The U.S. attorney had declined to prosecute him. The fraud was probably connected to his postwar use of the name William Bell and the fact that Company G had two men named John Williams. Williams/Bell died in the District of Columbia in 1902.[16]

Another soldier with a name change was Pvt. Alfred Owens, Company A. Owens was his slave master's last name, and after the war he assumed his father's name, Coleman. Coleman remained near Quincy and in neighboring Missouri and, although he could not write, stayed in touch with a large number of comrades, some of whom had "run off" to Illinois from slavery in Missouri with Coleman before the war. Owens/Coleman was confined in the Missouri State Penitentiary at Jefferson City in January 1877 and may have been jailed for shorter periods earlier. He had been a laborer in a lumber yard, driven an express wagon, and held other low-skill jobs in and around Hannibal before his sentence to two years imprisonment for "assault to kill," throwing a rock at another man. He died working as a prisoner in the Monserrat coal mines in November 1877, his wife claiming he "got smothered in the coal mine," the warden speculating, however, that he may have been killed trying to escape. A pension examiner wrote years later, "It is said that he would have been pardoned in a few days if he had not been accidentally killed." Using depositions from her husband's comrades, the widow successfully applied in 1904 for a pension, but the file contains papers expressing doubts about whether Owens and Coleman were the same man. As in several of these cases, the question seems to have been resolved in favor of the widow.[17]

A soldier engaged in fraud, although not only for his own claim, was Wagoner George Hawkins. He successfully applied to be pensioned for the accidental loss of his thumb at Quincy in late 1863. Hawkins was proficient in obtaining statements from many comrades, among them Sgts. John M. Perkins, William South, and George Templeton and Pvts. George Burke, James Jamison, John Wesley Logan, Peter Corsey, Thompson Kay, William Ross, and others. He even got statements from Captain Porter and Lieutenant Johnston. The number of depositions he obtained is explained by Hawkins's avocation some years after the war; he became a pension agent, helping others to file claims. A bureau examiner wrote in 1888 that "he has hitherttofore been involved in Crooked and fraudulent transactions in connection with arrears of pay, bounty, and pensions of colored clients"; he had been sentenced to prison by federal authorities at Jacksonville, Illinois, for taking illegal fees from clients, specifically Pvt. Charles Logan and the heirs of a soldier who died in the war. Hawkins had helped Logan to get 1877 pension approval for a wartime wound. The award was effective the date of the crater fight, so Logan collected $1,100.40, a large portion of which was extorted from him by Hawkins and another man—who also took Logan's wife. The pension office found Logan particularly vulnerable to such flimflam because of his illiteracy and "deep ignorance." After Logan's 1889 death at Quincy, a woman claiming to be Logan's second wife applied for a pension, but the examiner found that she had been convicted of stealing and had a generally bad reputation. Logan's sister testified for the woman, but the examiner discounted the sister's evidence; he found her to be "a low down colored prostitute and utterly unreliable." There was also evidence that Hawkins conspired with Company A Pvt. Harrison Williams, a three-time felon, in a false claim that was not completed. Despite all this, Hawkins was pensioned, and he collected payments until his 1927 death from tuberculosis in the Illinois Soldiers' and Sailors' Home.[18]

The Quincy pension agent James McGindley had a reputation as bad as Hawkins's. He usually preyed on widows and sometimes helped impostors to file for widows' pensions. He was certainly responsible for the confusion about the widow of Pvt. Martin Magruder, a soldier who died shortly after the crater fight. McGindley, it will be recalled, was suspected of fraud that resulted in the suspension of Magruder's wife's pension, and the agent also raised suspicions that a second woman, also representing herself as Magruder's wife, might be McGindley's accomplice or perhaps another victim. The same agent was suspected of similarly dubious maneuvers over a pension for the widow of Pvt. Jerry Morris. Morris died of pneumonia in July 1864, leaving a wife he married at Quincy early that year. She was pensioned without difficulty. In 1877, when she requested reinstatement following a suspension due to remarriage, a review showed that Morris had had an earlier wife from whom he was not divorced. The perpetrator of the suspected fraud was thought to be McGindley, who had conspired to conceal the first marriage.[19]

Pvt. James Harris, the Maryland soldier who saw General Lee surrender at Appomattox, was the object of a Baltimore agent's fraud. Approached in 1890 at a brickyard where he was working, Harris signed by his mark a number of affidavits and depositions. Comrades from army days, one or two of whom were employed at the same brickyard, also contributed depositions verifying Harris's in-service diseases. The agent, however, taking advantage of the men's gullibility, had falsified all the documents. The pension bureau detected this but, before the issue was resolved, in 1892, discovered a further complication: another man had been pensioned in Harris's name. He lived at Ottumwa, Iowa, and said that he had enlisted at Beakfield, Missouri, where he spent much of the war. The pension office took the Iowa man to Lincoln, Nebraska, to meet former commanding officer Captain Newton, who certified that he was the Company H soldier. Even so, pension officials were suspicious. The Iowa Harris died in March 1892, before he could be questioned in detail, and his widow made an application. It was obvious almost at once that the Iowa man was an imposter; he was the wrong age and claimed service where the Twenty-ninth USCT was never stationed. Unfortunately, the Baltimore Harris did not immediately benefit, although the false widow was finally rejected in 1897. Harris was denied because of the fraudulent certifications in his application, so he had to start the process from the beginning. Of course, pension examiners were now cautious. One asked Harris in 1893 if he were really the veteran. Harris answered: "I am not fool enough to fool with the government. I know what it does when you fool with it." Captain Newton was asked to look at photographs of both men. He refused this time to make a positive identification, favoring the Baltimore man, and explained that he had reached his first conclusion because of details the Iowa man knew about the company's service in Texas. Harris was finally granted his pension in 1899 (backdated to 1895), eleven years after the imposter was entered. Unfortunately, he never collected on it, for he died of ascites in March of the same year. He was a widower.[20]

Pvt. George H. Sherwood's less than truthful declarations at the time of enlistment caught up with him later. The New York–born soldier remained in Springfield for a short time after the war, drove a team to Fort Scott, Kansas, moved to Blue Jacket in Indian Territory, and returned to Fort Scott. He was pensioned for his Twenty-ninth Regiment service after 1891, but, when he sought an increase based on his age, in 1910, his record was reexamined. He was told he would need to produce written evidence of his date of birth, which he could not do, or, alternatively, ask the pension bureau to accept the date declared at enlistment. Since he had said he was ten years younger than he actually was when he entered the Twenty-ninth USCT, he offered what he said was correct information about his age from the Twenty-second New York Cavalry, the regiment he had deserted in Washington, D.C. Although records of desertion were frequently wiped clean by the army, the adjutant general denied Sherwood's application and would not give him an honorable discharge for the earlier service. The problem was that fraud was suspected with respect to substitute payments Sherwood had received, but, given that it had been so long since the alleged offense, Sherwood was never prosecuted; he died at Chetopa, Kansas, in 1919. One of his widows asked for a pension, but it was denied because Sherwood, who had been married three times, had at least one other living, undivorced wife.[21]

IDENTITY AND FAMILY PROBLEMS

Although several soldiers' identities were established by photography, one man's case largely depended on it. Pvt. James Gilmore was living in Vicksburg, Mississippi, after working at odd jobs in Quincy, Springfield, and Bloomington. He applied for a pension in 1904, citing rheumatism and adding old age. He could not prove his birth date, but the pension bureau was finally satisfied with the man's enlistment record entry. Another difficulty was verifying that the applicant was truly Gilmore. On this point the bureau circulated among his aged comrades a photograph from around 1905, but none could say more than that the face looked familiar. The identifications were enough to decide the matter, however, and he was pensioned. Gilmore died in 1911, survived by a widow.[22]

Why Gilmore waited so long to seek a pension is not known, but some soldiers filing late said that they simply did not know they were eligible. Pvt. John V. Thomas, a Baltimore hotel waiter, who was discharged with a disability, applied in 1894, explaining, "I had the idea that drafted men were not entitled to pension." Pvt. James Ringold, a soldier who took his discharge in New Orleans and spent his years as a farm laborer in Assumption Parish, made a claim in 1906, saying he had been unaware of the pension law until then.[23]

Although Pvt. Charles Sewell filed relatively early for a pension, his award was delayed. After serving in the regiment, he had returned to St. Mary's County, Maryland, and worked as a laborer, "renting such little houses from year to year as he could obtain." He could not, however, identify by name a single comrade who might support his claim. He had never asked their names, he said, because he was "not of an inquisitive disposition." He said that were he not awarded some payment, he would have to go to the "Poor House," so desperate was his condition. More common was the inability of veterans to verify their dates of birth when they were on in years and thus eligible for pensions based on age. This was because, being slaves at that time, they had never been told the information, and there were seldom written records of any kind. Former slave Andrew Sims had better information than many of his comrades. He recalled the day of his sale to a Kentucky man: "While on the 'block' I heard [from the auctioneer] that I was twenty one years of age." Occasionally, slave births were noted in the slave owner's family bible or those of slave families, if they had such books. More confusion arose when army records and depositions of soldiers and their family members were consulted, because the different sources were seldom in agreement. When Pvt. Peter Bernard applied from Alton in 1908 for an increase on reaching sixty-two, the pension examiner explained the method usually used to verify the matter: "Here we have an illiterate colored man, who, it is evident, does not know the date of his birth, his age being variously stated on the different declarations and other papers. In a case such as this we have to place most reliance upon the age at enlistment as shown by the War Dept. record."[24]

By far the most important want of information which bedeviled black veterans was a legacy of slave society: the nearly total lack of data on marriages. Since in slave states such information was never entered in official files, former soldiers and especially their widows, most of them illiterate and often without a strong memory of time and place, had a challenging task proving marriage. Because slave marriages were, by law and custom, informal, it is little wonder that many black men and women abandoned their spouses after the war and that this mind-set would long complicate pension requests. Pvt. Levi Marlow returned to Galesburg, Illinois, and separated from his wife, whom he found had been unfaithful during his absence. She married three more times in later years, and Marlow married again in 1880. He died of heart disease in 1903, and his first wife applied for the widow's pension. She was denied entry on the rolls because of her many marriages, not all of them legal. Marlow's second wife was not pensioned either, because he had not divorced his first. Pvt. William Arbuckle was also married many times. His first wife died in 1866 at Ridge Prairie, Illinois, where Arbuckle worked as a farmhand and as a fireman in Dunsteller's Flouring Mill. He moved to Mississippi, farming for wages and as a renter along the Yazoo River. He also worked in Louisiana on sugar and cotton farms, and he was married there in 1891. Arbuckle lived his last years at the Danville, Illinois, soldiers' home, and he married for the third time in 1904 while on leave from the home. He died in 1905, three months after his last marriage, but the last wife was not pensioned because both appeared to have been married three times and widowed or divorced but once.[25]

Pvt. John Abrams went to Indianapolis after his release from the army, working at cooking and other unskilled tasks. He married and divorced in 1880, remarried in 1882 but deserted his wife, Sarah, about 1887, and moved to Chicago. He married again in 1890 and was pensioned some years later for rheumatism and the effects of scurvy. He did not tell his last wife about Sarah, who from 1902 on received half his pension because she was a deserted wife. Abrams did not contest this award, and his Chicago wife recalled that he often complained about his low pension rate, not mentioning the reason. He died in 1911 of a cerebral hemorrhage at age sixty. His last wife, Julia, then requested a widow's pension but was rejected on the grounds that she had filed a "false statement." Only Sarah, who was by then insane and under care, received payment.[26]

A similar case, that of Cpl. George Easton (known after the war as George McLean), turned out differently because of a slave marriage complication. Married in slave fashion before the war at Henderson, Kentucky, Easton returned there in 1865. He moved after some years to Evansville, Indiana, working in a nursery and at other common labor jobs. What became of his first wife is not known, but Easton remarried in 1885. He may have been married again during the time between his two known marriages. He was pensioned in 1891 for a hernia and entered the Illinois soldiers' home at Danville in 1904, where he died in 1913. Two years before, his first wife, having located him, asked for half his pension because she had been deserted, but she was refused on grounds that their slave marriage was technically not lawful. Because the second wife's existence was never proved, Easton's third wife was pensioned after his death.[27]

Occasionally, government officials took some liberties with facts to permit what they saw as pensions for needy widows not otherwise entitled to consideration. Pvt. Alexander Morgan drowned one night in 1894 when he fell out of a boat on Coopers Creek in St. Mary's County, Maryland. Morgan's wife was initially rejected because he had been using the name of George Barnes, and no such soldier was found on the rolls of the Twenty-ninth U.S. Colored Infantry. This problem was overcome, but another remained: the validity of the marriage under Maryland law, which treated slaves and free men differently. Morgan and his wife claimed to have been free, "or at least they had that status at the date of inconception of their relationship." Therefore, a common-law marriage between them was legal. Had they been slaves, a ceremonial marriage would have had to have been documented. A pension examiner may have constructed the freed slave status of the couple because of the extremely poor condition in which he found the still unpensioned widow in 1909. "Her abode is a shack not over 5+ feet high and 8 feet square, in the piney woods. She is too feeble to work and looks half starved." The widow died, however, before being awarded the recommended payments.[28]

Pvt. Henry Powell was a Maryland native who chose to remain in the Midwest after being discharged. In 1866 he lived and was married at Mt. Vernon, Indiana, staying there until 1872. That same year he and his wife moved to Detroit, where Powell was employed by the Singer Sewing Machine Company until 1884. In October of the following year Powell told his wife he was going to Chicago to find work, and she never heard from him again. He was pensioned for rheumatism in 1899; the same year his wife claimed half his pension under the law allowing this payment for deserted wives. Powell protested on grounds that his wife was immoral, and he apparently prevailed. In 1902, however, he divorced her to prevent other claims. Powell died in the Quincy soldiers' home in 1907. Pvt. Thomas Nelson, a teamster at his native Hampton–Newport News, Virginia, area, also deserted a wife, and she was successful in securing half his pension. He divorced her because he said she had deserted him, and his pension was restored at the full rate. Nelson deserted a second wife later; she also petitioned for a share of his pension, but her claim was never entered.[29]

Sometimes a soldier was the abandoned party. Cpl. Samuel A. Arbuckle, who did not join the regiment until after Lee's surrender, returned to Alton after discharge. He was pensioned at two dollars monthly from the date of mustering out for stomach trouble that began in Virginia and deafness from fever that afflicted him while he was aboard the *Kennedy* on the way to Texas. Arbuckle farmed at Alton for five years and spent the next ten years in Iowa, Wisconsin, and Nebraska, working as a "speculator in horses." His first wife died, or he divorced her, and he married again in 1877. In all he had eleven children. Moving in 1890 to Los Angeles, California, he later lived in San Francisco and Portland, Oregon. He left his second wife in 1891 and was divorced two years later. As plaintiff in the case against her, he charged that "his wife shot him in 1890, at Lincoln, Neb., because she was seriously jealous of one Jenny Parker, causing a painful flesh wound. He also alleged that thereafter she lost all sense of decency, associated with all manner of disreputable people, and in 1891 attempted to poison him with Strychnine. She left him in Los Angeles, while he was absent at a Grand Army [of the Republic] celebration, moving all of the family furniture to Pasadena, Cal., where she now resides." The woman attempted to secure a half-pension as a deserted wife, but, since Arbuckle had divorced her on grounds of her desertion, she was unsuccessful. Arbuckle died in Portland in 1916.[30]

Similar jealousy seems to have led Pvt. John E. Barker, in 1889 at Jacksonville, Illinois, to abandon the woman he had married in 1855. She said she had broken up with him when he "got too fast with other women." Because he was not pensioned until 1900, the year he died, she did not get half the soldier's pension but did receive a widow's allowance. Pvt. Timothy A. Guard's second wife asked the government for half his pension that same year, claiming she was deserted in Saline County, Illinois. Guard made a successful counterclaim, asserting that he was the aggrieved party; his wife, according to him, "strolled about all over the country with an itinerate preacher."[31]

Perhaps the most unusual reason to desert a wife and family was offered by Pvt. Anthony Foggey. In 1892 at Quincy he was pensioned for the loss of an eye. Three years later the payment was reduced from twelve dollars a month to eight. Foggey deserted his wife and some of his six children in 1886 or 1887 and went to live with another woman. His excuse was that the pension reduction made it impossible to keep up house payments, and he added that his wife had deserted him. From 1895 on he was in and out of the Quincy soldiers' home and, apparently, did no further work. His wife tried to get a pension share, and she was finally admitted after the soldier's death (he was "run over by a train") at Quincy in 1905. In 1888 Pvt. Andrew Sims was deserted by his wife because, he said, he refused to live in St. Louis as she wished. He remarried at Centralia in 1891 and was pensioned the same year for a shoulder injury he had suffered at Dutch Gap. Having been a laborer all his life, Sims died at home in 1918 of senile debility. His second wife petitioned for a widow's payment but was refused because Sims still had an undivorced first wife when the two married in 1891. Although his first wife had died in 1911, that did not change the circumstances.[32]

The widow of a soldier who seemed to have been entitled to a pension refused to apply for an unusual reason. Pvt. William McKenney went back to Madison, Wisconsin, where he had enlisted and worked as a house servant. He later was a cook and steward "on freight steamers on the lake," out of Chicago and other Lake Michigan ports. He was pensioned in 1885 and died of a cerebral hemorrhage at Chicago in 1905. The woman he married in the year he was pensioned filed at once but was not accepted. McKenney, it turns out, already had another widow, unknown to this one. She was a white woman then living in Trout Lake, Washington. She married McKenney in 1872 at Oconomowoc, Wisconsin, moved with him to Milwaukee, and separated from him in Chicago, where he was a waiter at the Palmer House Hotel. The pension bureau had a difficult time reaching the first Mrs. McKenney in her remote home, and she initially denied any knowledge of or connection to the soldier. She may have been seeking to conceal the interracial marriage and did not apply for the widow's payment. The second wife, however, continued to seek it; her last unsuccessful attempt was in 1929. Another late application was filed in 1913 by a Mary Griffe claiming to be Margaret A. Griffin, the widow of Pvt. Joseph Griffin, who died at Sparta, Illinois, in 1891. The application and supporting papers were entirely fraudulent, but the U.S. attorney declined to prosecute on the basis of insufficient evidence. None of Griffin's widows was ever pensioned because the real Margaret and Griffin himself each had three spouses, some of them concurrently.[33]

Another unusual case was that of Pvt. Henry Clay, who settled in Illinois after the war. He died near Quincy about 1893, unmarried, at age forty-eight. The date of death is uncertain because of confusion about this man and another Henry Clay who lived in Quincy. The second Clay was never a soldier but became involved in the matter when it was found that someone had cashed Clay's quarterly pension checks for a year or so after his death. The pension bureau did not find the culprit, establishing that the second Clay died on 4 January 1892 and the soldier on 4 April 1893. In a bit of imaginative bookkeeping 4 January 1893 was designated the date of the soldier's death, a decision that somehow made all pension payments legal and ended the investigation.[34]

Soldiers whose own lives were led without scandal sometimes had difficulties with relatives. For example, Pvt. Philip Belden, a soldier from Quincy, divorced his first wife, according to the 1876 decree, for "habitual drunkenness . . . being in the habit of using very vulgar and profane language, and has been arrested and put in the calaboose by the citys authorys and fined for drunkenness." He married again the month following the divorce and lived with his second wife and their daughter until his death at Bloomington, Illinois, in 1905. He had been pensioned for the common complaints of rheumatism and chronic diarrhea, and his widow was qualified for payment later.[35]

An opposite case was that of Company A Sgt. William South, a Missourian, following the war. In later years he worked as a farmhand and was, the bureau examiner wrote, "a drunken fellow I am told." His wife and seven children left him in 1887. He had suffered a gunshot wound in the shin and sunstroke at the crater and claimed rheumatism caused "by working in rains and snows and exposure to the elements" in early 1865 on the Bermuda Hundred front. He died, a pensioned veteran, of what the coroner called "a stroke of apoplexy" in 1906 where he had lived since the war, Palmyra, Missouri, and his wife received a widow's pension.[36]

Pvt. John Carter, also a Missouri farmhand, did little with his life, living on his pension, and he was frequently arrested and confined for drunkenness. In 1893 the La Grange, Illinois, post of the Grand Army of the Republic unsuccessfully petitioned that Carter's pension be discontinued because he was a public scandal. The examiner agreed he was an alcoholic but also found that he was crippled from a spinal cord injury unrelated to drink. Hence, he remained on the rolls. He moved that year to Davenport, Iowa, possibly to escape his reputation. He seems to have taken with him Joanna, the pensioned widow of Company F Pvt. John Christine, who had died in 1886. After Christine's widow took up with Carter, an examiner was directed to determine "whether pensioner [Joanna] has been guilty of open Notorious Adultary & Cohabitation in violation of the act of Aug 9 1882" which defined such a disqualifying "vicious habit." The examiner was unable to verify the complaint, but the secretary of the interior approved dropping payments to the woman in June 1894, and Carter married her then, his third wife. Carter, likely unreformed, moved back to La Grange later and died there in 1915—and Joanna was pensioned again.[37]

Company F Second Lieutenant Wickham returned to New York, married, and read for the law. He asked for a pension on the grounds that he had been unable to work because of several maladies dating from military service, but what they were exactly is unclear. He moved to Rockford, Massachusetts, for a few years, lived at Ballston Spa near his New York birthplace, and spent some years in Binghamton, New York, possibly practicing law. He was found addicted to alcohol but claimed he was cured by 1894. It was probably this addiction, a "vicious habit," which prevented his pension claim for the effects of malaria and kidney troubles from being accepted. He succeeded, however, in obtaining congressional passage in 1902 of special legislation granting him sixteen dollars monthly. He died of arterial sclerosis in 1914 at Saratoga Springs.[38]

Company K commanding officer Captain Dunn was also ruined by drink. He returned to Marysville, Ohio, after discharge but did not resume his prewar occupation of schoolteacher, opening a hardware store instead. He had a stroke in 1883 brought on by "excessive use of intoxicating liquor." Dunn's wife left him; he lost his business and perhaps also his home. He later drove a wagon, selling coal oil door to door. Despite his addiction, he was pensioned for chronic diarrhea, rheumatism, and other maladies, and he died in 1901, survived by his widow and five children.[39]

Pvt. John Reed's record of what were judged "vicious habits" long delayed his pension. He was a Collinsville, Illinois, farmer, was married three times, and had nineteen children. His pension request was based on two postwar injuries. One was from a shotgun pellet wound gotten in an 1873 election dispute and the other a stab wound in the stomach. The latter was, he said, the result of his trying to maintain order at an 1886 Knights of Labor picnic at Bohemian Park in Collinsville. The pension bureau thought the claim suspicious and turned Reed down. He was later pensioned for ordinary disease and old age. He died in his hometown in 1930 at the age of one hundred and four.[40]

Pvt. Mackum McKeever, another victim of violence, was attacked by a highwayman in 1882 near Hamilton, Illinois, on his way home from work as a farm laborer. He lost sight in one eye and had a fractured jaw; both injuries were declared pensionable in 1892. Less fortunate was Pvt. Michael Taylor, who died of a fractured skull when assaulted in St. Mary's County, Maryland, by a man named Al Waters in 1906, but his widow was not pensioned because the couple had married after the 1890 cutoff. The third known victim of violence was the much married Pvt. George Ewing, who was returning from church at Greenville, Illinois, in 1900, when, he reported, "I was Suddenly Stabbed in the back and Thrown down and in an attempt to raise I was cut in the arm." Two men were sent to the penitentiary and another to reform school for assault with attempt to kill. Ewing was pensioned for these and other complaints, but he did not further explain the circumstances. His multiple and sometimes concurrent marriages meant that the mother of his children was not pensioned, and he left an impressive thousand-dollar estate, earned, according to his 1917 death certificate, while he was a "sand dealer" late in life.[41]

One soldier, Pvt. Charles South, who had been badly wounded at the crater, was given the benefit of the doubt and was considered totally disabled. He lived in Bowling Green, Missouri, for twenty years and then moved to Sedalia. Only his later years are chronicled, and accounts of them vary widely. Depositions in his record say that he ran a Sedalia dance hall and "was said to have conducted a house of prostitution . . . in said town." Furthermore, South "spent most of his money gambling." Bothered by his wounds, he was also said to have been addicted to narcotics, several citizens testifying that the drug was "probably cocaine" and one saying that "the soldier was a dope fiend." A pension examiner looking into these allegations suspected "vicious habits" in 1904 but found no real evidence beyond the affidavits. He said of South, "He is a physician, was at least twice a member of the Board of Examining Surgeons [for the pension office] here, and an unusually well posted and intelligent man." It seems likely that South's enemies were responsible for his problems, and his pension continued until his death from typhoid in 1918. South's brother Collins, six years younger, also lived in Bowling Green. He had no regular employment but worked as a common laborer. Although successful in convincing the pension bureau that he should be pensioned for an aneurism in his leg, he failed to get requested increases. Speaker of the U.S. House of Representatives Champ Clark of Missouri introduced a bill to pay South thirty-six dollars a month. The private legislation, changed to thirty dollars, was passed and approved in July 1918 but had no effect because South was then receiving thirty-five dollars, the rate authorized for veterans of his advanced years. He died in 1931 of senile dementia at the age of ninety-one.[42]

No doubt many more veterans were addicted to alcohol, had venereal diseases, or were guilty of moral misconduct than the pension files reveal, and a finding of disability caused by what the pension bureau called "vicious habits" could mean denial of compensation. In fact, the examining physicians and pension bureau officials appear to have gone out of their way to award deserved pensions, even to black men. They showed very little evidence of racism, and even their internal correspondence demonstrates tolerance and understanding, although providing the intricate documentation required by regulation was a challenge to the mostly illiterate applicants. Attorneys and others made a business of assisting a veteran's claim and were paid ten dollars per claim (later increased) only if it were successful. Thus, there was not much incentive to take on complicated applications, and veterans in remote areas could have overlooked their entitlements. It seems, however, that many of the soldiers of the Twenty-ninth U.S. Colored Infantry depended, in the years from 1890 until their deaths, on government payments, which were between two dollars and sixteen dollars monthly but which were greatly increased in later years.

DOCTORS AND PEACETIME SOLDIERS

An officer who could have been caught by morality considerations (but was not) was Surgeon David Mackay. He was a bigamist for much of the time after his arrival in the United States, in 1857 or 1858, from Glasgow, Scotland, a fact not revealed until after his death. Mackay took his discharge in New Orleans and was joined by a wife he married in 1861 at New Lebanon, Indiana. In Louisiana he was employed as a physician by the federal government, and later by the city government, and was widowed. He remarried in 1870 and began the practice of medicine the same year in Dallas, Texas, the marriage producing two sons. He was a member of the Board of Pension Examiners and was at some time superintendent of education for the city and sixteen other counties in the Fifth Congressional District. He was also surgeon general of the Grand Army of the Republic and active in the organization's national affairs. After 1890 he claimed a pension for the effects of exposure on 30 December 1864, when the regiment moved to Bermuda Hundred, spending the wet, cold night in the open. He said the cold caused catarrh, leading to the deafness and blindness that slowly incapacitated him. In September 1891 he was awarded a pension of twelve dollars a month. Dr. Mackay died in 1904, and his Texas widow filed for benefits. While the petition was pending, notice of Mackay's death was published in the London *Agnostic Journal* and the *Glasgow Weekly Mail,* alerting a woman in Scotland claiming to be Mackay's first wife, Mary. Mackay had fled to the United States to avoid his obligations in Scotland. The result was that Mary, being the first legal wife, was pensioned, and the wife in Texas was not.[43]

Two other Twenty-ninth Infantry doctors, Assistant Surgeons Ewen and Evans, had less colorful lives, the first as a career officer in the regular army, retiring in 1897, and the second, after a few years as an army contract surgeon, moving to San Bernardino, California, where he died of Bright's disease in 1896. Contract surgeon John Fee, who had been with the regiment from its recruiting days until August 1864, remained in public service after the war and was city physician in St. Louis, Oklahoma City, and Kansas City.[44]

The Twenty-ninth also had one future doctor, Lt. John C. Rollman, Company K, the native of Berlin, Prussia, who came to the United States just before the war. He described his occupation as a clerk when he enlisted in Ohio and New York volunteer regiments early in the war, but he also said that he was studying medicine and was employed as a druggist. Whatever his training, he was a practicing physician in 1866, first at Newport, Kentucky, and later at Burr Oak, Michigan, where he spent the rest of his life. He was pensioned for rheumatism that he claimed was caused by exposure when his company was on picket duty at Dutch Gap on a bad night, 18 March 1865, but not before questions were raised by his military record which stated that he had deserted the 108th Ohio Infantry in March 1863 before his Twenty-ninth Regiment service, a matter he seems to have clarified satisfactorily. He died in 1916, survived by a wife and three children.[45]

Each of the regiment's four doctors was called on in later years to support the pension applications of soldiers, certifying that injuries, wounds, and diseases had been incurred while in active service. Mackay, for one, sometimes charged ten dollars for each deposition, and the consequence was that he was not called on as much as he might have been.

Sometimes Mackay was unable to assist because all his records had been "burned by the Klu Klux[*sic*] in Louisiana on about the year 1870," when the doctor was working for the Freedmen's Bureau. Testimony from the other doctors did not carry the same weight, at least not that of Evans, who joined the unit late. Ewen was harder to find, being on the move with the regular army. Mackay treated one veteran regularly, Capt. Robert Porter of Company A, who relocated from Quincy to Texas. Badly wounded in the leg at the crater, he did not seek a pension until after 1890, claiming disability only from chronic diarrhea, a common complaint of veterans. Porter was a cattle herder in the Dallas vicinity and eventually became, probably because he was a wounded veteran, assistant postmaster at Millsap, a position from which he retired. He was pensioned but was constantly ill late in life, dying in 1914, a patient at the Government Hospital for the Insane at Washington, D.C., outliving his doctor by ten years.[46]

In addition to Assistant Surgeon Ewen, two other regimental officers choose careers in the regular army. James M. Smith was commissioned a second lieutenant in the Nineteenth U.S. Infantry in February 1866. He was promoted and transferred to the Twenty-eighth U.S. Infantry late the same year, serving in Kentucky, Arkansas, and Kansas until 1869, when he was appointed Indian agent at Washington, Texas. In late 1870, however, he was retired for service-related disabilities—malarial fever and chronic diarrhea. He weighed just one hundred and eighteen pounds. Smith lived in the District of Columbia until his death in 1893 of heart disease caused by "forced marches, just before the surrender" and common intestinal troubles. Lt. Col. Frederick E. Camp began a postwar military career as a second lieutenant in the Fourteenth U.S. Infantry. He was a captain by 1868 and resigned his commission in 1875. He died in 1891.[47]

Seven soldiers also thought that the army provided a better future than did civilian life. Sidney Northup, one of Company A's musicians, joined the Thirty-eighth U.S. Infantry a year after discharge and was soon transferred to the all-black Twenty-fourth Regiment. He was discharged at Fort Concho, Texas, in March 1870 and moved to Fort Leavenworth, possibly as an army civilian employee. He died of cancer in 1922. James Gibbs spent two years at his home in Delaware before enlisting in Company M, Tenth U.S. Colored Cavalry. He was sent to the Indian Territory with the "Buffalo Soldiers." In 1868 Gibbs was married by the post chaplain at Fort Gibson. Little more is known about his Tenth Cavalry service; he was once hospitalized at Fort Arbuckle, Indian Territory, with rheumatism and pneumonia. Gibbs was discharged at Fort Sill, Texas, in September

1872, and he moved back to Delaware, farming at Hartley, where he died in 1922.[48]

George Jackson, a former slave from Maryland, joined the Thirty-eighth Infantry at Springfield, Illinois, in April 1867. That regiment was consolidated with others, and he was transferred (as was Northup) to the Twenty-fourth Regiment. Having completed his enlistment, he was discharged at Fort Duncan, Texas, in 1870. He spent a few years at Fort Leavenworth and later in Cairo, declaring electrician as his occupation. He died in Chicago in 1927, having been brought there by his daughter. James Hawker (Wolflin) returned to his native Kentucky after being discharged from the Twenty-ninth USCT, but he left for Chicago, where he enlisted in the Ninth U.S. Colored Cavalry. His new regiment was assigned to Ringgold Barracks, where the Twenty-ninth USCT had been posted just after the war. Discharged in 1872, Hawker died at Danville, Illinois, in 1929.[49]

Edward C. Liggons was one of two soldiers from the Twenty-ninth USCT who spent more than the normal four-year enlistment in the postwar army. He joined the Tenth U.S. Colored Cavalry as a musician for duty in Texas. Having been in the army ten years, he was promoted to sergeant. Liggons was married at Fort Concha, Texas, in 1875 but had no children. He was discharged at Fort Grant, Arizona Territory, in 1886, not by choice but because he was found to have two venereal diseases. Liggons spent the next twenty-seven years at El Paso, working as a candy maker, and he moved to Sawtelle, California, where he died of heart failure in 1930. He was one of the most successful Twenty-ninth Regiment soldiers, leaving an estate valued at eighteen hundred dollars. Samuel Leonard returned to Baltimore after leaving the Twenty-ninth USCT. Work there and at Annapolis was hard to get, so he enlisted in the Tenth Cavalry as a bandsman. He was in the Tenth Cavalry for fifteen years and later served eight more years in the Twenty-fifth Infantry, another black unit. Discharged in 1888, he settled in Los Angeles. Leonard never married, and he died in Santa Monica in 1927.[50]

The seventh soldier with a postwar army enlistment was Lewis G. Lee, but his service did not end honorably. He joined the Thirty-eighth Regiment in Chicago sometime in 1867 and was sent to Jefferson Barracks, Missouri. Lee deserted his regiment at Fort Union, New Mexico, on 17 September 1867 and was absent until 8 October. A general court-martial sentenced him to a year's confinement at hard labor. Discharged at Fort Davis, Texas, he worked for a time on a railroad in Mexico then traveled to Walsenburg, Colorado, where he was a barber, to Fort Smith, Arkansas, and to Houston, Texas. He could write very well and so was in touch with many of his former Twenty-ninth Regiment comrades and with some of his officers, many of whom helped him secure a pension for deafness and other maladies. Lee was killed on 12 November 1892 in Houston, when he was struck by an International Great Northern Railroad train.[51]

Company E's Lieutenant Ferguson, who had fought at the crater before being commissioned, submitted a singular claim for injuries that he said were the result of postwar military service. He wanted compensation for a saber cut he received in Texas after the Twenty-ninth Regiment was mustered out at Brownsville and before it was shipped to New Orleans. Ferguson wrote that he was expecting to enter Mexican service and got caught up in a cavalry charge with Gen. Mariano Escobedo's republican army. The story is not very believable, and Ferguson's dates and sequences of events are faulty. In any event he was not compensated for the injury nor seriously suspected of fraud. He was eventually entered for the more common ailments of aging veterans: rheumatism, gastric problems, and kidney trouble. Ferguson left Louisiana, Missouri, and moved to Glenwood Springs, Colorado, where he had seventeen acres of land. He had little income beyond the pension, and he died with a small estate in 1902.[52]

A soldier who did not enter the postwar army but who spent his life in its employ was Pvt. Lewis Crisemen, a Virginian enlisted at Camp Casey. He went to Washington, D.C., after discharge and made his living as a barber. He was able to read and write very well, though it is not known how he acquired these skills. In 1884 he moved to Denver and later that year to the Fort Reno military post in the Indian Territory. He settled in Moscow, Nez Perce County, Idaho, by 1890, all the years working as a civilian barber with the army. He died in San Francisco in June 1902, perhaps still following the army. He apparently never married.[53]

SUCCESSFUL AND UNSUCCESSFUL VETERANS

Maj. T. Jefferson Brown, from Toledo, Ohio, made little of his life after the service, circumstances he attributed to the deterioration of his health as a result of army life. According to his own account, Brown suffered from chronic diarrhea after discharge, and he accepted a forty-dollars-a-month job as doorkeeper and cashier with a circus troupe touring Central America. He believed that the climate in that distant place would improve his physical condition. Three years later he returned, not much improved, to Elkhart, Indiana, where he worked for twelve years as a restaurant bookkeeper at the same low forty-dollar wage. Unable to continue working, he moved in with his brother, and his health declined further. An examining surgeon said of him in 1892, "He is a pitiful object physically being in abject poverty solely dependent on his relations for support." He weighed but eighty-five pounds. Since he was clearly eligible for a pension, one was granted, but he did not live to collect it; he died in June 1893.[54]

Other officers had equally hapless lives. All three of Company D's officers, for example, were poor men for all their days. Captain Knapp, who had been pensioned early after the war for losing a toe at Vicksburg before he was commissioned, was unable to work because of a back injury he said was the result of being trampled by his men at the crater. He returned to Rock Island, Illinois, after discharge, was hospitalized at St. Louis and Quincy, and moved to Fostoria, Kansas, in 1871, taking up the farming of two hundred acres. He constantly sought pension increases because he said he could not do the hard work needed to make his farm profitable. His neighbors, however, certified that in their opinion he was not as disabled as he said, so increases were long delayed. He died in 1897, still very poor, of Bright's disease at Fostoria, survived by his wife, Polly. Lieutenant Fickes went back to Pennsylvania, married, and settled in Iowa City, Iowa, where he made an inadequate living as a farmer. In 1879 his left arm was injured in a railway accident. Pensioned in 1890 for rheumatism, the arm injury, and effects of heat, he depended on government payments for his living. He described his work in 1898 as "caring for horse and cow." He died of cancer in 1906 at Iowa City. Lieutenant Eddowes went back to Philadelphia and to the wife he had married in 1855. He was pensioned from discharge (at four dollars monthly) for the arm wound he received when an enlisted man before being commissioned. Eddowes worked as a bookbinder until his death, always for someone else, and never had a business of his own. He died in 1893, leaving his widow a heavily mortgaged house and no other estate.[55]

Also unsuccessful was Captain Southwell, of Forest Lake, Pennsylvania, who found himself physically unable to go back to farming after the war. He was a mill worker for a time in New Hampshire, but he spent most of his life in Forest Lake, engaged, he said, in "wollen mfgr and wood alchol factory." He died at home in 1931 of prostate trouble. Captain Newton, on the other hand, had a better postwar start. After farming for twelve years at Wyanett, Illinois, he moved to Lincoln, Nebraska, where he established a hardware store and engaged in land speculation. The land deals ruined him, and he had to sell the business. He claimed a pension for injury from heavy lifting in the store, and he may never have worked again after 1888. He died in 1903 (perhaps in the Indian Territory), leaving his wife nothing except a small insurance policy.[56]

Major Hindekoper, who replaced Brown after the soldier's February 1865 resignation, did not apply for a pension, and the details of his life after muster out are not known. Chaplain George Barnes had a relatively rewarding postwar life, occupying Methodist Episcopal pulpits and settling in his retirement at Petosky, Michigan. His first wife died in 1880, and he was married a second time to Emma, a woman twenty years his junior. Passage of the 1890 law inspired him to build a case for a pension, though his health seems to have been good. He claimed disability based on the wound he received, bruises of the groin, from the explosion of a rebel shell before Richmond in December 1864, the same shell which cost Lieutenant Gosper his leg. He managed to locate Dr. Ewen, then an army surgeon and major in New York, to certify his injury, which was not, in fact, serious. It was not until 1907 that he received his first payment, twenty dollars monthly for being over seventy-five years old. Barnes died of jaundice in 1913, age eighty-three years and eleven months. His widow Emma married another war veteran years later and lived until 1929.[57]

The diminutive Lt. George G. Smith (he was 4', 11"), a seminary student before the war, returned to his studies in Allegheny, Pennsylvania, and was ordained a Presbyterian clergyman shortly thereafter. He lived in Williamsport in his home state until 1874, at Santa Fe, New Mexico; Helena, Montana; Adams, Rhode Island; again in Pennsylvania; and finally retiring in the District of Columbia. The pensioned clergyman lived to 1919, dying at Princeton, where his only son was on the faculty of the college.[58]

The most successful Twenty-ninth Regiment soldier was Lt. Albert S. Granger. He was a prewar graduate of Knox College, one of the handful of the regiment's officers and enlisted men with advanced formal education. He became a mining and oil promoter. Granger lived in Chicago, Joliet, and other Illinois cities, moving to Denver for two years and returning to Joliet. Until 1902 he owned a large house in the exclusive Romans Park section of the city and was president of the Joliet and New Mexico Oil and Coal Company. Pensioned for bronchitis, rheumatism, and stomach troubles, Granger died suddenly in Alhambra, California, in 1913.[59]

Few enlisted men appear to have done well in later life, only a scattering building estates of value in postwar America. Pvt. Henry Killion, a freeman from Collinsville, Illinois, farmed one hundred and six acres at Carlisle, where he died in 1898. The estate was estimated to be worth a substantial two thousand dollars. Company H's former first sergeant, William T. Demby, who was an illiterate former slave, overcame hardships at Chestertown, Maryland. He was primarily a farmer. He had a boat he used for fishing and crabbing, and he also sold melons. On his death in 1898 his property, consisting of a house, outbuildings, and farm land, was worth eighteen hundred dollars. A similarly high-value estate was left by Pvt. Jacob Cole, also a former Maryland slave, but it is uncertain how he accumulated this wealth, since his records show that all his life he was a common laborer at Cokeysville. The eighteen hundred dollars that Cole accumulated may have been partly savings, since he did not die until 1926, by which year pensions and wages were much elevated over late-nineteenth-century amounts. A number of veterans left estates worth several hundred dollars, usually houses and small parcels of land, but by far the overwhelming majority died as they had lived, desperately poor.[60]

Pvt. Nathan Ashby, one of several soldiers of that family from Peoria County, Illinois, was living largely on the pension he received in 1892 for rheumatism and lung disease. In a normal review by doctors employed by the pension bureau, his pension was discontinued in 1895 because Ashby was found to be able to perform manual labor. Although restored on appeal, Ashby suffered much without the income, and, when he died in 1899, he left his wife "two old mules" and no other property. Pvt. James Madison sought government payments beginning in 1891 but was rejected in 1897 and 1900, finally being accepted for rheumatism, heart trouble, and piles at eight dollars a month. He was refused raises but finally was paid more because of advanced age. Madison was entirely dependent on the pension. He entered the soldiers' home at Wood, Wisconsin, in 1908, remaining there until his death in late 1925. The veterans' home sold his personal property at auction. Appraised at thirty dollars and twelve cents, it brought thirteen.[61]

Other estates that were estimated to have had low cash values seem to have been more substantial. For example, Pvt. Charles Fields, once a slave, returned to Lignum, Virginia, and took up farming, mostly working for others. He and his wife had had children earlier "under the old system existing in the slave states." They married in 1881 because of rumors that the state would prosecute "colored people living together, but not married." Although he claimed that he could work only a few days a week, he managed to acquire an interest in what appears to have been substantial acreage. Fields was shot to death by a Clay Brown at Lignum in 1897. His estate, consisting of a one-third interest in a fifty-six-acre farm, was valued at only $146.67. Maryland Pvt. Benjamin Cooper, who died of tuberculosis in 1893, had a house and three acres in Kent County, but they were worth just $220.00. That appears to have been the approximate assessment of the estates of most propertied veterans, whether they lived in town or the country.[62]

Pvt. George Smith, wounded at the crater, was not pensioned immediately after the war. He did not return to Illinois but, instead, went to Kansas City, where he worked at whatever unskilled labor he could find. Hearing that there might be jobs with the Union Pacific Railroad, he traveled to Colorado, where he accidentally fell from a bluff overlooking a stone quarry and lost an eye. He was pensioned under the 1890 law for the eye and epileptic fits, which prevented him from doing manual labor. The pension was canceled in 1895 based on a finding that Smith could earn a living. He appealed and got a partial restoration, which was insufficient. From that time until his death at Kansas City in 1897, "He handled roots and herbs and made his living by being a kind of Doctor." He earned, he said, "not more than a dollar or a dollar and a half a week." Pvt. Frank McAllister also joined the regiment early but was sick for much of his service and was discharged in March 1865 at a New York hospital. Joining his wife, whom he married at Chicago in 1862, he was soon accepted for disability payments based on back injuries incurred in the line of duty, while constructing breastworks at the front. He was dropped from the pension rolls in 1875 because a surgeon found him no longer to be disabled. He had no regular and little other income from then until he died "suddenly in a saloon" on South Clark Street in Chicago in May 1879, leaving his widow, who gave birth to their son two months later. The widow sought to be pensioned but had a difficult time proving McAllister's death, which she did not hear about for some time. In addition, she was unable to produce his papers, which had been lost, as were the documents of several Twenty-ninth Regiment soldiers, in the great Chicago Fire of October 1871. A comrade's affidavit said that McAllister "had become very poor and dissipated and but little attention was paid to him at the time of his death more than to get rid of his corpse about like a dead dog." The widow and son were finally pensioned.[63]

Perhaps the saddest story of a former soldier completely degraded by his life in poverty was written by a pension bureau examiner about Pvt. John Copeland, whose postwar employment in Baltimore was at a brickyard and as an "oyster shucker." He asked to be pensioned in 1890 but was rejected because the medical examiner found "all disability described is in all probability [the] result of syphilis." When he was sixty-five Copeland applied again on the basis of age, and he ultimately was entered. An examiner wrote of his circumstances in 1910, "He lives in the most vicious part of Baltimore [at 860 Raborg Street], in the heart of the 'red light' district." Another said, "Claiment [*sic*] is desperately poor. He had just walked a dozen blocks to dispose of a load of junk for which he received three cents, which he invested at once in bread, which he was devouring ravenously when I found him." The pension saved his life, perhaps, and it may have been the reason Copeland lived until 1920. He was then ninety-five.[64]

On the other hand, Pvt. Joseph H. Downes found steady employment working for prominent citizens. Downes was discharged at New Orleans on 20 December 1865, long after his regiment was broken up at Springfield, and he went directly home to Baltimore. More than a year later he recovered from the illness that had kept him in the Corps d'Afrique hospital. Because his mother had worked during the war as a house servant for the former Army of the James commanding general, he had been given a special opportunity; from February 1867, as he put it:

> I was employed by Gen. Benj. F. Butler as valet and accompanied him to Lowell Mass, residing at Belveder[e], An[d]over St, in that city. I remained with Gen'l Butler until Nov.-1870, residing with the General in Washington during the sessions of Congress, of which he was a member. In Nov. 1870, I entered the employ of U.S. Senator Zachariah Chandler of Detroit, Mich as groom for blooded stallions, remaining with him [at Detroit] until Mar.-1874. . . . In March. 1874 I entered service of Mrs. Hamilton [Julia Kean] Fish serving her invalid mother [at Garrison, New York] until Nov.-1874. In Nov.-1874, I entered the service of Mr. H. M. Hutchinson, Washington, D.C., as coachman, and still [1891] remain in the service of his widow in that capacity.

Pensioned in 1892 for several disorders, Downes may have become a janitor in the District of Columbia public schools shortly thereafter. He died in Washington in 1924, leaving behind a widow.[65]

A wide variety of motivating factors and circumstances existed among the veterans who traveled far from their places of enlistment as they sought peacetime lives. Cpl. Henry Clay apparently thought Quincy too confining after a few years of living on his pension for the disabling war wound he received at the Bermuda Hundred in December 1865. He relocated to St. Louis in 1873 and to Eatonsville, El Paso County, Colorado, in 1891. For twelve years he operated a farm outside Colorado Springs, where he was married for the fourth time, moving then to Pasadena, California, where he died in 1915. California also attracted a few other enlisted men and one officer, Lieutenant Gosper. The officer, who had lost his leg from a wound received at the front in early December 1865, returned after discharge to Illinois, entirely dependent on his pension. He relocated to Prescott, Arizona, where, either through marital connections or because of his wound, he was for some time secretary of the territory. He eventually moved to Los Angeles, without permanent employment, where he died in 1913. Willis Easley, Company C first sergeant, worked in the Chicago area for fourteen years at a variety of jobs—store porter, Pullman porter, and train conductor, the last two for the Illinois Central Railroad. Railway work took him to San Diego in 1879 where he was employed for a short time with the Denver and Rio Grande Railroad. He followed this labor with raising poultry until 1911, when he relocated to Port Jefferson, New York; he died there in 1921, outliving two wives and all four of his children. Pvt. Henry Mason lived out his later years in California. He was a Maryland recruit who decided to remain in the Midwest, settling in Memphis after a year at Springfield. Marrying in 1874, he and his wife lost three children to "the Fever" in the winter of 1878–79. He filed for a pension in 1892 and left Memphis for Lodi and Stockton, California, the same year. Mason was a whitewasher, house cleaner, and laborer. He made several further pension applications, claiming a wide variety of sicknesses and disabilities, but without success. A pension examiner sent in 1896 to check on the validity of the oaths in his applications, as was the practice with black applicants whose witnesses usually signed by mark, said, "He is an innocent, rather ignorant sort of fellow." He continued to be rejected until 1903, when he was pensioned for the loss of an eye. Part of the delay was due to the discovery of another pensioned Henry Mason from the regiment, a twenty-five-year-old St. Mary's County, Maryland, draftee. Mason died at Stockton in 1911, and his widow was pensioned.[66]

Because he never married might have been why Pvt. George A. Henderson was free to travel more widely than most of his Twenty-ninth Regiment comrades. He seemed settled in Jacksonville, Illinois, working as a coachman until 1876, then moved to Quincy, where he was employed for two years in a livery stable. For the next ten years he lived and worked as a laborer in Nashville, Charleston (S.C.), New York, Massachusetts, Connecticut, Trenton, Newark, and Indianapolis. He was pensioned in 1891 for rheumatism, which he said he contracted first at Ringgold Barracks, and heart trouble. He died in Jacksonville in late 1892. Other former soldiers, such as Pvts. Thomas Mudd, a Marylander who remained in the Midwest; Charles Jones, originally a Virginian enlisted at Quincy who returned to Chicago; James I. Winyard, a deserter and malingerer; and Charles Hunter, a native Illinoisan, all became ministers of black religious denominations and traveled extensively in Illinois, Wisconsin, Indiana, Kansas, Iowa, and Kentucky. None of them recorded encounters with wartime comrades, although there must have been some.[67]

AN INCOMPLETE STORY

These sparse stories of the postwar lives of the soldiers of the Twenty-ninth U.S. Colored Troops are the best chronicles available. Not one of the officers and men is known to have left a more complete personal account of his military experiences and later postwar circumstances. The war service of these men changed little in their lives, understandable since, except for the officers, few of them were in uniform for more than a year. It cannot be determined if any of the men learned to read or write in the regiment, and it seems unlikely that many were given the opportunity.

What is clear, however, is that without government pensions few of the veterans would have been able to support themselves and would have had to depend on the limited local public assistance available in late-nineteenth- and early-twentieth-century America. It is to the government's credit that the same pension system was used for blacks as for whites, even whites with four years in the ranks and with many hard campaigns behind them. Even so, the pension amount, which was paid quarterly, was not sufficient to support families and was easily spent before the next check arrived. Perhaps pensions prolonged lives, but the lives were, it seems, without luxury, often without necessities, and frequently full of misery.

Civil War soldiers did not learn trades transferable to civilian life, but very few skilled workers were needed by the businesses and farms of the

United States' low-technology, labor-intensive economy. An unscientific review of the files of two hundred of the pensioned black soldiers who reported their occupations to the government shows that military service gave few if any of them an advantage in the work market. The declared occupation of over 70 percent of these men was common laborer working for wages on a day-to-day basis. (No distinction is made between urban and farm laborers, because both groups were equally unskilled.) And this was the case twenty-five years and longer after the regiment was mustered out in 1865.

Some soldiers reported variations on the common, or day, laborer category, but these work descriptions are usually another way of saying the same thing. Some examples are: "running short errons[sic] around the eating house"; "light chores" such as "blackening shoes, cooking, dish washing"; "Cutting or Mowing yards with a sickle cleaning yards & windows"; "Gathering rags and junk and gardening"; "Oystering when able"; "Laborer & Job about"; and "nothing Specially. Whatever I can get to do."

Ten men were in the elevated trade of barbering, and a few others likely had steady jobs as waiters at the Palmer House Hotel in Chicago, policeman in the city, and aboard steamboats on rivers and lakes. Two were miners, one did office work, and a scattering reported themselves as express drivers and teamsters. The most prominently employed were the musician Thompson Kay, who may have been a lawyer, and the physician Pvt. Charles South, but entry into those professions then was considerably less formal than it is now.[68]

It can be said that most black Civil War veterans themselves benefited very little by their army service, even though generally it was completed with devotion and competence. What the soldiers accomplished was the beginning of a long line of black men serving in the nation's military, a line that is unbroken to this day. For much of the time, however, blacks were in segregated units, having not earned the right, according to the War Department, to be treated the same as white soldiers. Indeed, for the most part black soldiers were thought to be inferior and unworthy of equality, as they had been when the black soldier experiment began in the Civil War. The situation merely reflected the state of race relations in the United States; treatment of black soldiers was no worse and often better than law and custom established for most blacks in the nation. For ninety years, until they were accepted into the armed forces as equals with other citizens, black soldiers continued to do their military duties effectively.

When they were allowed to be part of the fighting forces, which was seldom, they performed with similar proficiency.

The veterans of the Twenty-ninth U.S. Colored Infantry and all their comrades in the other 148 black regiments and artillery batteries should be remembered for their sacrifices but also for their faithful service. Notwithstanding exemplary performance by black soldiers in the Revolution and War of 1812, black Civil War veterans began the continuous service of black soldiers in the U.S. Army—a proud tradition to be honored and respected.

Appendix
SOME STATISTICS

I choose the men of two companies as representative of all the regiment's enlisted soldiers. Company A, raised initially at Quincy, had the longest service of all the ten companies, and Company I was one of the last enlisted, made up mostly of draftees and paid substitutes from Maryland, Virginia, and Delaware, with a scattering of men found in or near Illinois. My aim was to determine the number of men who were former slaves and the number who were free men.

The men of Company A were recruited in two groups, the first group numbering the minimum required before the company could be mustered into the service of the United States. In the second group were those enlisted after the regiment's combat experience at the Battle of the Crater at Petersburg, and they came to the regiment from replacement pools in Illinois and at the theater of war in the East. The original Company A veterans had the longest service and, consequently, the most casualties from war and illness. The veterans of Company A were very like the original soldiers in Companies B, C, D, and F. The "recruits," those men enlisted as replacements and to fill up Company A, were similar to recruits in the other battle-tested companies and to the entire complement of Companies G, H, I, and K.

The sample made up of all Company I's soldiers consists almost entirely of draftees and paid substitutes, as were the soldiers in all the companies mustered in after the crater fight and the later recruits in the veteran companies.

I sought to determine earlier occupations of the soldiers in the two companies, but enlistment and other records proved unreliable because recruiting officials did not seek out accurate information from the new men and listed the same work using a variety of labels. Many differences were found between the occupations shown on enlistment records and in the regiment's descriptive books and what the veterans gave after the war as their occupations before entering the army. Other than a few of the handful of free men who were enlisted and made noncommissioned officers at once, most soldiers had no experience except as agricultural workers while they were slaves. Among those freed by the army or by their own initiative, only laborers from rural areas and unskilled day workers from urban areas can be identified. In fact, few of them had other occupations after the war and until their deaths.

Because recruits often concealed their backgrounds as slaves for fear of being returned to their former owners, a sizable number cannot be categorized as slave or free. A survey using just enlistment records would show more of them in an uncertain status, but after the war many were no longer constrained by the threat of renewed bondage, and they freely described their prewar status on pension applications and related documents.

Company A was made up of eighty-one original enlisted men who joined the company from November 1863 to January 1864. Of these, fifty-six can positively be identified as slaves or slaves recently freed by their owners or by fleeing bondage. Only six were listed as free men, but it is not clear whether several of these might have earlier been slaves. The status of nineteen original recruits remains unsure, but almost certainly most of them were former slaves.

The places of birth of the Company A original recruits, as recorded by the army, with adjustments from pension file information, follow. Other than those from Missouri, most of the men were not resident in their home states at the time of enlistment, and most of them were recruited in Missouri or Illinois:

MO 45
KY 10
VA 8
AL 3
IL 2
MD 2
SC 2
AR, DC, IA, NY, OH, one each

Since these Company A soldiers had the longest service of any in the regiment, they also had the highest number of casualties—four killed in action, nine dying of poor treatment and disease while prisoners of war, and fourteen of disease. Two men deserted the company, one was discharged for wounds, and two were found by army doctors to be disabled by injury or disease and were discharged early.

Company A had seventy-eight recruits enlisted from late August to February 1865, of which fifty-eight were slaves and eleven were free men, most of the latter attracted by bounties. The status of nine men is uncertain. Places of birth are shown as:

VA 23
MO 10
TN 10
IL 8
MI 6
AR, Canada, GA, KY, LA, MD, NC, NY, OH, PA, 1 to 3 each

Even though these late recruits served in the regiment for more than a year, some months under severe conditions over the winter before Petersburg/Richmond, during the final pursuit of General Lee, and in Texas, only four succumbed to disease, and none were killed or wounded by enemy action.

Company I enlisted 111 men from November to December 1865, a few of whom were signed up a month or so earlier or later. Eight-five of the men were former slaves, thirteen free men, and another thirteen cannot be accurately categorized. Their places of birth were:

MD 41
VA 22
DE 10
MO 8
TN 7
PA 6
IL 2
Canada, Cuba, England, GA, Jamaica, KY, MI, SC, 1 to 3 each

Company I casualties, like those of the Company A late recruits, were light. Nine died of disease, and four deserted.

Joseph T. Glatthaar, in *Forged in Battle*, went further in statistical sampling of the officers of a number of black regiments, including prewar and postwar occupations, estates at death, rank as enlisted men before commissioning, and so on. Few of these measures could be duplicated with enlisted men, so he limited his study of them to places of birth and occupations of soldiers in a substantial number of randomly chosen infantry and cavalry companies and artillery batteries. His results and mine are about the same, although he distinguished between more different types of laborers and farmworkers than I found could be verified in Twenty-ninth U.S. Colored Infantry records. He also did not tally the number of slaves and free men—except for one South Carolina company—and he made no note of casualties. The National Archives are currently making a database of parts of the Compiled Service Records of all black soldiers in the Civil War. When it is completed, sampling soldiers' characteristics may be simpler—if less accurate—than undertaking a record-by-record review.

Notes

PREFACE

1. Available in several editions, the 1994 version contains *The Life of Johnny Reb* in the same volume (1951; reprint, New York: Book-of-the-Month Club, 1994).

2. Recent examples are Edwin S. Redkey, ed., *A Grand Army of Black Men: Letters from African-American Soldiers in the Union Army, 1861–1865* (New York: Cambridge University Press, 1992), letters written to black publications, primarily the *Christian Recorder* (Phila.); and Virginia M. Adams, ed., *On the Altar of Freedom: A Black Soldier's Civil War Letters from the Front* (Amherst: University of Massachusetts Press, 1991), a collection of letters to a New Bedford newspaper by Cpl. James Henry Gooding, Fifty-fourth Massachusetts Infantry (Colored).

CHAPTER 1: FINDING A PLACE

1. General Orders no. 27, 21 March, and no. 91, 29 July 1862, Adjutant General's Office, "The Negro in the Military Service of the United States, 1609–1889," 7 vols., Records of the Office of the Adjutant General, Record Group 94, U.S. National Archives, Washington, D.C. (hereafter cited as "Negro in the Military Service," NA), 2:486, 912–16; report, Provost Marshal General's Bureau, to secretary of war, 17 March 1866, U.S. Department of War, *A Compilation of the Official Records of the Union and Confederate Armies in the War of the Rebellion*, 127 vols. (Washington, D.C.: Government Printing Office, 1880–1902) (hereafter cited as ORA), ser. 3, vol. 5: 632–33, 654–55; Howard C. Westwood, "Lincoln's Position on Black Enlistments," *Black Troops, White Commanders and Freedmen during the Civil War* (Carbondale: Southern Illinois University Press, 1992), 1–20; Bernard C. Nalty, *Strength for the Fight: A History of Black Americans in the Military* (New York: Free Press, 1986), 27.

2. ORA, ser. 3, vol. 5: 656, 660–61. Rebel North Carolina and Tennessee were not listed, but the first was added later.

3. Howard C. Westwood, "Generals David Hunter and Rufus Saxton and Black Soldiers," *South Carolina Historical Magazine* 86 (1985): 165–81; James M. McPherson, *The Struggle for Equality: Abolitionists in the Civil War and Reconstruction* (Princeton: Princeton University Press, 1964), 208 n; *Thomas's report, 5 October 1865*, ORA, ser. 3, vol. 5: 124.

4. James D. Richardson, ed., *A Compilation of the Messages and Papers of the Presidents* (New York: Bureau of National Literature, 1897), 7:3297–99, 3358–60; *ORA,* ser. 3, vol. 3: 215–16 (General Orders no. 143, Adjutant General's Office, 22 May 1863), 5:656, 661. Regimental numbers were assigned sequentially by date of mustering into U.S. service. Some regiments retained state designations for some time in federal service; most were renumbered USCT regiments or were folded into other units. The Twenty-ninth Connecticut (Colored) Volunteers retained its number throughout the war and is sometimes confused with the Illinois regiment. The Fifty-fourth and Fifty-fifth Regiments of Massachusetts Volunteers (Colored) were organized and officered by state authorities until mustered out, the only exceptions among black army units.

5. Margaret Leech. *Reveille in Washington, 1860–1865* (New York: Harper and Brothers, 1941), 258; Fred Albert Shannon, *The Organization and Administration of the Union Army, 1861–1865,* 2 vols. (Cleveland: Arthur H. Clarke Co., 1928), 1:233–34; George F. Sutherland, "The Negro in the Late War," Wisconsin Commandery, Military Order of the Loyal Legion of the United States, *War Papers* (Milwaukee: Brudick, Armitage and Allen, 1891), 1:174. Sutherland was a captain in the Thirteenth U.S. Colored Heavy Artillery.

6. Telegram, Yates to Lincoln, 11 July 1862, Ira Berlin et al., eds., *Freedom: A Documentary History of Emancipation, 1861–1867,* ser. 2: The Black Military Experience (New York: Cambridge University Press, 1982), 848; Arthur Charles Cole, *The Era of the Civil War, 1848–1867,* Cultural History of Illinois series (1919; reprint, Freeport, N.Y.: Books for Libraries Press, 1971), 282; letter to the secretary of war, 19 July 1862, "Negro in the Military Service," NA, 2:898; Norwood P. Hallowell, *The Negro As a Soldier in the War of the Rebellion* (Boston: Little, Brown, 1897), 8; David W. Blight, *Frederick Douglass' Civil War: Keeping Faith in Jubilee* (Baton Rouge: Louisiana State University Press, 1989), 148, 157, 165, 167–70.

7. Extract of editorial, Berlin et al., *Freedom,* 94–95.

8. Editorial and note, Medill to Stanton, 15 June 1863, and Stanton endorsement, n.d., Berlin et al., *Freedom;* telegrams, Yates to Stanton and Stanton to Yates, both 28 July 1863; letter, Yates to Stanton, 28 August 1863; letter, assistant adjutant general Maj. C. W. Foster, Washington, D.C., to Yates, 25 September 1863, Special Orders no. 15, Adjutant General's Office, 4 May 1861, *ORA,* vol. 3: 584, 736, 838, ser. 3, vol. 1: 151–52; *Chicago Daily Tribune,* 31 October 1863, the latter with a description of specified regimental organization and excerpts from "Revised Mustering Regulations" concerning appointment of officers. The same information was reprinted on 6 November 1863.

9. Letter, Illinois adjutant general, Brig. Gen. Allen C. Fuller, to Foster, 6 October 1863, and letter, Foster to Fuller, 12 October 1863, *ORA,* ser. 3, vol. 3: 864–65, 876; Shannon, *Organization and Administration of the Army,* 1:165; General Orders no. 44, Springfield, 26 October 1863, Box 3, Application for Appointments (in the colored units), 1863–1865, RG 94, NA; Victor Hicken, *Illinois in the Civil War* (Urbana: University of Illinois Press, 1966), 137; Illinois,

Military and Naval Department, *Report of the Adjutant General of the State of Illinois,* 9 vols. (Springfield: Baker, Bailache & Co., 1867), 8:778–79.

10. Robert B. Howard, *Illinois: A History of the Prairie State* (Grand Rapids, Mich.: William B. Eerdmans Publishing Co., 1972), 129–31, 188; Eugene H. Berwanger, *The Frontier against Slavery: Western Anti-Negro Prejudice and the Slavery Extension Controversy* (Urbana: University of Illinois Press, 1969), 8–33.

11. Howard, *Illinois,* 188–90; Cole, *Era of the Civil War,* 226–28, 333–35, 389; *Harper's Weekly,* 22 April 1865, reporting the law's repeal, said that two years before two blacks were convicted of being "persons of color" in Illinois, and "they were sold, one for fifty-five and the other for ninety-five years."

12. Berwanger, *Frontier against Slavery,* 34–35, 138; Forrest G. Wood, *Black Scare: The Racist Response to Emancipation and Reconstruction* (Berkeley: University of California Press, 1968), 13, 21; George Washington Williams, *A History of Negro Troops in the War of the Rebellion, 1861–1865* (1888; reprint, New York: Bergman Publishers, 1968), 232; James M. McPherson, *The Negro's Civil War: How American Negroes Felt and Acted during the Civil War for the Union* (1965; reprint, Urbana: University of Illinois Press, 1982), 252–54; McPherson reprints the petition in *Marching toward Freedom: The Negro in the Civil War, 1861–1865* (New York: Alfred A. Knopf, 1965), 134–35; Leon F. Litwack, *North of Slavery: The Negroes in the Free States, 1790–1960* (Chicago: University of Chicago Press, 1961), 264; the legislature overturned the black codes in the same session in which it approved the Thirteenth Amendment ending slavery, the first state to ratify (Elmer Gertz, "The Black Laws of Illinois," *Journal of the Illinois State Historical Society* [hereafter cited as *JISHS*] 60 [Autumn 1967]: 472); [Arthur Swazey], *Memorial of Colonel John Bross, Twenty-ninth U.S. Colored Troops* (Chicago: Tribune Book and Job Office, 1865), 8–9.

13. Bell Irvin Wiley, *The Life of Billy Yank: The Common Soldier of the Union* (Baton Rouge: Louisiana State University Press, 1971), 109, 112, 120–121; General Thomas noticed the attitude of ethnic groups, recommending to Stanton that no recruits from slave states be sent north because there "prejudice is particularly the case with those of Irish and German descent" (letter, 1 April 1863, "Negro in the Military Service," NA, 3:1157); Jacque V. Voegeli, *Free but Not Equal: The Midwest and the Negro during the Civil War* (Chicago: University of Chicago Press, 1967), 100–101.

14. Undated reports, *Chicago Times* and *Chicago Daily Tribune, Daily Illinois State Journal* (Springfield), 12 and 13 January 1863; the same newspaper, 28 January 1863, printed a *Missouri Democrat* letter from Col. N. Niles, 130th Illinois Volunteers, in which the colonel complained that many from home were encouraging soldiers to be disloyal; the 109th was disbanded on 12 April 1863 for "having lost 237 by desertion and officers (excepting those of Company 'K') having proved themselves incompetent," and the 128th, raised at Springfield, mustered out on 1 April 1863 "by order of Gen. Grant, having lost in 5 months over

700 men, principally by desertion, and the Officers having proved themselves utterly incompetent" (Frederick H. Dyer, *A Compendium of the War of the Rebellion* [1908; reprint, Dayton, Ohio: Press of Morningside Bookshop, 1978], 1092, 1100); Victor Hicken, "The Record of Illinois' Negro Soldiers in the Civil War," *JISHS* 56 (Autumn 1963): 538; Thomas's report, 10 June 1863, "Negro in the Military Service," NA, 3:1262.

15. Thomas's report, 10 June 1863, "Negro in the Military Service," NA, 3:1262; Hicken, "Illinois' Soldiers," *JISHS* 56:538–39, quoting letters, Ira Payne, 27 February 1863, and David Giver, 14 February 1863, originals in Illinois State Historical Library, Springfield; *Chicago Daily Tribune,* 6 August 1863. Of the garrison's 262 blacks just over 20 percent were made prisoner, but 60 percent of the fort's 295 whites survived (John Cimprich and Robert C. Mainfort, "Fort Pillow Revisited: New Evidence about an Old Controversy," *Civil War History* 28 [December 1982]: 94; Page Smith, *Ordeal by Fire* [New York: McGraw-Hill Book Co., 1982], 320).

16. Report, C. W. Foster, assistant adjutant general, Bureau for Colored Troops, 20 October 1865, *ORA,* ser. 3, vol. 5: 138; Indiana, Adjutant General's Office, *Report of the Adjutant General of the State of Indiana, 1861–1865, Containing Indiana in the War of the Rebellion and Statistics and Documents,* 8 vols. (Indianapolis: Alexander H. Connor, 1865–69), 1:80–81; proclamation, 24 October 1863, *Daily Whig and Republican* (Quincy), 27 October 1863. Apparently, Yates's proclamation was not observed, because he found it necessary to issue another like it on 6 August 1864 (*Daily Illinois State Journal,* 8 August 1864).

17. Hicken, "Illinois' Negro Soldiers," *JISHS* 56:536; Augustin Chetlain, *Recollections of Seventy Years* (Galena: Gazette Publishing Co., 1899), 70–79, 100; report, 5 October 1865, letter, 13 December 1864, both Thomas to Stanton, *ORA,* ser. 3, vol. 5: 122, vol. 4: 995; John Wesley Blassingame, "The Organization and Use of Negro Troops in the Union Army, 1863–1865" (Master's thesis, Howard University, 1963), 27–28.

18. Delany's Chicago assistant was John Jones, a wealthy black man who was the founder of the earlier "Repeal Association" (Blassingame, "Negro Troops in the Union Army," 26). Delany, born free in Virginia in 1812, studied medicine at Harvard and was active from 1850 on as an abolitionist and advocate of black emigration to Africa—he even negotiated a treaty for Niger Valley settlements.

19. Letter, Fuller to Col. James B. Fry, provost marshal general, Washington, D.C., 10 January 1864; final report of acting assistant provost marshal general Bvt. Brig. Gen. James Oakes, Springfield, 5 August 1865, *ORA,* ser. 3, vol. 6: 20, vol. 5: 837–38. Oakes was lieutenant colonel of the regular Fourth U.S. Cavalry and was detailed to Illinois for the entire war (Howard, *Illinois,* 313).

20. Letter, Census Office, Department of the Interior, to adjutant general, February 1863, "Negro in the Military Service," NA, 2:394, 3:1092–93; Herbert Aptheker, *The Negro in the Civil War* (New York: International Publishers, 1938), 11.

21. Letter, Fuller to Lt. Col. James Oakes, superintendent, Recruiting Service, Springfield, 29 October 1863, Miscellaneous Letters, Twenty-ninth USCT, RG 94, NA (hereafter cited as Miscellaneous Letters, NA); Swazey, *Memorial of Colonel Bross*, 3–7; David B. Dick, "Resurgence of the Chicago Democracy, April–November, 1861," *JISHS* 56 (Autumn 1967): 140; Dumas Malone, ed., *Dictionary of American Biography* (New York: Charles Schribner's Sons, 1927), s.v. "Bross, William"; Joseph T. Glatthaar, *Forged in Battle: The Civil War Alliance of Black Soldiers and White Officers* (New York: Free Press, 1990), 17; letter, William Strawn to J. B. Turner, 18 November 1863, Hicken, "Illinois' Black Soldiers," *JISHS* 56:541, original in Illinois State Historical Library.

22. Bross, Compiled (Military) Service Records, Twenty-ninth USCT, RG 94, NA (hereafter cited as CMSR, NA); order, Colonel Oakes to Capt. Charles C. Pomeroy, Chicago disbursing and mustering officer, 7 November 1863, Miscellaneous Letters, NA; War Department General Orders no. 61, 19 August 1861, and no. 82, 21 July 1862, in Francis A. Lord, *They Fought for the Union* (New York: Bonanza Books, 1960), 15; General Orders no. 110, 29 April 1963, in Hondon B. Hargrove, *Black Soldiers in the Civil War* (Jefferson, N.C.: McFarland and Co., 1988), 125; letter, Edwin M. Stanton to Gov. John Brough, Ohio, 2 August 1864, *ORA*, ser. 3, vol. 4: 569–70; Fred Albert Shannon, "The Federal Government and the Negro Soldier, 1861–1865," *Journal of Negro History* 11 (October 1926): 578.

23. *ORA*, ser. 3, vol. 5: 746–47; *Chicago Daily Tribune*, 3 January 1864; certified copy of news item, *Henry County Dial* (Kewanee, Ill.), 4 February 1864, in Lewis, pension record, Case Files of Approved Pension Applications of Veterans Who Have Served in the Army and Navy Mainly in the Civil War and the War with Spain, 1861–1934, Civil War and Later Pension Files, Records of the Veterans Administration, RG 15, NA (hereafter cited as pension record, NA); Ward, Carroll, Hopson, and Bolden, CMSR and pension records, NA.

24. List of Commissioned Officers in Descriptive Book (Twenty-ninth USCT), RG 94, NA; *Chicago Daily Tribune*, 31 October and 6 November 1863; letter, adjutant general, U.S. Army, to Yates, 25 September 1863, *ORA*, ser. 3, vol. 3: 838; letter, Fuller to Foster, 23 December 1863, asking permission to send Porter, Brown, and Isaac M. Strickler to St. Louis, Box 4, Applications for Appointment, NA; Porter and Brown, CMSR and pension records, NA; Muster Rolls, box 5399, RG 94, NA (hereafter cited as Muster Rolls, NA).

25. Hazell, Thomas, Heithman, and Perkins, CMSR and pension records, NA.

26. Tinker, CMSR, NA; Golden, CMSR and pension record, NA.

27. Hawkins, Burke, Jamison, and Plegett, CMSR and pension records.

28. Bletcher, CMSR, NA; Corsy, Logan, and Washington, CMSR and pension records, NA.

29. Dudley, Gilmore, and Lewis, CMSR and pension records, NA; Franklin and Johnson, CMSR, NA.

30. Magruder, Perry, and Williams, CMSR and pension records, NA.

31. McCoslin, ibid.

32. Descriptive Book, NA; McCoslin, Heithman, Thomas, CMSR and pension records, NA. Since compiled service records rarely contain enlistment papers, clothing records requiring signatures were reviewed to determine literacy rates, admittedly an imperfect measure (Clothing Account Books, Twenty-ninth USCT, file nos. 141-159–144-162, Moorland Springarn Research Center, Howard University, Washington, D.C. [hereafter cited as Clothing Account Books, Howard]). These books were made at muster out, so X marks may have been made by company officers instead of searching out soldiers for signatures, unlike on regimental payroll records that were destroyed. Pension records, like service records, seldom show whether a soldier's literacy went beyond writing his name, and some veterans learned this skill in the service or many years later.

33. Allen, CMSR and pension record, NA.

34. Millander, Rickman, Scott, and Turpin, CMSR and pension records, NA; Needham and Williams, CMSR, NA.

35. Griffin, CMSR and pension record, NA.

36. Johnson (Porter's 25 June 1864 letter), Moss, Morris, and Williams, ibid.

37. Morgan, ibid.; *ORA,* ser. 3, vol. 5: 657.

38. Markell and McDowell, CMSR and pension records, NA.

39. *Chicago Daily Tribune,* 12 November 1863.

40. Ibid., 13 November, 10 and 14 December 1863; *ORA,* ser. 3, vol. 5: 855; Descriptive Book, NA; Litwack, *North of Slavery,* 265–26; Hicken, "Illinois' Negro Soldiers," *JISHS* 56:533, 538.

41. *Daily Whig and Republican,* 20 November (reprinting letter from *Chicago Evening Journal*), 24 and 30 November 1863.

42. Ibid., 8 December 1863, 26 January 1864, citing the *Journal,* and the *St. Joseph* (Mo.) *Herald;* Landry Genosky, *People's History of Quincy and Adams County, Illinois: A Sesquicentennial History* (Quincy: Jost and Kiefer Printing Co., 1976), 476.

43. Aiken, CMSR, NA, Aiken was enlisted on 8 January but not mustered in until 11 May 1864; Miscellaneous Letters, NA; Stephen Longstreet, *Chicago, 1860–1919* (New York: David McKay Co., 1973), 37; Descriptive Book, NA; *Illinois Adjutant General's Report,* 8:781–82.

44. Mills, Long, and James and Jordon Stewart, CMSR and pension records, NA.

45. Griffin and Bogart, ibid.

46. Brooks, Grayson, and Graves, ibid.

47. *Chicago Daily Tribune,* 3 and 13 January 1864; *Illinois Adjutant General's Report,* 8:781–85; *Chicago Evening Journal,* 5, 7, and 12 January 1864.

48. *Chicago Daily Tribune,* 13 January 1864; *Chicago Times,* 31 January 1864.

49. Brockway, Easley, Griffin, Davis, CMSR and pension records, NA; Muster Rolls, NA; Descriptive Book, NA; *Illinois Adjutant General's Report,* 8:783–84; Clothing Account Books, Howard.

50. Carr and Daniels, CMSR and pension records, NA.

51. Gaskins may have been living in Kankakee when enlisted but was credited to Chicago (Gaskins, Flowers, Jones, and Williams, CMSR and pension records, NA).

52. Blakely, CMSR and pension record, NA.

53. *Chicago Evening Journal,* 5 January 1864; Longstreet, *Chicago,* 38; *Illinois Adjutant General's Report,* 1:126; Warren Wilkinson, *Mother, May You Never See the Sights I Have Seen: The Fifty-seventh Massachusetts Veteran Volunteers in the Army of the Potomac, 1864–1865* (New York: Harper and Row, 1990), 10.

54. Knapp, W. H. Flint, Daggett, Chapman, Gosper, and W. W. Flint, CMSR and pension records, NA, Knapp was mustered in on 28 May, W. H. Flint on 12 May, Daggart on 25 July, Chapman on 22 July, Gosper on 1 July, and W. W. Flint on 12 May 1864; Morning Reports, Twenty-ninth Regiment of USC Troops, by Month, U.S. Colored Troops, Adjutant General's Office, RG 94, NA (hereafter cited as Morning Reports, NA); *Chicago Daily News* and *Chicago Daily Tribune,* both 29 April 1864. W. W. Flint, age twenty-two, may have been related to his company commander; both were from Alton.

55. Carroll, Elliott, and Hunter, CMSR and pension records, NA.

56. Liggons, Patton, Frank and Jefferson Gash, and David (Logan), ibid.

57. Perryman, ibid; Milion, Sexton, and Riden, CMSR, NA.

58. Singleton, O'Fallon, Smith, White, Hunter, and Alexander, CMSR and pension records, NA.

59. Brooks and Jackson, ibid.; letters, John A. (?) Black, commissioner, Pension Office, Washington, D.C., to Sharp, Montgomery City, 17 April, and Sharp to Black, 28 April 1886, Gardiner, pension record, NA.

60. Batty (Webb), CMSR and pension record, NA.

61. Conrad J., Joseph, Joseph C., John P., Robert S., Samuel A., and William Arbuckle, ibid.

62. Pension Records and Descriptive Book, NA; *Illinois Adjutant General's Report,* 8:786–93; *Chicago Daily Tribune,* 29 April 1864.

63. Williams, Weaver, and Walmslee, CMSR and pension records; Stark, CMSR, NA. Four of seven corporals were enlisted from January to April 1864, and the company's two musicians and wagoneer were also signed on early (CMSR, NA).

64. Long and Taylor, CMSR and pension records, NA.

65. Descriptive Book, NA; *Illinois Adjutant General's Report,* 8:791–93; Swazey, *Memorial of Colonel Bross,* 14.

66. Yates to Stanton, 26 January 1864, and Stanton to Yates, 27 January 1864, *ORA*, ser. 3, vol. 4: 55; Fuller to Oakes, 27 October 1863, Miscellaneous Letters, NA; *Daily Whig and Republican*, 3 December 1863; Blassingame, "Negro Troops in the Union Army," 24, 60; Descriptive Book, NA; CMSR, NA.

67. Thomas W. Higgenson, "Regulars and Volunteers," *Atlantic Monthly* 14 (September 1864): 348–57; letter, 30 April 1864, Edward G. Longacre, ed., "'Would to God That War Was Rendered Impossible,' Letters of Captain Roland M. Hall, April–July 1864," *Virginia Magazine of History and Biography* 89 (October 1981): 455; Wiley, *Billy Yank*, 313–14; Hicken, "Illinois' Negro Soldiers," *JISHS* 56:533; Joseph Mark Califf, *Record of Service of the Seventh Regiment United States Colored Troops, from September, 1863, to November, 1866, by an Officer in the Regiment* (1878; reprint, Freeport, N.Y.: Books for Libraries Press, 1971), 19; letter, Casey to the adjutant general, 23 February 1863, forwarding the revised manual, "Negro in the Military Service," NA, 3:1107.

68. *Herald-Whig* (Quincy, Ill.), 15 June 1990,; Maurice G. Baxter, *Orville H. Browning: Lincoln's Friend and Critic* (Bloomington: Indiana University Press, 1957), 166–67; letters, John Wood and others to Browning, 5 January, Bross to Oakes, 12 January, Fee to Bross (?), 5 April 1864, Miscellaneous Letters, NA.

69. General Orders no. 117, Adjutant General's Office, 14 March 1864, sent the regiment to Annapolis, and General Orders no. 48, Headquarters, Ninth Army Corps, Annapolis, 18 April 1864, assigned the corps' colored troops to the Fourth Division, "Negro in the Military Service," NA, 4:2423, 2489.

70. Shannon, *Organization and Administration of the Union Army*, 1:66; report, Bross to Fuller, 15 April 1864, letter, Adjutant General's Office, Washington, D.C., to Fuller, 16 April 1864, Special Orders no. 193, Adjutant General's Office, 23 April 1864, Miscellaneous Letters, NA; Morning Reports, NA; Compiled Service Records Showing Service of Military Units in Volunteer Union Organizations, U.S. Colored Troops, RG 94, NA (hereafter cited as Record of Events, NA); *Illinois Adjutant General's Report*, 8:778–79, 790; Ward, Freeman, Hawkins, and Winyard, CMSR and pension records, NA. Another soldier, Ralph Adkins from Alton, died prior to muster and was "buried in his clothing [military uniform]" at Quincy (Clothing Account Books, Howard); Long tried for a pension years after the war, citing a hernia, but his claim was disallowed on grounds that the injury was sustained while he was a deserter (Long, pension record, NA).

71. William H. Collins and Cicero F. Perry, *Past and Present of the City of Quincy and Adams County* (Chicago: S. J. Clark Publishing Co., 1905), 295; Brown and Daggert, CMSR, NA.

72. Morning Reports, NA; Howard, *Illinois*, 319; Alfred Theodore Andreas, *History of Chicago*, 3 vols. (1884–85; reprint, New York: Arno Press, 1975), 2:312–13; *Chicago Daily Tribune*, 29 April 1864. The *Chicago Evening Journal*, 28 April 1864, did not report the arrival or ceremony but did print an editorial calling for equal pay for black and white soldiers.

73. Quoting *Chicago Daily Tribune,* 29 April, 1864, the horse and outfit were valued at four hundred dollars. The *Chicago Evening Journal,* which had followed recruiting in the city, did not report the Twenty-ninth USCT's arrival or the ceremony but on that day, 28 April 1864, printed an editorial asking equal pay for black soldiers.

74. Swazey, *Memorial of Colonel Bross,* 11; *Daily Whig and Republican,* 18 and 23 April 1864; *Chicago Daily Tribune,* 28 April 1864.

75. Brainerd Dyer, "The Treatment of Colored Union Troops by the Confederates, 1861–1865," *Journal of Negro History* 20 (July 1935): 282, citing Statutes at Large, Confederate States, 1 May 1863, 167–68. Davis's 12 January 1863 statement alluding to the Emancipation Proclamation said he would deliver captured officers to states for "punishment [as] criminals engaged in exciting servile insurrection" ("Negro in the Military Service," NA, 7:4408–9, 4530–32).

76. Lincoln's 30 July 1863 order in General Order no. 252, Adjutant General's Office, 31 July 1863, *ORA,* ser. 2, vol. 6: 163.

77. *Richmond Examiner,* 23 April 1864; *Chicago Times,* 8 May 1864; *Richmond Record,* n.d., but probably late 1864, quoted in William T. Alexander, *The History of the Colored Race in America* (1887; reprint, Westport, Conn.: Negro Universities Press, 1986), 340–41; *Chicago Daily Tribune,* 29 April 1864.

78. *Chicago Daily Tribune,* 29 April 1864; "A Regiment of Africans on Their Way to the War—Reception and Entertainment by Ladies of Chicago—Strange Scenes at the Cars," *Daily Age* (Phila.), 3 May 1964, quoting the *Tribune,* n.d.

79. Morning Reports, NA; McCoslen's letter, 26 July 1864, *Christian Recorder* (Phila.), 27 August 1864.

CHAPTER 2: CAMPAIGNS IN VIRGINIA

1. Frank J. Welcher, *The Union Army, 1861–1865, Organization and Operations,* 2 vols. (Bloomington: Indiana University Press, 1989), 1:428; *Chicago Daily Tribune,* 28 and 30 April 1864; Ezra J. Warner, *Generals in Blue: Lives of the Union Commanders* (Baton Rouge: Louisiana State University Press, 1964), 150.

2. Compiled Service Records Showing Service of Military Units in Volunteer Union Organizations, and Morning Reports, Twenty-ninth Regiment of USC Troops, by Month, U.S. Colored Troops, Records of the office of the Adjutant General, Record Group 94, National Archives (hereafter cited as Record of Events and Morning Reports, NA, respectively); telegram, Adjutant General's Office, Washington, D.C., to Bross, 30 April 1864, Miscellaneous Letters, Twenty-ninth USCT, RG 94, NA (hereafter cited as Miscellaneous Letters, NA); Thomas, pension record, Case Files of Approved Pension Applications of Veterans Who Have Served in the Army and Navy Mainly in the Civil War and the War with Spain,

1861–1934, Civil War and Later Pension Files, Records of the Veterans Administration, RG 15, NA (hereafter cited as pension record, NA).

3. Letter, Casey to assistant adjutant general, Washington, D.C., 2 May 1864, Miscellaneous Letters, NA; [Arthur Swazey], *Memorial of Colonel Bross*, Twenty-ninth U.S. Colored Troops (Chicago: Tribune Book and Job Office, 1865), 12; *ORA*, ser. 1, vol. 36: 364.

4. General Orders nos. 1 and 2, 3 May, and no. 4, 15 May 1864, Order Book, Twenty-ninth USCT, Adjutant General's Office, RG 94, NA; Morning Reports, NA; quoting Francis A. Lord, *They Fought for the Union* (New York: Bonanza Books, 1960), 33. Evidence that Winyard's wound was not thought to have occurred in the line of duty is that he was not immediately pensioned, was several times denied a pension for disability, and was not entered until 1899 when he qualified as over sixty-two (Winyard, pension record, NA).

5. Bross's letter, n.d., Swazey, *Memorial of Colonel Bross*, 13; General Orders no. 10, Headquarters First Provisional Brigade, Camp Casey, 21 May 1864, Issuances, Regimental Papers, Twenty-ninth USCT, box 26, RG 94, NA (hereafter cited as Issuances, NA); Morning Reports, NA; Francis B. Heitman, *Historical Register and Dictionary of the United States Army, from Its Organization, September 29, 1789, to March 2, 1903*, 2 vols. (1903; reprint, Urbana: University of Illinois Press, 1965), 2:852; Indiana, Adjutant General's Office, *Report of the Adjutant General of the State of Indiana in the War of the Rebellion and Statistics and Documents*, 8 vols. (Indianapolis: Alexander H. Connor, 1865–69), 3:379.

6. Brown's file, Compiled (Military) Service Records, Twenty-ninth USCT, RG 94, NA (hereafter cited as CMSR, NA); *Chicago Daily News*, 30 April 1864; letter, Pomeroy to Oakes, 9 July 1864, Miscellaneous Letters, NA;Illinois, Military and Naval Department, *Report of the Adjutant General of the State of Illinois*, 9 vols. (Springfield: Baker, Bailache and Co., 1867), 8:791–93; *Daily Whig and Republican*, 26 April 1864.

7. Christian, Foggey, Rice, Sink, Weaver, and McKinney, CMSR and pension records, NA.

8. Johnson, Phoenix, and Phillips, ibid.; Wood, CMSR, NA

9. List of Commissioned Officers in Descriptive Book (Twenty-ninth USCT), RG 94, NA; Conant, CMSR, NA; Monthly Report of New Organizations of Volunteers, 30 June 1864, Miscellaneous Letters, NA; report, Bross to Adjutant General's Office, Washington, D.C., 17 May 1864, Special Orders no. 10, Headquarters, First Provisional Brigade, 21 May 1864, Issuances, NA.

10. The regimental history says only of this period: "Remained at Camp Casey having daily drills up to 30 May" (Record of Events, NA). Morning Reports, NA.

11. Mackay's American family lived in St. Louis during his army service (Mackay, CMSR and pension record, NA); J. W. Wells and N. A. Strait, *Roster of All the Regimental Surgeons and Assistant Surgeons in the Late War and Hospital*

Service (1883; reprint, San Francisco: Norman Publishing, 1990), 208, 309; Mackay may have embellished his resume, his obituary claiming he graduated from the University of Glasgow in 1855 and followed this with service as a surgeon on a British warship during the Crimean War, but these accomplishments are doubtful, "Death of Dr. David Mackay," *Dallas Morning News*, 24 March 1904.

12. McCoslin's letter, 26 July 1864, *Christian Recorder* (Phila.), 27 August 1864; Morning Reports, NA; Record of Events, NA; Ferrero's report, 1 August 1864, U.S. Department of War, *A Compilation of Official Records of the Union and Confederate Armies in the War of the Rebellion*, 127 vols. (Washington, D.C.: Governmant Printing Office, 1880–1902) (hereafter cited as *ORA*) ser. 1, vol. 36 (pt. 1): 990; Todd, White, Carter, and Dotson, CMSR and pension records, NA.

13. Carter, Casey, Couch, and Hunter, CMSR and pension records, NA.

14. Ulysses Simpson Grant, *Memoirs of Ulysses S. Grant*, 2 vols., (New York: Charles L. Webster and Co., 1885), 2:178, 196. Ferrero was assigned to the Sixth Corps on 6 May (*ORA*, ser. 1, vol. 36 [pt. 1]: 988–90).

15. George Agassiz, ed., *Meade's Headquarters, 1863–1864; Letters of Colonel Theodore Lyman, From Wilderness to Appomattox* (Boston: Atlantic Monthly Press, 1922), 102.

16. Selden Conner, "The Colored Troops," Commandery of the State of Maine, Military Order of the Loyal Legion of the United States, *War Papers*, 3 vols. (Portland: Lefavor-Tower Co., 1908), 3:78; Noah Andre Trudeau, *Bloody Roads South: The Virginia Campaign, 1864–1865* (New York: Charles Schribner's Sons, 1989), 110, 163, 209, citing Freeman S. Bowley, *A Boy Lieutenant* (Philadelphia: Henry Altemus Co., 1906); Joseph T. Wilson, *The Black Phalanx: A History of Negro Soldiers in the United States in the Wars of 1776–1810, 1861–'65* (Hartford: American Publishing Co., 1892), 392.

17. Letter, 23 May 1864, in David S. Sparks, ed., *Inside Lincoln's Army: The Diary of Marsena Rudolph Patrick, Provost Marshal General, Army of the Potomac* (New York: Thomas Yoseloff, 1864), 376; Grant, *Memoirs*, 2:289; Welcher, *Union Army*, 1:429.

18. Warner, *Generals in Blue*, 502; Heitman, *Historical Register*, 1:954; Thomas Holdup Stevens Hamersly, comp. and ed., *Complete Regular Army Register of the United States for One Hundred Years (1779–1879)* (Washington, D.C.: Thomas H. S. Hamersly, 1880), 805. The Nineteenth, with Lt. Col. Joseph G. Perkins as acting commander, was made up almost entirely of former slaves from Maryland's eastern shore; the Twenty-third, Col. Clarence J. Campbell, also primarily former slaves, was organized at Camp Casey; the Thirty-first, Lt. Col. W. E. W. Ross, was raised at Hart's Island, New York; the Twenty-seventh, Lt. Col. Charles J. Webster, was organized at Camp Delaware, Ohio; the Thirtieth, Col. Delevan Bates, and Thirty-ninth, Col. Ozora P. Stearns, were Maryland regiments similar to the Nineteenth; and the Forty-third, Lt. Col. H. Seymour Hall, was from Philadelphia (Henry Goddard Thomas, "The Colored Troops at Petersburg,"

in *Battles and Leaders of the Civil War*, ed. Robert U. Johnson and Clarence Buel, 4 vols. [1887–88; reprint, Secaucus, N.J.: Castle, 1989], 4:563).

19. Welcher, *Union Army*, 1:430; *ORA*, ser. 1, vol. 40 (pt. 1): 549; Sparks, *Patrick Diary*, 384.

20. Ferrero's report, 1 August 1864, *ORA*, ser. 1, vol. 40 (pt. 1): 594; Griffin's 10 June 1864 letter, pension record, NA.

21. Charles Wilson, "Exploding a Mine," *National Tribune* (Washington, D.C.), 14 May 1896; William Freeman Fox, *Regimental Losses in the American Civil War, 1861–1865* (Albany: Albany Publishing Co., 1889), 83; Freeman S. Bowley, *The Petersburg Mine*. Paper read before the California Commandery, Military Order of the Loyal Legion of the United States, War paper no. 3 (San Francisco: for the commandery, 1889), 4; Warren Wilkinson, *Mother, May You Never See the Sights I Have Seen: The Fifty-seventh Massachusetts Veteran Volunteers in the Army of the Potomac, 1864–1865* (New York: Harper and Row, 1990), 199; William H. Powell, "The Battle of the Petersburg Crater," *Battles and Leaders*, 4:559; Warren Wilkinson,"Bury Them If They Don't Move," *Civil War Times Illustrated* 29 (March–April 1990): 34; U.S. Congress, Joint Committee on the Conduct of the War, *Report of the Joint Committee . . . on the Attack on Petersburg, on the 30th Day of July, 1864*, Senate Report no. 114, 38th Cong., 2d sess., 15 December 1864, 159; General Orders no. 21, Fourth Division, 9 July 1864, Issuances, NA.

22. Wilson, *Black Phalanx*, 389.

23. Powell, "Battle of the Crater," *Battles and Leaders*, 4:547–48, 559.

24. Henry Pleasants Jr., *The Tragedy of the Crater* (1938; reprint, Washington, D.C.: Eastern National Park and Monument Association, 1975), 62; Horace Porter, *Campaigning with Grant* (New York: Century Co., 1897), 219; Agassiz, *Lyman Letters*, 180. Ferrero, as it happened, spoke French.

25. Porter, *Campaigning with Grant*, 253–56.

26. Record of Events, NA.

27. McCoslin's 26 July 1864 letter, *Christian Recorder*, 27 August 1864.

28. Thomas, "Colored Troops at Petersburg," *Battles and Leaders*, 4:563.

29. Porter, Morris, Williams, and Lee, CMSR and pension records, NA; McGrundy, CMSR, NA.

30. Houston, pension record, NA.

31. Company A information is the result of review of the CMSR and available pension records of every soldier in the unit; soldiers' records for companies B through F were selectively reviewed, and the sample shows a similar pattern of illness and accident (Bernard, Campbell, Golden, Kay, Scott, Washington, G. Williams, and W. Williams, CMSR and pension records, NA). Details were hospital, quartermaster, provost guard, teamsters, and engineers, and the most common was construction of fortifications.

32. Wood, Brown, and Scott, ibid.

33. Arbuckle, pension record, NA.

34. *Illinois Adjutant General's Report,* 8:778–93; List of Commissioned Officers, Descriptive Book, NA; Hassler, Ferguson, Johnston, CMSR and pension records, NA.

CHAPTER 3: TEST OF BATTLE

1. *Army and Navy Journal and Gazette of the Regular and Volunteer Forces* (Washington, D.C.), 2 and 9 July 1864.

2. Ferrero had objected to his division being "constantly employed on fatigue duties" and asked that "sufficient time be given for rest and to clean their arms, &c., before taking part in the proposed assault," a request Meade granted a few days later (letter, Ferrero to Ninth Corps, 17 July 1864, with endorsements, U.S. Department of War, *The War of the Rebellion: A Compilation of the Official Records of the Union and Confederate Armies,* 127 vols.[Washington, D.C.: Government Printing Office, 1880–1902], ser. 1, vol. 40 [pt. 3]: 304 [hereafter cited as *ORA* and ser. 1, unless indicated]).

3. The movement practiced by the black regiments was for the regiments in columns "to take half distance, and as soon as the leading regiment of the right brigade to come into line perpendicular to the enemy's line by the 'right companies on the right into line, wheel,' 'the left companies on the right into line, . . . and the leading regiment in the left brigade to execute the reverse movement to the left" (letter, Burnside to Meade, July 26, 1864, William H. Powell, "Battle of the Petersburg Crater," in *Battles and Leaders of the Civil War,* 4 vols. [1887–88; reprint, Secaucus, N.J.: Castle, 1989], ed. Robert U. Johnson and Clarence Buel, 4:546–47).

4. Henry Pleasants Jr., *The Tragedy of the Crater* (Washington, D.C.: Eastern National Park and Monument Association, 1975), 61; William Marvel, *Burnside* (Chapel Hill: University of North Carolina Press, 1991), 330; H. Seymour Hall, "Mine Run to Petersburg," in Kansas Commandery, Military Order of the Loyal Legion of the United States, *War Talks in Kansas* (Kansas City: Franklin Hudson Publishing Co., 1906), 220; Henry Goddard Thomas, "The Colored Troops at Petersburg," *Battles and Leaders,* 4:563.

5. Warren Wilkinson, *Mother, May You Never See the Sights I Have Seen: The Fifty-seventh Massachusetts Veteran Volunteers in the Army of the Potomac, 1864–1865* (New York: Harper and Row, 1990), 197; *Daily Express* (Petersburg, Va.), 1 August 1864; quoting John Sergeant Wise, *The End of an Era,* ed. Curtis Carroll Davis (1899; reprint, New York: Thomas Yoseloff, 1965), 351–52.

6. Timothy H. Donavan Jr. et al., *The American Civil War,* West Point Military History series (Wayne, N.J.: Avery Publishing Group, 1987), 227; *Harper's Weekly,* 20 August 1864; *ORA,* 40 (pt. 3): 46, quoting Richard Wheeler, *On Fields of Fury, from the Wilderness to the Crater: An Eyewitness History* (New York: HarperCollins, 1991), 280.

7. Meade's 29 July 1864 order, *ORA*, 40 (pt. 3): 596–97.

8. Ezra J. Warner, *Generals in Blue: Lives of the Union Commanders* (Baton Rouge: Louisiana State University Press, 1964), 277; Stephen Minot Weld, *War Diary and Letters of Stephen Minot Weld, 1861–1865*, 2d ed. (Boston: Massachusetts Historical Society, 1979), 317, 344, 353; Weld, "The Petersburg Mine," in *Papers of the Military Historical Society of Massachusetts*, 7 vols. (Boston: By the Society, 1906), 5:218; Daniel R. Ballou, "The Petersburg Mine," *National Tribune* (Washington, D.C.), 5 June 1913; *New York Daily Tribune*, 2 August 1864; Charles Wilson, "Exploding a Mine," *National Tribune*, 14 and 23 May 1896; Horace Porter, *Campaigning with Grant* (New York: Century Co., 1897), 262.

9. Burnside's order, telegram, 29 July 1864, Letters, Telegrams and Orders Received and Issued, Ninth Army Corps, box 7, U.S. Army Continental Commands (1821–1920), Record Group 393, National Archives; *ORA*, 40 (pt. 3): 611–12 (emph. added).

10. Order to Brig. Gen. J. B. Carr, Third Division, Eighteenth Army Corps, 29 July 1864, *ORA*, 40 (pt. 3): 47, 635; Ledlie's instructions described by Capt. Thomas W. Clark, Twenty-ninth Massachusetts Volunteers, in Wilkinson, *Mother, May You Never See*, 238; Donavan, *American Civil War*.

11. Michael Arthur Cavanaugh and William Marvel, *The Petersburg Campaign, The Battle of the Crater, "Horrid Pit," June 25–August 6, 1864*, Virginia Civil War Battles and Leaders series (Lynchburg: H. E. Howard, 1989), 33; [Arthur Swazey], *Memorial of Colonel John Bross, Twenty-ninth U.S. Colored Troops* (Chicago: Tribune Book and Job Office, 1865), 16; *New York Daily Tribune*, 6 August 1864; Henry Goddard Thomas, "The Colored Troops at Petersburg," *Battles and Leaders*, 4:563; Delavan Bates, "A Day with the Colored Troops," *National Tribune*, 30 January 1908.

12. James Judson Chase, *The Charge at Daybreak: Scenes and Incidents at the Battle of the Mine Explosion, Near Petersburg, Va, July 30th, 1864* (Lewiston: Lewiston Journal, 1875), 13; Swazey, *Memorial of Colonel Bross*, 16, 78 (Mackay's letter, 22 September 1864); List of Commissioned Officers, Descriptive Book (Twenty-ninth USCT), Records of the Office of the Adjutant General, RG 94, NA; Colonel Russell's (he commanded the Twenty-ninth USCT's brigade at the time) history of the Twenty-ninth, 16 November 1864, Miscellaneous Letters, Twenty-ninth USCT, RG 94, NA.

13. Swazey, *Memorial of Colonel Bross*, 16; Wilkinson, *Mother, May You Never See*, 247–50; Freeman S. Bowley, *The Petersburg Mine*, paper read before the California Commandery, Military Order of the Loyal Lefion of the United States, War paper no. 3 (San Francisco: for the Commandery, 1889) 5–6; Philippe Regis de Trobriand, "Burnside Fumbles His Chance to Take Petersburg," in *The Blue and the Gray: The Story of the Civil War As Told by Participants*, ed. Henry S. Commager (New York: Bobbs-Merrill, 1950), 1019–20; Wise, *End of an Era*, 357; *ORA*, 40 (pt. 1): 126.

14. Thomas, "Colored Troops at Petersburg," *Battles and Leaders,* 4:564–65; Noah Andre Trudeau, *The Last Citadel, Petersburg, Virginia, June 1864–April 1865* (Boston: Little, Brown, 1991), 115–16; Porter, *Campaigning with Grant,* 268.

15. Burnside's 13 August 1864 report on the action, Adjutant General's Office, "The Negro in the Military Service, of the United States, 1609–1889," 7 vols., RG 94, NA, 4:3212–13.

16. William Mahone, *The Battle of the Crater* (facsimile reprint of original) (Collingswood, N.J.: C. W. Historicals, n.d.), 4; Wise, *End of an Era,* 355, 677.

17. James C. Coit, "The Battle of the Crater, July 30, 1864," *Southern Historical Society Papers* 10 (1882): 126–27; Wise, *End of an Era,* 360; testimony, Surgeon H. E. Smith, Twenty-seventh Michigan Volunteers, *ORA,* 40 (pt. 1): 103–4, 113; Wilkinson, *Mother, May You Never See,* 249–52; Charles W. Walton, "The Battle of the Mine," *National Tribune,* 20 November 1884.

18. *ORA,* 40 (pt. 1): 103, 595; George Kilmer, "The Dash into the Crater," *Century Illustrated Magazine* 12 (September 1887): 775; James M. Guthrie, *Camp-Fires of the Afro-American* (1899; reprint, Boston: Johnson Reprint Co., 1970), 528.

19. Cavanaugh and Marvel, *Petersburg Campaign,* 56–58; Ferrero's 31 August 1864, testimony, *ORA,* 40 (pt. 1): 93; James H. Rickart, "Service with Colored Troops in Burnside's Corps," Rhode Island Soldiers and Sailors Historical Society, *Personal Narratives* (Providence: Providence Press, 1894), ser. 5, no. 1, 43; Bowley, *Petersburg Mine,* 9; Hall, "Mine Run to Petersburg," *War Talks,* 238; Harry F. Jackson and Thomas F. O'Donnell, eds., *Back Home in Oneida: Herman Clark and His Letters* (Syracuse: Syracuse University Press, 1965), 27.

20. Jackson and O'Donnell, *Back Home in Oneida,* 10.

21. Thomas's 2 August 1864 report, *ORA,* 40 (pt. 1): 598; Thomas, "Colored Troops at Petersburg," *Battles and Leaders,* 4:564–65; Northup's letter to editor, *News-Press* (St. Joseph, Mo.), n.d., in Peter Coleman, pension record, U.S. Veterans Administration, RG 15, Civil War and Later Survivor Certificates, Civil War and Later Pension Files, NA (hereafter cited as pension record, NA); George Agassiz, ed., *Meade's Headquarters, 1863–1864: Letters of Colonel Theodore Lyman, from Wilderness to Appomattox* (Boston: Atlantic Monthly Press, 1922), 199; Wise, *End of an Era,* 366.

22. Ferrero's order, Bowley, *Petersburg Mine,* 10; Thomas, "Colored Troops at Petersburg," *Battles and Leaders,* 4:565; Thomas's 2 August 1864 report, *ORA,* 40 (pt. 1): 598; Rickard, "Service with Colored Troops," *Narratives,* 27–28; Thomas's 20 August 1864 report, "Negro in the Military Service," NA, 4:3281. Two Eighteenth Corps brigades were also ordered in; they captured some trenches on the right front but were soon driven into the crater (Wilkinson, *Mother, May You Never See,* 255). Stevens, Compiled (Military) Service Records of Volunteer Soldiers Who Served during the Civil War, RG 94, NA (CMSR, NA); Bailey, Brown

and Maxon, CMSR and pension records, NA; Swazey, *Memorial of Colonel Bross*, 17–18; Wise, *End of an Era*, 364; George T. Rodgers, "The Crater Battle, July 30, 1864," *Confederate Veteran* 3 (January 1893): 12; Joseph T. Glatthaar, *Forged in Battle: The Civil War Alliance of Black Soldiers and White Officers* (New York: Free Press, 1990), 275–76; letter, Ferrero to assistant adjutant general, Ninth Army Corps, 7 November 1864, "Negro in the Military Service," NA, 4:2820. While most regiments had two colors, the United States standard, supplied by the army, and a regimental flag, often provided by citizens from where the regiment was raised, it does not seem that the Twenty-ninth had more than the U.S. color at the battle.

23. Trudeau, *Last Citadel*, 118; Wheeler, *On Fields of Fury*, 284–85; report, Maj. Gen. Bushrod R. Johnson, commanding Confederate forces at Petersburg, 20 August 1864, "Negro in the Military Service," NA, 4:3286–87; Thomas's 2 August 1864 report, *ORA*, 4 (pt. 1): 104, 498–99; Thomas, "Colored Troops at Petersburg," *Battles and Leaders*, 4:567; Freeman S. Bowley, "The Crater," *National Tribune*, 6 November 1884; Bowley, *Petersburg Mine*, 12; George S. Bernard, "The Battle of the Crater," *War Talks of Confederate Veterans* (Petersburg, Va.: Fenn and Owen Publishers, 1892), 159; *Army and Navy Journal*, 6 August 1864; de Trobriand, "Burnside Fumbles His Chance," *Blue and Gray*, 1920.

24. *Harper's Weekly*, 29 August 1864; Thomas's 20 August 1864 report, "Negro in the Military Service," NA, 4:3282–83.

25. Grant to H. W. Halleck, chief of staff, Washington, D.C., 10 A.M., and Meade's retreat order, 9:30 A.M., 30 July 1864, *ORA*, 40 (pt. 3): 636, 662; Burnside's 13 August 1864, report, "Negro in the Military Service," NA, 4:3264; Wilkinson, *Mother, May You Never See*, 256.

26. Bowley, *Petersburg Mine*, 12; Kilmer, "Dash into the Crater," *Century Magazine* 22:775–6; James I. Robertson Jr., "Negro Soldiers in the Civil War," *Civil War Times Illustrated* 7 (October 1968): 31; *ORA*, 40 (pt. 1): 113.

27. *ORA*, 40 (pt. 1): 93, 119; Pleasants, *Tragedy of the Crater*, 81.

28. Bowley, *Petersburg Mine*, 13; William Miller Owen, *In Camp and Battle with the Washington Artillery of New Orleans* (Boston: Ticknor and Co., 1885), 343; *New York Daily Tribune*, 6 August 1864.

29. John C. Fetherstone, "Graphic Account of the Battle of the Crater," *Southern Historical Society Papers* 33 (1905): 363; and *Battle of the Crater*, Eyewitness Accounts of the Civil War (1906; reprint; Birmingham: Birmington Public Library Press, 1987), 21; J. H. Stine, *History of the Army of the Potomac* (Philadelphia: J. B. Rogers Publishing Co., 1892), 680; Bowley, *Petersburg Mine*, 14.

30. Bowley, *The Petersburg Mine*, 14–16; Marvel, *Burnside*, 405–6; Joseph T. Wilson, *The Black Phalanx: A History of Negro Soldiers in the United States in the Wars of 1776–1810, 1861–'65* (Hartford: American Publishing Co., 1892), 417; Wilkinson, *Mother May You Never See*, 258; Benjamin Spear, "In Front of Petersburg," *National Tribune*, 20 June 1889; Fetherston, "Graphic Account,"

Southern Historical Society Papers 33:363; Fetherston, *Battle of the Crater,* 21; Wise, *End of an Era,* 366; Stine, *History of the Army of the Potomac,* 689.

31. Gaskins, "A Colored Soldier's Experience How Rebels Treated Prisoners in the Southern Prisons" (clipping), *Journal* (Chicago?), (n.d. but about mid-1880s) in Gaskins, pension record, NA.

32. Letter, W. C. McClellan, 15 August 1864, Bell Irvin Wiley, *The Life of Johnny Reb: The Common Soldier of the Confederacy* (Baton Rouge: Louisiana State University Press, 1943), 314–15; letter, Private Henry Biggs, n.d., Randall C. Jimerson, *The Private Civil War: Popular Thought during the Sectional Conflict* (Baton Rouge: Louisiana State University Press, 1988), 114; Bowley, *Petersburg Mine,* 16; Shelby Foote, *The Civil War: A Narrative,* 3 vols. (New York: Vintage Books, 1986), 3:538.

33. *Daily Dispatch* (Richmond), 1 and 2 August 1864; *Daily Express* (Petersburg), 1 August 1864; W. A. Day, "The Breastworks at Petersburg, *Confederate Veteran* 29 (May 1921): 175; *Richmond Daily Enquirer,* 1 and 2 August 1864; *Army and Navy Journal,* 6 August 1864.

34. Rickard, "Service with Colored Troops," *Narratives,* 29; Owen, *In Camp and Battle,* 345; *Daily Express,* 1 August 1864; *Daily Dispatch,* 2 August 1864; affidavit, Surgeon F. J. D'Avignon, Ninety-sixth New York Volunteers, 13 October 1864, "Negro in the Military Service," NA, 7:4371, Bowley, *Petersburg Mine,* 16; Wise, *End of an Era,* 368; R. K. Beechem, "Adventures of an Iron Brigade Man," *National Tribune,* 27 November 1902.

35. Report of Casualties, Ferrero to Ninth Corps, 31 July 1864, letter, Thomas to adjutant general, Fourth Division, 10 August 1864, "Negro in the Military Service," NA, 4:3274, 2736; Report of the Casualties in 2d Brigade 4th Division 9AC in the Action of July 30, 1864, Weekly Reports of Losses and Gains (March 1864–July 1865), Stations of the Troops, 10, 31 August 1864, Ninth Army Corps, box 7, RG 393, NA; *Chicago Evening Journal,* 3 August (dispatches, Brig. Gen. Julius White and Gosper, both 2 August 1864) and 4 August, 1864; *Chicago Daily Tribune,* 2 August 1864; *Daily Whig and Republican,* 9 August 1864; CMSR, NA; Pension Records, NA; *New York Daily Tribune,* 3 August 1864; Swazey, *Memorial of Colonel Bross,* 17, 33, 35; promotion order, Adjutant General's Office, 27 July 1864, Colonel Russell's 16 November 1864 history, Miscellaneous Papers, NA.

36. David S. Sparks, ed., *Inside Lincoln's Army: The Diary of Marsena Rudolph Patrick, Provost Marshal General, Army of the Potomac* (New York: Thomas Yoseloff, 1964), 407; *New York Daily Tribune,* 3 August 1864; *ORA,* 40 (pt. 3): 707; William Howell Reed, *Hospital Life in the Army of the Potomac,* 2d ed. (1866; reprint, Boston: n.p., 1891), 80–81; L. P. Brockett and Mary C. Vaughn, *Women's Work in the Civil War: A Record of Heroism, Patriotism and Patience* (Philadelphia: Zeigler, McCurdy & Co., 1868), 133–47; Edward A. Miller Jr. "Angel of Light: Helen L. Gilson, Army Nurse," *Civil War History* 43 (March

1997), 33–34. Benjamin Quarles, *The Negro in the Civil War* (Boston: Little, Brown, 1953), 304.

37. Burnside to Meade, 31 July, Grant to Meade, 30 July, Burnside to Meade, 6 P.M., 31 July 1864, *ORA*, 40 (pt. 3): 640, 702; letter, Capt. George Barton, 31 July 1864, Wilkinson, *Mother, May You Never See,* 266; *New York Daily Tribune,* 5 August 1864; Henry Goddard Thomas, "Twenty-Two Hours a Prisoner of War in Dixie," Maine Commandery, Military Order of the Loyal Legion of the United States, *War Papers,* 3 vols. (Portland: published by the Order, 1898), 1:29; journal entry, 1 August 1864, Owen, *In Camp and Battle,* 346; *Charleston* (S.C.) *Daily Courier,* 8 August 1864; Fetherstone, *Battle of the Crater,* 25; Day, "Breastworks at Petersburg," *Confederate Veteran* 29:175; Agassiz, *Lyman Letters,* 203 n.

38. Owen, *In Camp and Battle,* 347; Fetherstone, "Graphic Account," *Southern Historical Society Papers* 33:368; Thomas, "Twenty-Two Hours," *War Papers,* 1:37–41; Rickard, "Service with Colored Troops," *Narratives,* 30.

39. *New York Daily Tribune, Daily Illinois State Journal,* both 4 August; and *Daily Dispatch, Daily Express,* both 1 August 1864; Clifford Dowdey, ed., *The Wartime Papers of R. E. Lee* (Boston: Little, Brown, 1961), 502 (telegram, 6:30 P.M., 30 July 1864), 827 (Lee's 1 August 1864 report); James W. Beller, "The Crater," *National Tribune,* 20 June 1889.

40. *ORA*, 40 (pt. 1): 55, 60, 248; William Freeman Fox, *Regimental Losses in the American Civil War, 1861–1865* (Albany: Albany Publishing Co., 1889), 55, 60; U.S. Army, Adjutant General's Office, *Official Army Register of the Volunteer Forces of the United States Army for the Years 1861, '62, '63, '64, '65* (Washington, D.C.: Government Printing Office, 1865), pt. 8, 200; Powell, "Battle of the Petersburg Crater," *Battles and Leaders,* 4:559; Cavanaugh and Marvel, *Petersburg Campaign,* 113.

41. Morning Reports, Twenty-ninth Regiment of USC Troops, by Month; Compiled Military Service Records Showing Service of Military Units in Volunteer Union Organizations, Record of Events, Twenty-ninth U.S. Colored Inf. (Record of Events); Descriptive Book; all RG 94, NA; Illinois, Military and Naval Department, *Report of the Adjutant General of the State of Illinois,* 9 vols. (Springfield: Baker, Bailache & Co., 1867), 8:781–82, 786–87; Aiken, Crawford, Lee, Darson, and Hughes, CMSR, NA; Green, Simpson, Watts, Stewart, E. Carter, Long, H. Carter, and Griffin, CMSR and pension records, NA.

42. Morning Report, NA; Gale, CMSR and pension record, NA; Chapman and Hassler, CMSR, NA.

43. Morning Report, NA; Asher, CMSR, NA; Duffin, CMSR and pension record, NA.

44. Green, Jordan, Maloney, Sidnor, and Williams, CMSR, NA; Burnett, Boston, and Summerfield, CMSR and pension records, NA.

45. Knapp and Marlow, CMSR and pension records, NA. The Company D

Morning Report, NA, says two officers were at the battle, but, other than Knapp, no other officer can be identified.

46. Lewis, CMSR, NA; Lancaster, Markell, and Thornton, CMSR and pension records, NA.

47. Hazell, CMSR and pension record, NA; Washington, CMSR, NA.

48. Dudley, Dyer, and Lewis, CMSR, NA; Green and Jamison, CMSR and pension records, NA.

49. Louis Williams, CMSR, NA; George Williams and Corsey, CMSR and pension records, NA.

50. Millender, Perkins, Logan, and Johnson, CMSR and pension records, NA.

51. Franklin, CMSR, NA; Doolin, Fonsey, Rickman, Rogers, Smith, South, Washington, and Magruder, CMSR and pension records, NA.

52. Clipping, "A Colored Soldier's Experience," *Journal*, n.d.; and other documents in Gaskins, pension record, NA.

53. Williams, CMSR and pension record, NA.

54. Robertson and Richardson, CMSR, NA; Bibb, Mosely, and Rue, CMSR and pension records, NA.

55. Butler, Broaddy, Jones, and Carr, CMSR and pension records, NA.

56. Brockway, CMSR, NA. Brockway was pensioned in 1866; Gosper and Conant, CMSR and pension records, NA.

57. Maxon and Blakely, CMSR and pension records, NA.

58. Brown, ibid.

59. Wilson, ibid. Flint apparently had no dependents.

60. Higlon and Parker, CMSR, NA; J. White, Route, Walker, Scott, Brown, Hammons, and Perkins, CMSR and pension records, NA.

61. W. W. Flint, CMSR, NA; Martin, S. White, Ferguson, and Sexton, CMSR and pension records, NA.

62. Odin, MacKay, Jackson, Stark, Allen, Price, Ross, Robinson, and Strander, CMSR, NA; Tinsley and Thrasher, CMSR and pension records, NA. Thrasher's pension record includes the April 1870 letter from Royce, then in Scranton, Pennsylvania.

63. Tinsley, CMSR and pension record, NA.

64. Sink and Charles and Collins South, ibid. Underhill, CMSR, NA.

65. Hammon, Smith, and Rice, CMSR and pension records, NA.

66. Clothing Account Books, Twenty-ninth USCT, Moorland Spingarn Research Center, Howard University, Washington, D.C.; *Illinois Adjutant General's Report*, 8:791.

67. Ferrero's casualty report, 31 July 1864, "Negro in the Military Service," NA, 4:3274.

68. *ORA*, 40 (pt. 1): 177–78, 569, 599; letter, Pvt. Willis A. Bogart to Mrs. Bross, *Memorial of Colonel Bross*, 31. Colonel Bross's brother William has a more lasting monument: Mt. Bross, a 14,185-foot peak in the Colorado Rockies, is

named after him (Alfred Theodore Andreas, *History of Chicago*, 3 vols. [1884–85; reprint, New York: Arno Press, 1975], 2:492–93). An impressive monument to Bross erected by his family still stands at Graceland Cemetery, Chicago.

69. Ulysses Simpson Grant, *Memoirs of Ulysses S. Grant*, 2 vols. (New York: Charles L. Webster and Co., 1885), 2:313, 315; Marval, *Burnside*, 409; "Report of the Court of Inquiry on the Mine Explosion," *ORA*, 40 (pt. 1): 128–29; Mark Mayo Boatner III, *The Civil War Dictionary* (New York: David McKay Co., 1959), 474; Warner, *Generals in Blue*, 150.

70. U.S. Congress, Joint Committee on the Conduct of the War, *Report of the Joint Committee . . . on the Attack on Petersburg, on the 30th Day of July, 1864*, Senate Report no. 114, 38th Cong., 2d sess., 15 December 1864, 5, 10, 23; Burnside's 10 August testimony before the court of inquiry, *ORA*, 40 (pt. 1): 73.

71. Barton's letters, Wilkinson, *Mother, May You Never See*, 255, 266; Jackson and O'Donnell, *Back Home in Oneida*, 27; letter to Boyd Hamilton, 3 August, and letter to mother, 29 August 1864, William Hamilton Papers, Documents Division, Library of Congress, Washington, D.C.; letters, 31 July and 10 November 1864, Agassiz, *Lyman Letters*, 199–200, 262; *Washington* (D.C.) *Star*, 1 August 1864.

72. Reports, Ledlie, 4 August; Brig. Gen. S. G. Griffin, 31 July; Brig. Gen. R. B. Potter, 1 August; Lt. Col. Gilbert P. Robinson, all 1864; and Colonels Potter and Sigfried, 31 July and 20 August 1864, who did not fix blame ("Negro in the Military Service," NA, 4:3211–82); Weld, *War Diary*, 353–54.

73. *Chicago Evening Journal* and *Daily Whig and Republican*, both 3 August 1864; *Worcester* (Mass.) *Daily Spy*, 2 August 1864; *Harper's Weekly*, 20 August 1864; editorial, *New York Evening Express*, 2 August 1864.

74. Ervin T. Case, "Battle of the Mine," Rhode Island Soldiers and Sailors Historical Society, *Personal Narratives of Events in the War of the Rebellion* (Providence: Sidney S. Rich, 1879), ser. 1, no. 10, 28; Squire D. Rhodes, "The Battle of the Crater," and James E. Catlin, "The Battle of the Crater," *National Tribune*, 8 October 1903, 22 January 1903, respectively; Powell, "Battle of the Petersburg Crater," *Battles and Leaders*, 4:556; letter to editor, Charles Wilson, *National Tribune*, 3 July 1919.

75. Letter, Carter, to "Friend Charles," 3 December 1864 (MS from a private collection, Fort Ward Museum and Historical Park, Alexandria, Va.). Carter survived the war and was discharged as the first sergeant of Company G, Twenty-eighth USCT

76. Donavan et al., *American Civil War*, 229; *New York Daily Tribune*, 6 August 1864; letter, Ferrero to Burnside, 4 August 1864, "Negro in the Military Service," NA, 4:3275.

CHAPTER 4: FURTHER WAR SERVICE

1. Report, provost marshal general, U.S. Department of War, *The War of*

the Rebellion: A Compilation of the Official Records of the Union and Confederate Armies, 127 vols. (Washington, D.C.: Government Printing Office, 1880–1902), ser. 3, vol. 5: 633 (hereafter cited as *ORA* and ser. 1, unless indicated); General Orders no. 227, Adjutant General's Office, 9 July 1864, implementing conscription act of 4 July, Adjutant General's Office, "The Negro in the Military Service of the United States, 1609–1889," 7 vols., office of the Adjutant General, Record Group 94, National Archives, 4:2673; John Wesley Blassingame, "The Organization and Use of Negro Troops in the Union Army" (Master's thesis, Howard University, Washington, D.C., 1963), 30.

2. *Daily Illinois State Journal,* 4 May 1864; Compiled (Military) Service Records (CMSR), Twenty-ninth USCT, RG 94, NA; Fred Albert Shannon, *The Organization and Administration of the Union Army, 1861–1865,* 2 vols. (Cleveland: Arthur H. Clark Co., 1928), 2:168; Circular no. 27, Provost Marshal General's Office, 19 July 1864, "Negro in the Military Service," NA, 4:2696; *ORA,* ser. 3, vol. 5: 659 (sec. 14, act of 4 July 1864), ser. 3, vol. 4: 564 (Circular no. 60, Adjutant General's Office, 1 August 1864). The pay raise was even more significant for noncommissioned officers who earlier got the same ten dollars as privates. A sergeant now was paid twenty dollars and a corporal eighteen (Thomas Holdup Stevens Hamersly, ed. comp., *Complete Regular Army Register of the United States: For One Hundred Years [1779–1879]* [Washington, D.C.: Thomas H. S. Hamersly, 1880], 192).

3. Washington, James, Campbell, Bhillet, Crayon, Gilworth, and Williams, CMSR, NA.

4. Lumpkins, CMSR and pension record, Case Files of Approved Veterans Who Served in the Army and Navy Mainly in the Civil War and the War with Spain, 1861–1934, Civil War and Later Pension Files, Records of the Veterans Administration, RG 15, NA (hereafter cited as pension record, NA); Johnson and Hubbard, CMSR, NA.

5. Descriptive Book, Twenty-ninth USCT, RG 94, NA; Illinois, Military and Naval Department, *Report of the Adjutant General of the State of Illinois,* 9 vols. (Springfield: Baker, Bailache and Co., 1867), 8:785–86; Berlin, CMSR and pension record, NA.

6. *Illinois Adjutant General's Report,* 8:787–94; Williams, Rowens, Desha, and Elam, CMSR and pension records, NA; Indiana, Adjutant General, *Report of the Adjutant General of the State of Indiana, 1861–1865, Containing Indiana in the War of the Rebellion and Statistics and Documents,* 8 vols. (Indianapolis: Alexander H. Conner, 1865–69), 7:670–82.

7. Stanley, Easton, and Williams, CMSR and pension records, NA.

8. Gregory and Wilson, ibid.

9. Douglas, ibid.

10. Sherwood, ibid.

11. *Illinois Adjutant General's Report,* 8:778–96; letter, 27 August 1864,

Miscellaneous Letters, Twenty-ninth USCT, RG 94, NA; Compiled Service Records Showing Service of Military Units in Volunteer Organizations, U.S. Colored Troops, Record of Events, Twenty-ninth U.S. Col'd Inf., RG 94, NA (Record of Events, NA); Frank J. Welcher, *The Union Army, 1861–1865: Organization and Operations*, 2 vols. (Bloomington: Indiana University Press, 1989), 1:435; *New York Times*, 21 August 1864; *Forney's War Press* (Phila.), 27 August 1864; Joseph Mark Califf, *Record of Service of the Seventh Regiment United States Colored Troops . . .* (1878; reprint, Freeport, N.Y.: Books for Libraries Press, 1971), 45; Robert A. Webb, "The Heights of Glory," *Washington Post*, 18 February 1990.

12. Letters, Lee to Grant, 1 October; Grant to Lee, 2 October; Lee to Grant, 3 October; Grant to Lee, 3 October; Butler to Robert Olds, 12 October; Lee to Seddon, ? October; Lee to Grant, 19 October; Grant to Butler, 20 October 1864, *ORA*, ser. 2, vol. 7: 206–7, 909, 914, 967, 970, 991, 1010–12, 1015; Jack D. Foner, *Blacks and the Military in American History: A New Perspective* (New York: Praeger Publishers, 1974), 44; General Orders no. 252, Adjutant General's Office, 31 July 1863, "Negro in the Military Service," NA, 7:1097.

13. Letters, Butler to Grant, 19 August; Grant to Butler, 20 August; Meade to Grant; 26 August 1864, "Negro in the Military Service," NA, 5:2753–54, 2756; *Forney's War Press*, 17 September 1864.

14. Record of Events, NA.

15. Ibid.

16. *Illinois Adjutant General's Report*, 8:780–81; Mitchell, Burke, and Foreman, CMSR, NA; Clark, Winston, Frazier, Lee, and Turner, CMSR and pension records, NA.

17. *Illinois Adjutant General's Report*, 8:781–82; Ellsworth, CMSR and pension record, NA; Carter, Davenport, and Shores, CMSR, NA.

18. *Illinois Adjutant General's Report*, 8:785–86; Smith (Young), CMSR and pension record, NA.

19. Washington, CMSR and pension record, NA.

20. *Illinois Adjutant General's Report*, 8:787–88; Hughes, CMSR and pension record, NA.

21. Descriptive Book, NA, and Morning Reports, Twenty-ninth Regiment of USC Troops, by Month, RG 94, NA.

22. *Illinois Adjutant General's Report*, 8:789–96; N. Ashby and W. J. Ashby, CMSR and pension records, NA; M. Ashby and W. H. Ashby, CMSR, NA.

23. Demby, Costley, and Polk, CMSR and pension records, NA; Wilson and Ford, CMSR, NA; Clothing Account Books, Howard.

24. Tross and Dorsey, CMSR and pension records, NA.

25. Lindsey, ibid.

26. McCabe (Mitchell), ibid.

27. A. Ewing, G. Ewing, J. Ewing, J. R. Green, and A. Green, ibid.

28. *Illinois Adjutant General's Report*, 8:796–802.

29. Ibid., 3:694–988, 8:802–5.

30. Ibid., 8:779, 782, 792; Williams, Cofield, Robinson, CMSR, NA; Hopson and Bird, CMSR and pension records, NA.

31. Burke and Mitchell, CMSR and pension records, NA.

32. Bogart, ibid.

33. Alexander, Baynard, and Ender, ibid.

34. Murry, Douglas, Howard, and Stewart, ibid.

35. Special Orders no. 19, Ninth Army Corps, 13 September 1864, Ferrero's battle report, 29 October 1864, "Negro in the Military Service," NA, 4:3359–3403; Welcher, *Union Army,* 1:437; *ORA,* 40 (pt. 1): 159, (pt. 3): 888; Noah Andre Trudeau, *The Last Citadel, Petersburg, Virginia, June 1864–April 1865* (Boston: Little, Brown, 1991), 225.

36. Descriptive Book and Morning Reports, NA; Aiken, Eddowes, Hassler, Heusted, Johnston, Palmer, Sanders, G. Smith, and J. Smith, CMSR and pension records, NA; Brownell, CMSR, NA; Muster Rolls, Twenty-ninth USCT, box 5399, RG 94, NA; Applications for Appointments (in the Colored Units), 1863–1865, Boxes 9–10, RG 94, NA.

37. Descriptive Book and Morning Reports, NA; Southwell, Fickes, Granger, Newton, Ferguson, Wentz, CMSR, NA; Applications for Appointments, Boxes 9–10, NA.

38. Miscellaneous letters, NA; Chapman, Little, CMSR and pension records, NA; *Illinois Adjutant General's Report,* 8:777, 796; Descriptive Book, NA.

39. Descriptive Book, NA; Barnes, Gosper, CMSR, NA; Muster Rolls, NA; Edwin S. Redkey, "Black Chaplains in the Union Army," *Civil War History* 33 (December 1987): 331–50; Francis B. Heitman, *Historical Register and Dictionary of the United States Army, from Its Organization, September 29, 1789, to March 2, 1903,* 2 vols. (1903; reprint, Urbana: University of Illinois Press, 1965), 1:411; Roster of Commissioned Officers of the Twenty-ninth USCT, 7 December 1864, Miscellaneous Letters, NA.

40. *Illinois Adjutant General's Report,* 8:778–96; Gunnell, CMSR, NA; Geter, Day, and Carroll, CMSR and pension records, NA.

41. Miller, Senia, and Ringold, CMSR and pension records, NA.

42. Morgan, Scott, and Hogan, ibid. Scott's widow was pensioned in 1867, the award dating from the day the regiment was mustered out, absent any information on the time of the soldier's death.

43. The men were David Bell, Henry Ellis, John Washington, Sidney Jones, Thomas Tyler, Josiah Woolsey, Thomas Queen, and John Williams (CMSR, NA); Scott, CMSR and pension record, NA.

44. Benson, CMSR and pension record; Telford, Berbo, and Wallace, CMSR, NA.

45. Hawkins, Smith, Mabree, and Newton, CMSR and pension records, NA; Miller, CMSR, NA.

46. Jackson, Yugando, Brown, Washington, and Wright, CMSR, NA; Jefferson and Limehouse, CMSR and pension records, NA.

47. Davis and Watkins, CMSR, NA.

48. Descriptive Book, NA; Sanders and Hipwell, CMSR and pension records, NA; Applications for Appointments, box 10, NA.

49. Lee and Bell, CMSR and pension records, NA.

50. Lee, Bell, Curtis, Cutchimber, Downes, Morgan, and Murray, ibid.

51. Descriptive Book, NA; Dunn and Rollman, CMSR and pension records, NA; Application for Appointments, box 9, NA.

52. *Illinois Adjutant General's Report,* 8:779; Buckner, Freeman, and Mumford, CMSR and pension records, NA.

53. *Illinois Adjutant General's Report,* 8:782–88; Patterson (King), CMSR and pension record, NA.

54. *Illinois Adjutant General's Report,* 8:790–98; Bradyman, CMSR and pension record, NA; Clevis, CMSR, NA.

55. *Illinois Adjutant General's Report,* 8:798–802; Arbuckle, Robinson, Settles, and Watkins, CMSR and pension records, NA.

56. Letter to the regiment and General Orders no. 5, Adjutant General's Office, 10 and 25 February 1865, respectively, Miscellaneous Papers, NA.

57. Special Orders no. 27, Adjutant General's Office, 18 January 1865, Issuances, Regimental Papers, Twenty-ninth USCT, box 26, RG 94, NA; Descriptive Book, NA; Royce, CMSR, NA.

58. Descriptive Book, NA; Brown, Camp, Hindekoper, CMSR, NA; Heitman, *Historical Register,* 1:276; *Illinois Adjutant General's Report,* 8:777; Muster Rolls, NA.

59. Scott, Brown, Wood, and Blue, CMSR and pension records, NA; Francis, CMSR, NA.

60. *ORA,* 40 (pt. 1): 71, (pt. 3): 888, 1113; Welcher, *Union Army,* 1:437, 504; Trudeau, *Last Citadel,* 378; General Orders no. 297, Adjutant General's Office, 3 December 1864, "Negro in the Military Service," NA, 4:2840; Ezra J. Warner, *Generals in Blue: Lives of the Union Commanders* (Baton Rouge: Louisiana State University Press, 1964), 1015; 6 December 1864, dispatch, R. J. M. Blackett, ed., *Thomas Morris Chester, Black Civil War Correspondent: His Dispatches from the Virginia Front* (Baton Rouge: Louisiana State University Press, 1989), 201–2.

61. General Orders no. 3, Second Division, Twenty-fifth Army Corps, 8 December 1864, Issuances, NA; *ORA,* 40 (pt. 1): 143; Record of Events, NA; Porter's 2 February 1892 affidavit in Mackay, pension record, NA.

62. Williams, Heusted, and Lilly, CMSR and pension records, NA.

63. Clay, Campbell, and Wilson, ibid.

64. Record of Events, NA; Richard Wayne Lykes, *Petersburg National Military Park, Virginia,* National Park Service Historical Handbook Series no. 13 (1951; reprint, Washington, D.C.: Government Printing Office, 1961), 29; Inspector General's Report for March and April 1865, Washington, D.C., May 1865, Letters, Orders, Circulars and Miscellaneous Reports Received, box 2, Twenty-fifth Army Corps, U.S. Army Continental Commands (1821–1920), RG 393, NA.

65. General Orders, no number, but bound between nos. 20 and 21, 20 February 1865, Letter Book, Twenty-fifth Army Corps, vol. 9, RG 393, NA.

66. Morning Reports and Record of Events, NA; George Washington Williams, *A History of the Negro Troops in the War of the Rebellion, 1861–1865* (1888; reprint, New York: Bergman Publishers, 1968), 293.

67. Smith, CMSR and pension record, NA; *Illinois Adjutant General's Report,* 8:777–78, 783, 786, 794.

68. J. Brown (Shorter) and Young, CMSR and pension records, NA; J. Brown, Demby, Reed, and White, CMSR, NA.

CHAPTER 5: WAR'S END AND FINAL SERVICE

1. Granger, Conant, Parker, Wicham, and Broderick, Compiled (Military) Service Records, Records of the Office of the Adjutant General, Record Group 94, National Archives (CMSR, NA); Muster Rolls, Twenty-ninth USCT, box 5399, RG 94, NA; Endorsements and Letter Book, Twenty-fifth Army Corps, vol. 7, U.S. Army Continental Commands (1821–1920), RG 393, NA.

2. Morning Reports, Twenty-ninth Regiment of USC Troops, by Month, RG 94, NA; Patton, pension record, Case Files of Approved Veterans Who Served in the Army and Navy in the Civil War and the War with Spain . . . , 1861–1934, Records of the Veterans Administration, RG 15, NA (hereafter cited as Morning Reports, NA, and pension record, NA, respectively).

3. Hughes and Wood, CMSR and pension records, NA.

4. Morning Reports, NA; Descriptive Book of the Twenty-ninth Regiment, U.S. Colored Troops, RG 94, NA (Descriptive Book, NA); Clothing Account Books, Twenty-ninth USCT, Moorland Springarn Research Center, Howard University, Washington, D.C.; Horace Porter, "Five Forks and the Pursuit of Lee," *Battles and Leaders of the Civil War,* ed. Robert U. Johnson and Clarence Buel, 4 vols. (1887–88; reprint, Secaucus, N.J.: Castle, 1989), 4:708–9.

5. Chaplain Barnes's report for April 1865, Miscellaneous Letters, Twenty-ninth USCT, RG 94, NA; U.S. Department of War, *The War of the Rebellion: A Compilation of the Official Records of the Union and Confederate Armies,* 127 vols. (Washington, D.C.: Government Printing Office, 1880–1902) (hereafter cited as *ORA*), ser.1, vol. 40 (pt. 1): 143 (Colonel Woodward's report, 27 April 1865), vol. 42 (pt. 3): 213, 697; Compiled Military Records, Showing Service of Military Units in Volunteer Military Organizations, U.S. Colored Troops, Record of Events, Twenty-ninth U.S. Col'd Inf., RG 94, NA (Record of Events, NA).

6. Descriptive Book, NA; Beeson, and Cassels, CMSR and pension records, NA; Shipman, CMSR, NA.

7. Vantrece, Harris, Cole, Williams, and King, CMSR and pension records, NA.

8. Cole, ibid.; Martin and Wilson, CMSR, NA.

9. Harris, Williams, and Costley, CMSR and pension records, NA.

10. Collins, ibid.

11. Turpin and Curtis, ibid.; Fisher and Holland, CMSR, NA.

12. Record of Events, NA.

13. *ORA,* ser. 1, vol. 40 (pt. 1): 143 (Woodyard's 27 April 1865 report), vol. 46 (pt. 3): 990 (Hallack's 1 May 1865 letter); "Negro in the Military Service of the United States," RG94, NA, 4:3631, 3638.

14. Blackett, *Chester Dispatches,* 341; General Orders no. 17, 28 April 1865, Headquarters, Twenty-ninth USCT, Order Book, RG 94, NA.

15. Washington, CMSR and pension record, NA; Gilworth and Green, CMSR, NA. A field officer court was used to deal with minor offenses and could not impose severe sentences. A general court made up of several officers judged all serious infractions and officers charged with any offense.

16. Ulysses Simpson Grant, *Memoirs of Ulysses S. Grant,* 2 vols. (New York: Charles L. Webster and Co., 1885), 2:546; report, Sheridan to chief of staff, 14 November 1866, U.S. House of Representatives, *Annual Report of the Secretary of War* (1866), Exec. Doc. no. 1, 39th Cong., 2d sess., 1867, 44–46.

17. Califf, *Record of Service,* 71; General Orders no. 50, Headquarters, Department of Virginia, 1 May 1865, "Negro in the Military Service," NA, 4:3635; *ORA,* vol. 46 (pt. 3): 1062; Frederick H. Dyer, *A Compendium of the War of the Rebellion* (1908; reprint, Dayton, Ohio: Press of the Morningside Bookshop, 1978), 1728; Blackett, *Chester Dispatches,* 331; Frederick W. Browne, *My Service in the U.S. Colored Cavalry,* Paper read before the Ohio Commandery, Military Order of the Loyal Legion of the United States, 4 March 1908, *Sketches of War History, 1861–1865* (Cincinnati: R. Clark and Co., 1908), 11.

18. Joseph T. Glatthaar, *Forged in Battle: The Civil War Alliance of Black Soldiers and White Officers* (New York: Free Press, 1990), 218–19; Adjutant General's Office, letter, 20 May 1864, *ORA,* ser. 3, vol. 5: 28–29; Adjutant General's Office, letter, 29 April 1865, Issuances, Regimental Papers (box 26), RG 94, NA; Blackett, *Chester Dispatches,* 342; Williams, CMSR and pension record, NA. The only soldiers shot in Texas were Kentuckians 1st Sgt. William Kease and Sgt. Doctor Moore, 116th U.S. Colored Infantry, executed at Ringgold Barracks on 11 August 1865 for mutiny at Petersburg about 12 May (Robert I. Alotta, *Civil War Justice: Union Army Executions under Lincoln* [Shippensburg, Pa.: White Mane Publishing Co., 1989], 172).

19. Special Orders no. 134, 18 May 1865, Special Orders from the Headquarters, Twenty-fifth Army Corps, 1865–66, vol. 683, RG 94, NA; *ORA,* vol. 48 (pt. 3): 1168.

20. Annual report, Quartermaster Department to Stanton, 8 November 1865, *ORA,* ser. 3, vol. 5: 228, ser. 1, vol. 40 (pt. 1): 143, vol. 48 (pt. 3): 1253; Record of Events, NA; telegram, 24 May 1865, Quartermaster, City Point; report, Lt. Col. H. B. Blood, chief quartermaster, Twenty-fifth Army Corps, n.d.; Report of Animals and Material for Transportation, n.d.; Statement of Embarkation and Sailing of the Second Division Twenty-fifth Army Corps from Hampton Roads,

Va., Brig. Gen. R. H. Jackson, n.d., Letters, Orders, Circulars and Miscellaneous Reports Received (January 1865–66), box 2, RG 393, NA; Brown's diary, Civil War Miscellaneous Collection, U.S. Army Military History Institute, Carlisle Barracks, Pennsylvania (USAMHI).

21. Browne, *Service in Colored Cavalry,* 11; Alexander H. Newton, *Out of the Briars: An Autobiography and Sketch of the Twenty-ninth Connecticut Volunteers* (Philadelphia: AME Book Concern, 1910), 69–70. The Twenty-ninth's Chaplain Barnes also complained about profanity, but he blamed the poor example of the regiment's officers which gave "increased license" to the enlisted men (Monthly Chaplain's Report, 31 May 1865, Miscellaneous Letters, NA).

22. Morning Reports, NA; letter, Weitzel to adjutant general, Washington, D.C., 30 March 1865, Endorsements and Letter Book, Twenty-fifth Army Corps, vol. 7, RG 393, NA; Henry, Ridley, and Evans, CMSR and pension records, NA.

23. *Illinois Adjutant General's Report,* 8:778–802.

24. Record of Events, NA; *ORA,* vol. 46 (pt. 1): 143; Daggett, CMSR, NA. Brazos de Santiago is at Port Isabel, near the south end of Padre Island; it was the site of General Taylor's supply base in 1846 during the war with Mexico.

25. S. Hemenway, "Observations on Scurvy, and Its Causes among U.S. Colored Troops of the 25th Army Corps, during Spring and Summer of 1865," *Chicago Medical Examiner* 7 (October 1866): 582, 585; Sepp, Clemens, and Marks, CMSR, NA; Easley, CMSR and pension record, NA.

26. Monthly Chaplain's Report, 30 June 1865, Miscellaneous Letters, NA; Newton, *Out of the Briars,* 71–73; Smith and Joseph Griffin (Company I), CMSR and pension records, NA.

27. *Illinois Adjutant General's Report,* 8:778–802; Robinson, Wilson, White, and Ash, CMSR, NA; Shaw, Anderson, Colwell, and Buchanan, CMSR and pension records, NA.

28. Griffin (25 August 1865 letter to his family), Heithman, Barker, Ross, Carter, Locks, and Gash (Mackay's 1886 affidavit), CMSR and pension records, NA; *Military Medical and Surgical Essays* (Philadelphia: J. B. Lippincott and Co., 1864), 176.

29. Grant's 21 May 1865, order, Joseph T. Wilson, *The Black Phalanx: A History of Negro Soldiers in the United States in the Wars of 1776–1810, 1861–'65* (Hartford: American Publishing Co., 1892), 461; Sheridan's report, 11 November 1866, *Annual Report of the Secretary of War* (1866), 46–47; Califf, *Record of Service,* 74.

30. Sheridan's report, 11 November 1866, 48; Newton, *Out of the Briars,* 78; letters from soldiers to editor, *Christian Recorder,* 29 July and 9 September 1865; Ringold, Polland, and Butler, CMSR, NA; Johnson, CMSR and pension record, NA.

31. Royce's report, 5 July 1865, inspection report, Headquarters, Twenty-fifth Army Corps, 11 July 1865, Royce's letter, 8 October 1865, Miscellaneous Letters, NA; Company F's 28 June 1865, entry, Morning Reports, NA; Daggett

and Brownell, CMSR, NA; Court Martial Order no. 3, Department of the South, 10 October 1865; General Orders no. 16, Third Brigade, mid-June 1865, Royce's undated roster, Issuances, NA.

32. Record of court-martial, Punch, CMSR and pension record, NA; Cotton, OMSR, NA.

33. Record of Events, NA.

34. Cooper, Arbuckle, Cole, and Cruthers, CMSR and pension records, NA.

35. Monthly Chaplain's Reports, 31 July and 31 August 1865, Miscellaneous Letters, NA; Newton, *Out of the Briars,* 82; Brown Diary, USAMHI; *Illinois Adjutant General's Report,* 8:778–802.

36. *Illinois Adjutant General's Report,* 8:778–802; Sandy and Harris, CMSR and pension records, NA; Price, CMSR, NA.

37. *Illinois Adjutant General's Report,* 8:778–802; Parker, CMSR, NA; Yates, CMSR and pension record, NA.

38. *Illinois Adjutant General's Report,* 8:778–802; letter, Royce to Bureau for Colored Troops, 7 September 1865, Letters and Endorsements Book, Twenty-ninth USCT, RG 94, NA.

39. Grant, *Memoirs,* 2:546; telegrams, Adjutant General's Office to Sheridan, New Orleans, 1 August and 8 September 1865, *Annual Report of the Secretary of War* (1866), 75, 77; Special Orders no. 29, Department of Texas, Galveston, 16 September 1865, Miscellaneous Letters, NA.

40. General Orders no. 63, Twenty-fifth Army Corps, 28 September 1865, Letter Book, Twenty-fifth Army Corps, vol. 9, RG 393, NA; Special Orders no. 250, Twenty-fifth Army Corps, 8 October 1865, Issuances, NA; Circular no. 19, Adjutant General's Office, 16 May 1865, *Annual Report of the Secretary of War* (1866), 67; *Illinois Adjutant General's Report,* 1:133, 161; General Orders no. 65, Twenty-fifth Army Corps, 5 October 1865, General Orders no. 2, Adjutant General's Office, 6 January 1866, "Negro in the Military Service," NA, 4:3638, 3735; Morning Reports, NA; report, Second Division, Twenty-fifth Army Corps, to assistant adjutant general, Washington, D.C., (20?) October 1865, General Orders no. 94, Adjutant General's Office, 15 May 1865, Miscellaneous Letters, NA; Special Orders no. 263, Twenty-fifth Army Corps, 25 October 1865, Special Orders from the Twenty-fifth Army Corps, 1865–66, vol. 683, RG 94, NA.

41. Cowan, Henderson, and Jones, CMSR, NA.

42. Telegram, assistant adjutant general, Military Division of the Gulf, 8 November 1866, Miscellaneous Letters, NA; *Daily Illinois State Journal,* 13 November 1865; General Orders no. 101, Adjutant General's Office, 30 May, and no. 114, 15 June 1865, *Annual Report of the Secretary of War* (1866), 64–65; Special Orders no. 263, Twenty-fifth Army Corps, 25 October 1865, Special Orders, vol. 683, RG 94, NA.

43. *Illinois Adjutant General's Report,* 1:80–81, 84, 8:777–802; letter to Adjutant General's Office, Washington, D.C., 21 November 1865, Miscellaneous Letters, NA; Wells and McCabe, CMSR and pension records, NA; Ezra J. Warner,

Generals in Blue: Lives of the Union Commanders (Baton Rouge: Louisiana State University Press, 1964), 9.

44. Provost Marshal Order to commander of "Police Jail," New Orleans, 11 November 1865, letter, Twenty-ninth USCT to mustering officer, Springfield, 25 October 1865, Miscellaneous Letters, NA; letter, Adjutant General's Office to Oglesby, 20 May 1865, *ORA*, ser. 3, vol. 5: 28–29.

45. Daily Illinois State Journal, 21, 22, and 23 November 1865; Robert B.Howard, *Illinois: A History of the Prairie State* (Grand Rapids, Mich.: William B. Eerdmans Publishing Co., 1972), 323–24.

46. Douglas and Dorsey, pension records, NA; receipt for colors and records from Royce signed by Brigadier General Oakes, 24 November 1865, Miscellaneous Letters, NA. The colors do not appear in later state adjutant general flag inventories.

47. Hill, Nelson, and Hawkins, CMSR and pension records, NA.

48. Report, Bureau for Colored Troops, 18 November 1865, *ORA,* ser. 3, vol. 5: 138; vol. 4: 1270; CMSR, NA; *Illinois Adjutant General's Report,* 8:694–98.

49. *Illinois Adjutant General's Report,* 8:777–802; Descriptive Book, NA; Clothing Records, Howard; Dyer, *Compendium,* 1728; Fox, *Regimental Losses,* 591; reports, Adjutant General's Office, Washington, D.C., 17 March and 14 November 1866, *ORA,* ser. 3, vol. 5: 669–70, 1030.

50. Report, Adjutant General's Office, 14 November 1866, *ORA,* ser. 3, vol. 5: 668–69; George F. Sutherland, "The Negro in the Late War," Wisconsin Commandery, Military Order of the Loyal Legion of the United States, *War Papers* (Milwaukee: Burdick, Armitage and Allen, 1891), 1:180; Joseph K. Barnes, ed., *The Medical and Surgical History of the War of the Rebellion (1861–65),* 6 vols. (Washington, D.C.: Government Printing Office, 1870–88), vol. 1.1:664–65, 685, 705, 712. There were thirty homicides, nine suicides, and thirty-nine executions among black troops.

51. *ORA,* ser. 3, vol. 5: 668–69; Indiana, Adjutant General's Office, *Report of the Adjutant General of the State of Indiana, 1861–1865, Containing Indiana in the War of the Rebellion and Statistics and Documents,* 8 vols. (Indianapolis: Alexander H. Connor, 1865–69), 1:5, 31.

52. George M. Fredrickson, *The Black Image in the White Mind: The Debate on Afro-American Character and Destiny, 1817–1914* (New York: Harper and Row, 1971), 168.

CHAPTER 6: THE LATER YEARS

1. William Henry Glasson, *Federal Military Pensions in the United States* (New York: Oxford University Press, 1918), 124, 234.

2. Ibid., 234–36, 244. Widows who had married a veteran after 1890 were not eligible, but there were exceptions.

3. Pension records for individual soldiers are in the series Case Files of Approved Veterans Who Served in the Army and Navy Mainly in the Civil War and the War with Spain ("Civil War and Later Survivors' Certificates"), 1861–1934, Civil War and Later Pension Files, Records of the Veterans Administration, Record Group 15, National Archives (pension record, NA). An individual soldier's file contains all applications made by him or his dependent wife, minor children, and other dependent relatives, primarily mothers. Files are indexed on microfilm by soldiers' names and also by companies in regiments. A file always has an application number or numbers and will have a certificate number for each approved application. Generally, the file with an application that did not result in a pension often cannot be retrieved. A soldier's file in Compiled (Military) Service Records, Records of the Office of the Adjutant General, 1780–1917, RG 94, National Archives (CMSR, NA), usually contains only sketchy information. At the time the regiment's soldiers applied for pensions the Bureau of Pensions, Department of the Interior, was the responsible agency that created and maintained the files in Record Group 15

4. Quoting "Stay of Embezzlement Revived: While Treasurer of the Veterans' Home, He Appropriated the Fund of that Institution," *San Francisco Daily Call,* 2 October 1897, Royce, pension record, NA. The widow Isabella Annetta Mason Bross and her son, Nelson Mason, born in 1860, both living on Michigan Avenue in Chicago, were pensioned effective the day of Lieutenant Colonel Bross's death at the crater (Bross, pension record, NA).

5. Smith, pension record, NA.

6. Rogers, ibid.

7. The soldier used the name under which he had entered the army until, he said, "I was arrested in Kansas City Kans. then I gave my name as Chuset Wells [he was imprisoned as Chary Wells]" (Wells, ibid.).

8. Daggett, ibid. Daggett's military record contains a note, Record and Pension Office, War Department, 31 October 1899, "The notation of May 24, 1884 [not found], is canceled for the reason that the sentence of the general court martial in the case . . . was never carried into effect" (Daggett, CMSR, NA). Whether Daggett was actually dismissed remains in doubt.

9. Kelly, CMSR and pension record, NA.

10. Coleman, pension record, NA.

11. "'Ben Turner' Stricken from Pension Rolls," *Taylorville Breeze,* 27 April 1909; Turner, ibid.

12. Douglas, ibid.

13. Dorsey, Limehouse, and Lewis, ibid.

14. Steward, ibid.

15. Cole, ibid.

16. Williams(Bell), ibid.

17. Owens(Coleman), ibid.

18. Hawkins, Logan, and Adam Plegatt, ibid. Williams has no pension file

(Williams, CMSR, NA).

19. Magruder and Morris, pension records, NA.

20. Harris, ibid.

21. Sherwood, ibid.

22. Gilmore, ibid. Although the envelope is in the file, the photograph is missing.

23. Thomas and Ringold, ibid.

24. Sewell, Sims, and Bernard, ibid.

25. Marlow and Arbuckle, ibid.

26. Abrams, ibid.

27. Easton/McLean, ibid.

28. Morgan/Barnes, ibid.

29. Powell and Nelson, ibid.

30. Arbuckle, ibid.

31. Barker and Guard, ibid.

32. Foggery and Sims, ibid.

33. McKenney and Griffin, ibid.

34. Clay, ibid.

35. Belden, ibid.

36. South, ibid.

37. Carter and Christine, ibid.

38. Wickham, ibid.

39. Dunn, ibid.

40. Reed, ibid.

41. McKeever, Taylor, and Ewing, ibid.

42. Charles South changed his name in 1884 to Charles S. Walden on the grounds that when he joined the army he used "the name of the white man to whom I belonged and did not know what my proper name was at that time." His preferred name was "from old Dr. Walden, now dead," who was no relation but might have trained South in medicine (Charles South, ibid.). Collins South, ibid.

43. Mackay, ibid.; *Dallas Daily News,* 24 March 1904.

44. Francis B. Heitman, *Historical Register and Dictionary of the United States Army, from Its Organization, September 29, 1789, to March 2, 1903* (1903; reprint, Urbana: University of Illinois Press, 1965), 1:411; Evans, pension record, NA. Fee's service is reconstructed from several depositions he made supporting pension applications of soldiers of the Twenty-ninth USCT.

45. Rollman, CMSR and pension record, NA.

46. Mackay quoted in McKenney, pension record, NA; Porter, ibid.

47. Heitman, *Historical Register,* 276, 899; Smith, pension record, NA.

48. Northup and Gibbs, pension records, NA.

49. Jackson and Hawker(Wolfin), ibid.

50. Liggons and Leonard, ibid.

51. Lee, ibid.
52. Ferguson, ibid.
53. Criseman, ibid.
54. Brown, ibid.
55. Knapp, Fickes, and Eddows, ibid.
56. Southwell and Newton, ibid.
57. Barnes, ibid.
58. Smith, ibid.
59. Granger, ibid.
60. Killion, Demby, and Cole, ibid.
61. Ashby and Madison, ibid.
62. Fields and Cooper, ibid.
63. Smith and McAllister, ibid.
64. Copeland, ibid.
65. Downes, ibid.
66. Clay, Gosper, Easley, and Mason, ibid.
67. Henderson, Mudd, Jones, Winyard, and Hunter, ibid. Pvt. Henry Johnson, an Anne Arundel County, Md., draftee, went to work for his old master after release from the army; moving to the District of Columbia, he sometimes did chores for Lieutenant Sanders, who was a retired minister there (Johnson, ibid.).
68. Kay and South, ibid.

Bibliography

UNPUBLISHED MATERIAL

Blassingame, John Wesley. "The Organization and Use of Negro Troops in the Union Army, 1863–1865." Master's thesis, Howard University, Washington, D.C., 1961.

Drinkard, Dorothy Lee. "A Regimental History of the Twenty-ninth Infantry, United States Colored Troops, 1864–1865." Master's thesis, Howard University, 1963.

Fort Ward Museum and Historical Park, Alexandria, Virginia, Morgan W. Carr MS letter from a private collection.

Moorland Spingarn Research Center, Howard University, Washington, D.C., Clothing Account Books, Twenty-ninth Infantry, U.S. Colored Troops (USCT).

U.S. Library of Congress, Washington, D.C., Documents Division, William Hamilton Papers.

U.S. National Archives, War Records Division, Washington, D.C.

Records of the Office of the Adjutant General, 1780–1917, Record Group 94.

Applications for Appointments (in the Colored Units), 1863–1865, boxes 3, 4, 9–11.

Compiled (Military) Service Records Twenty-ninth USCT, boxes 41262–81.

Compiled Military Records, Showing Service of Military Units in Volunteer Military Organizations, U.S. Colored Troops, Record of Events, Twenty-ninth U.S. Colored Infantry.

Descriptive Book of the Twenty Ninth Regiment, U.S. Colored.

Issuances, Regimental Papers, box 26, Twenty-ninth USCT.

Letters and Endorsements Book, Twenty-ninth USCT.

List of Commissioned Officers by Regiment, USCT.

Morning Reports—Twenty-ninth Regiment of USC Troops, by Month.

Miscellaneous Book, Twenty-ninth USCT.

Miscellaneous Letters, Twenty-ninth USCT.

Muster Rolls, Twenty-ninth USCT.

Order Book, Twenty-ninth USCT.

"The Negro in the Military Service of the United States, 1607–1889," 7 vols., microfilm.

Bibliography

Special Orders from the Headquarters of the Twenty-fifth Army Corps, and other Records of the Ninth and Twenty-fifth Army Corps.
——— U.S. Army Continental Commands (1821–1920), Record Group 393. Orders, letters, and inspection and station reports for Ninth and Twenty-fifth Army Corps.
Compiled (Military) Service Records, Twenty-ninth USCT, boxes 41262–81.
———U.S. Army Continental Commands (1821–1920), Record Group 393 Orders, letters, and inspection and station reports for Ninth and Twenty-fifth Army Corps.
———. Records of the Veterans Administration, Record Group 15, Case Files of Approved Veterans Who Served in the Army and Navy in the Civil War and the War with Spain ("Civil War and Later Survivor Certificates"), 1861–1934.

BOOKS

Agassiz, George, ed. *Meade's Headquarters, 1863–1865: Letters of Colonel Theodore Lyman from Wilderness to Appomattox.* Boston: Atlantic Monthly Press, 1922.

Alexander, William T. *History of the Negro Race in America.* 1887. Reprint. Westport: Negro Universities Press, 1986.

Alotta, Robert I. *Civil War Justice: Union Army Executions under Lincoln.* Shippensburg, Pa.: White Mane Publishing Co., 1989.

Aptheker, Herbert. *The Negro in the Civil War.* New York: International Publishers, 1938.

Berlin, Ira, Barbara J. Fields, Thaviola Glymph, Joseph P. Reedy, and Leslie S. Rowland, eds. *Freedom: A Documentary History of Emancipation, 1861–1867.* Ser. 2: "The Black Military Experience." New York: Cambridge University Press, 1982.

Berwanger, Eugene H. *The Frontier against Slavery: Western Anti-Negro Prejudice and the Slavery Extension Controversy.* Urbana: University of Illinois Press, 1967.

Billings, Charles H. *Hardtack and Coffee; or, The Unwritten Story of Army Life.* 1889. Reprint. Gettysburg: Civil War Times, 1974.

Blackett, R. J. M., ed. *Thomas Morris Chester, Black Civil War Correspondent, His Dispatches from the Virginia Front.* Baton Rouge: Louisiana State University Press, 1989.

Blight, David W. *Frederick Douglass' Civil War: Keeping Faith in Jubilee.* Baton Rouge: Louisiana State University Press, 1989.

Boatner, Mark Mayo, III. *The Civil War Dictionary.* New York: David McKay Co., 1959.

Brockett, L. P., and Mary C. Vaughn. *Woman's Work in the Civil War: A Record of Heroism, Patriotism and Patience.* Philadelphia: Zeigler, McCurdy and Co., 1868.

Bibliography

Bowley, Freeman S. *The Petersburg Mine*. Paper read before the California Commandery, Military Order of the Local Legion of the United States, 6 November 1889. War paper no. 3. San Francisco: for the Commandery, 1889.

Brown, William Willis. *The Negro in the American Rebellion: His Heroism and Fidelity*. Boston: Lee and Shepard, 1867.

Browne, Frederick W. *My Service in the U.S. Colored Cavalry*. Paper read before Ohio Commandery, Military Order of the Loyal Legion of the United States, 4 March 1908. Sketches of War History, 1861–1865. Cincinnati: R. Clark and Co., 1908.

Califf, Joseph Mark. *Record of Service of the Seventh Regiment, U.S. Colored Troops, from September, 1863, to November, 1866, by an Officer of the Regiment*. 1878. Reprint. Freeport, N.Y.: Books for Libraries Press, 1971.

Catton, Bruce. *Grant Takes Command*. Boston: Little, Brown, 1968.

Cavanaugh, Mitchael Arthur, and William Marvel. *The Petersburg Campaign, The Battle of the Crater, "The Horrid Pit," June 25–August 6, 1864*. Vol. 10 of the Virginia Civil War Battles and Leaders series. Lynchburg: H. E. Howard, 1989.

Chase, James Judson. *The Charge at Day-Break: Scenes and Incidents at the Battle of the Mine Explosion, Near Petersburg, Va, July 30th, 1864*. Lewiston, Maine: Lewiston Journal, 1875.

Chetlain, Augustus L. *Recollections of Seventy Years*. Galena, Ill.: Gazette Publishing Co., 1899.

Cole, Arthur Charles. *The Era of the Civil War, 1848–1870*. Cultural History of Illinois series.1919. Reprint. Freeport, N.Y.: Books for Libraries Press, 1971.

Collins, William H., and Cicero F. Perry. *Past and Present of the City of Quincy and Adams County, Illinois*. Chicago: S. J. Clark Publishing Co., 1905.

Cornish, Dudley T. *The Sable Arm: Black Troops in the Union Army, 1861–1865*. Lawrence: University of Kansas Press, 1987.

Donovan, Timothy H., Jr., et al. *The American Civil War*. West Point Military History series. Wayne, N.J.: Avery Publishing Group, 1987.

Dowdey, Clifford, ed. *The Wartime Papers of R. E. Lee*. Boston: Little, Brown, 1961.

Dyer, Frederick H. *A Compendium of the War of the Rebellion*. 1908. Reprint. Dayton, Ohio: Press of Morningside Bookshop, 1978.

Foner, Jack D. *Blacks in the Military in American History: A New Perspective*. New York: Praeger Publisher, 1974.

Foote, Shelby. *The Civil War: A Narrative*. Vol. 3: *Red River to Appomattox*. New York: Vintage Books, 1986.

Fox, William Freeman. *Regimental Losses in the American Civil War, 1861–1865*. Albany: Albany Publishing Co., 1889.

Frassanito, William A. *Grant and Lee: The Virginia Campaign, 1864–1865*. New York: Charles Scribner's Sons, 1983.

Genosky, Landry. *People's History of Quincy and Adams County, Illinois: A Sesquicentennial History*. Quincy: Jost and Kiefer Printing Co., 1976.

Bibliography

Glatthaar, Joseph T. *Forged in Battle: The Civil War Alliance of Black Soldiers and White Officers.* New York: Free Press, 1990.

Grant, Ulysses Simpson. *Memoirs of Ulysses S. Grant.* Vol. 2. New York: Charles L. Webster and Co., 1885.

Guthrie, James M. *Camp-Fires of the Afro-American.* 1899. Reprint. New York: Johnson Reprint Corp., 1970.

Hamersly, Thomas Holdup Stevens. Ed. and comp. *Complete Army Register of the United States: For One Hundred Years (1779–1879).* Washington, D.C. Thomas H. S. Hamersly, 1880.

Hargrove, Hondon B. *Black Union Soldiers in the Civil War.* Jefferson, N.C.: McFarland and Co., 1988.

Heitman, Francis B. *Historical Register and Dictionary of the United States Army, from Its Organization, September 29, 1789, to March 2, 1903.* 2 vols. 1903. Reprint. Urbana: University of Illinois Press, 1965.

Hicken, Victor. *Illinois in the Civil War.* Urbana: University of Illinois Press, 1966.

Hollowell, Norwood P. *The Negro As a Soldier in the War of the Rebellion.* Boston: Little, Brown, 1897.

Howard, Robert P. *Illinois: A History of the Prairie State.* Grand Rapids, Mich.: William B. Eerdmans Publishing Co., 1972.

Illinois. Military and Naval Department. *Report of the Adjutant General of the State of Illinois.* 9 vols. Vols. 1 and 8. 1877. Reprint. Springfield: Phillips Bros., 1900–1901.

Indiana. Adjutant General. State of Indiana. *Report of the Adjutant General of the State of Indiana, 1861–1865, Containing Indiana in the War of the Rebellion and Statistics and Documents.* 8 vols. Vols. 1, 3, 6, and 7. Indianapolis: Alexander H. Conner, 1865–69.

Jackson, Harry F., and Thomas F. O'Donnell, eds. *Back Home in Oneida: Hermon Clark and His Letters.* Syracuse: Syracuse University Press, 1965.

Jimerson, Randall C. *The Private Civil War: Popular Thought during the Sectional Conflict.* Baton Rouge: Lousiana State University Press, 1988.

Leech, Margaret. *Reveille in Washington, 1860–1865.* New York: Harper and Brothers, 1941.

Litwack, Leon F. *North of Slavery: The Negro in the Free States, 1790–1860.* Chicago: University of Chicago Press, 1961.

Longstreet, Stephen. *Chicago, 1860–1919.* New York: David McKay Co., 1973.

Lord, Francis A. *They Fought for the Union.* New York: Bonanza Books, 1960.

Lykes, Richard Wayne. *Petersburg National Military Park, Virginia.* National Park Service Historical Handbook series no. 13. 1951. Reprint. Washington, D.C.: Government Printing Office, 1961.

McPherson, James M. *Marching toward Freedom: The Negro in the Civil War, 1861–1865.* New York: Alfred A. Knopf, 1965.

———. *The Negro's Civil War: How American Negroes Felt and Acted during the War for Union.* Rev. ed. 1965. Reprint. Urbana: University of Illinois Press, 1982.

———. *Ordeal by Fire: The Civil War and Reconstruction.* New York: Alfred A. Knopf, 1982.

———. *The Struggle for Equality: Abolitionists in the Civil War and Reconstruction.* Princeton: Princeton University Press, 1964.

McWhiney, Grady, and Perry D. Jamieson. *Attack and Die: Civil War Military Tactics and the Southern Heritage.* Tuscaloosa: University of Alabama Press, 1982.

Mahone, William. *The Battle of the Crater.* Facsimile reprint of original. Collingswood, N.J.: C. W. Historicals, n.d.

Marvel, William. *Burnside.* Chapel Hill: University of North Carolina Press, 1991.

Mays, Joe H. *Black Americans and Their Contributions toward Union Victory in the American Civil War, 1861–1865.* Lanham, Md.: University Press of America, 1984.

Nalty, Bernard C. *Strength for the Fight: A History of Black Americans in the Military.* New York: Free Press, 1986.

Newton, Alexander H. *Out of the Briars: An Autobiography and Sketch of the Twenty-ninth Connecticut Volunteers.* Philadelphia: AME Book Concern, 1910.

Owen, William Miller. *In Camp and Battle with the Washington Artillery of New Orleans.* Boston: Ticknor and Co., 1885.

Pleasants, Henry, Jr. *The Tragedy of the Crater.* 1938. Reprint. Washington, D.C.: Eastern National Park and Monument Association, 1975.

Porter, Horace. *Campaigning with Grant.* New York: Century Co., 1897.

Quarles, Benjamin. *The Negro in the Civil War.* Boston: Little, Brown, 1953.

Redkey, Edwin S., ed. *A Grand Army of Black Men: Letters from African-American Soldiers in the Union Army, 1861–1865.* New York: Cambridge University Press, 1992.

Reed, William Howell. *Hospital Life in the Army of the Potomac.* 2d ed. 1866. Reprint. Boston: N.p., 1891.

Richardson, James D., ed. *A Compilation of the Messages and Papers of the Presidents.* Vol. 7. New York: Bureau of National Literature, 1897.

Shannon, Fred Albert. *The Organization and Administration of the Union Army, 1861–1865.* 2 vols. Cleveland: Arthur H. Clark Co., 1928.

Smith, Page. *Trial by Fire.* Vol. 5 of *A People's History of the Civil War and Reconstruction.* New York: McGraw-Hill, 1982.

Sommers, Richard J. *Richmond Redeemed: The Siege of Petersburg.* Garden City, N.Y.: Doubleday, 1981.

Sparks, David S., ed. *Inside Lincoln's Army: The Diary of Marsena Rudolph Patrick, Provost Marshal General, Army of the Potomac.* New York: Thomas Yoselff, 1964.

Stine, J. H. *History of the Army of the Potomac.* Philadelphia: J. B. Rodgers Publishing Co., 1892.

Bibliography

[Swazey, Arthur]. *Memorial of Colonel John A. Bross, Twenty-ninth U.S. Colored Troops*. Chicago: Tribune Book and Job Office, 1865.

Trudeau, Noah Andre. *Bloody Roads South: The Wilderness to Cold Harbor, May–June 1864*. Boston: Little, Brown, 1989.

———. *The Last Citadel: Petersburg, Virginia, June 1864–April 1865*. Boston: Little, Brown, 1991.

U.S. Army. Adjutant General's Office. *Official Army Register of the Volunteer Forces of the United States Army for the Years 1861, '62, '63, '64, '65*. Pt. 8. Washington, D.C.: Government Printing Office, 1865.

U.S. Congress. Joint Committee on the Conduct of the War. *Report of the Joint Committee on the Conduct of the War on the Attack on Petersburg, on the 30th Day of July, 1864*. Senate Report no. 114, 38th Cong., 2d sess., 15 December 1864.

U.S. House of Representatives. *Annual Report of the Secretary of War*, 1866, 14 November 1866, Exec. Doc. no. 1, vol. 1, 39th Cong., 2d sess., 1867.

———. *Report of the Secretary of War*, 1865, 22 November 1865. Exec. Doc. no. 1, pts. 1–2, 39th Cong., 1st sess., 1866.

U.S. War Department. *The War of the Rebellion: A Compilation of the Official Records of the Union and Confederate Armies*. 128 vols. Washington, D.C.: U.S. Government Printing Office, 1880–1902.

Voegeli, V. Jacques. *Free but Not Equal: The Midwest and the Negro during the Civil War*. Chicago: University of Chicago Press, 1967.

Warner, Ezra J. *Generals in Blue: Lives of the Union Commanders*. Baton Rouge: Louisiana State University Press, 1964.

Welcher, Frank J. *The Union Army, 1861–1865, Organization and Operations*. Vol 1: *The Eastern Theater*. Bloomington: Indiana University Press, 1989.

Weld, Stephen Minot. *War Diary and Letters of Stephen Minot Weld, 1861–1865*. 2d ed. Boston: Massachusetts Historical Society, 1979.

Wells, J. W., and N. A. Strait. *Roster of All the Regimental Surgeons and Assistant Surgeons in the Late War and Hospital Service*. 1888. Reprint. San Francisco: Norman Publishing, 1990.

Westwood, Howard C. *Black Troops, White Commanders, and Freedmen during the Civil War*. Carbondale: Southern Illinois University Press, 1992.

Wheeler, Richard. *On Fields of Fury: From the Wilderness to the Crater, An Eyewitness History*. New York: HarperCollins, 1991.

Wiley, Bell Irvin. *The Life of Billy Yank: The Common Soldier of the Union*. Baton Rouge: Louisiana State University Press, 1971.

———. *The Life of Johnny Reb: The Common Soldier of the Confederacy*. Baton Rouge: Louisiana State University Press, 1943.

Wilkinson, Warren. *Mother, May You Never See the Sights I Have Seen: The Fifty-seventh Massachusetts Veteran Volunteers in the Army of the Potomac, 1864–1865*. New York: Harper and Row, 1990.

Williams, George Washington. *A History of the Negro Troops in the War of the Rebellion, 1861–1865.* 1888. Reprint. New York: Bergman Publishers, 1968.

Wilson, Joseph T. *The Black Phalanx: A History of Negro Soldiers of the United States in the Wars of 1775–1812, 1861–'65.* Hartford: American Publishing Co., 1892.

Wise, John Sergeant. *The End of an Era.* Ed. Curtis Carroll Davis. 1899. Reprint. New York: Thomas Yoseloff, 1965.

Wood, Forrest G. *Black Scare: The Racist Response to Emancipation and Reconstruction.* Berkeley: University of California Press, 1968.

ARTICLES

Abbott, Abial. "The Negro in the War of the Rebellion." Illinois Commandery, Military Order of the Loyal Legion of the United States. *Military Essays and Recollections,* 3:373–84. Chicago: Dial Press, 1899.

Ballou, Daniel R. "The Petersburg Mine." *National Tribune* (Washington, D.C.), 5 June 1913.

Bates, Delevan. "A Day with the Colored Troops." *National Tribune,* 30 January 1908.

Beller, James W. "The Mine Explosion." *National Tribune,* 20 June 1889.

Bernard, George S. "The Battle of the Crater." *Southern Historical Society Papers* 18 (1890): 1–38.

Blassingame, John Wesley. "Negro Chaplains in the Civil War." *Negro History Bulletin* 27 (October 1963): 23–24.

Bowley, Freeman S. "The Crater." *National Tribune,* 6 November 1884.

———. "The Petersburg Mine." California Commandery, Military Order of the Loyal Legion of the United States. *War Papers No. 3.* San Francisco: 1889.

Browne, Frederick W. "My Service in the U.S. Colored Cavalry." Ohio Commandery, Military Order of the Loyal Legion of the United States. *Sketches of War History, 1861–1865,* 4:. Cincinnati: R. Clark and Co., 1908.

Burbank, Horace H. "The Battle of the Crater." Maine Commandery, Military Order of the Loyal Legion of the United States. *War Papers,* 1:283–94. Portland: Thurston Press, 1898.

Carter, Solon A. "Fourteen Months' Service with Colored Troops." Massachusetts Commandery, Military Order of the Loyal Legion of the United States. *Civil War Papers,* vol. 1, no. 8, 155–79. Boston: For the Commandery, 1890.

Case, Ervin T. "Battle of the Mine." Rhode Island Soldiers and Sailors Historical Society. *Personal Narratives of the War of the Rebellion.* Ser. 2, no. 10. Providence: Sidney S. Rich, 1879.

Coit, James C. "The Battle of the Crater, July 30, 1864." *Southern Historical Society Papers* 10 (1882): 123–30.

Conner, Selden. "The Colored Troops." Maine Commandery, Military Order of the Loyal Legion of the United States. *War Papers,* 3:61–82. Portland: Lefavor-Tower Co., 1908.

Bibliography

de Trobriand, Regis. "Burnside Fumbles His Chance to Take Petersburg." In *The Blue and the Gray: The Story of the Civil War As Told by Participants,* ed. Henry S. Commager, 1017–21. New York: Bobbs-Merrill, 1950. Excerpted from *Four Years with the Army of the Potomac,* trans. George K. Dauchy, 608 ff. Boston: Ticknor and Co., 1889.

Dick, David B. "Resurgence of the Chicago Democracy, April–November, 1861." *Journal of the Illinois State Historical Society* 56 (Autumn 1963): 139–49.

Dyer, Brainerd. "The Treatment of Colored Union Troops by the Confederates, 1861–1865." *Journal of Negro History* 20 (July 1935): 273–86.

Fetherstone, John C. *Battle of the Crater.* Eyewitness Accounts of the Civil War. 1906. Reprint. Birmingham: Birmingham Public Library Press, 1987. Also published as "Battle of the Crater through Southern Eyes." *National Tribune,* 19 November 1925.

———. "Graphic Account of the Battle of the Crater." *Southern Historical Society Papers* 33 (1905): 358–74.

Furness, William Elliot. "The Negro As a Soldier." Illinois Commandery, Military Order of the Loyal Legion of the United States. *Military Essays and Recollections,* 2:457–88. Chicago: A. C. McClung and Co., 1894.

Gertz, Elmer. "The Black Laws of Illinois." *Journal of the Illinois State Historical Society* 56 (Autumn 1963): 454–73.

Hall, H. Seymour. "Mine Run to Petersburg." Kansas Commandery, Military Order of the Loyal Legion of the United States. *War Talks in Kansas,* 206–49. Kansas City, Mo.: Franklin Hudson Publishing Co., 1906.

Hemenway, S. "Observations on Scurvy, and Its Causes among U.S. Colored Troops of the 25th Army Corps, during Spring and Summer of 1865." *Chicago Medical Examiner* 7 (October 1866): 582–86.

Hicken, Victor. "The Record of Illinois' Negro Soldiers in the Civil War." *Illinois State Historical Society Journal* 56 (Autumn 1963): 529–51.

Higgenson, Thomas W. "Regular and Volunteer Officers." *Atlantic Monthly* 14 (September 1864): 348–57.

Houghton, Charles H. "In the Crater." In *Battles and Leaders of the Civil War,* ed. Robert U. Johnson and Clarence C. Buel, 4:561–62. New York: Century, 1887–88.

Kilmer, George. "The Dash into the Crater." *Century Illustrated Magazine* 11 (September 1887): 774–76.

Longacre, Edward G., ed. "'Would to God That War Was Rendered Impossible,' Letters of Captain Roland M. Hall, April–July 1864." *Virginia Magazine of History and Biography* 89 (October 1981): 448–66.

Matson, Dan. "The Colored Man in the Civil War." Iowa Commandery, Military Order of the Loyal Legion of the United States. *War Sketches and Incidents,* 1:236–54. DeMoines, Iowa: Kenyon Press, 1898.

McMaster, Fitz William. "The Battle of the Crater, July 30, 1864." *Southern Historical Society Papers* 10 (1882): 119–23.

Bibliography

Miller, Edward A. Jr. "Angel of Light: Helen L. Gilson, Army Nurse." *Civil War History* 43 (March 1997), 17–37.

Montgomery, Horace. "A Union Officer's Recollection of the Negro As a Soldier." *Pennsylvania History, Quarterly Journal of the Pennsylvania Historical Association* 27 (April 1960): 156–86.

Powell, William H. "The Battle of the Petersburg Crater." In *Battles and Leaders of the Civil War,* ed. Robert U. Johnson and Clarence C. Buel, 4:545–60. New York: Century, 1887–88.

Redkey, Edwin S. "Black Chaplains in the Union Army." *Civil War History* 33 (December 1987): 331–50.

Rhodes, Squire D. "The Battle of the Crater." *National Tribune,* 20 November 1884.

Rickard, James H. "Service with Colored Troops in Burnside's Corps." Rhode Island Soldiers and Sailors Historical Society. *Personal Narratives of Events in the War of the Rebellion.* Ser. 5, no. 1. Providence: Providence Press, 1894.

Robertson, James I., Jr. "Negro Soldiers in the Civil War." *Civil War Times Illustrated* 7 (October 1968): 21–32.

Rogers, George T. "The Crater Battle, 30th July, 1864." *Confederate Veteran* 3 (January 1895): 12–14.

Shannon, Fred A. "The Federal Government and the Negro Soldier, 1861–1865." *Journal of Negro History* 11 (October 1926): 574–83.

Shaw, James. "Our Last Campaign and Subsequent Service in Texas." Rhode Island Soldiers and Sailors Historical Society. *Personal Narratives of Events in the War of the Rebellion.* Ser. 6, no. 9. Providence: Providence Press, 1905.

Spear, Benjamin. "In Front of Petersburg." *National Tribune,* 20 June 1889.

Stewart, William H. "The Charge of the Crater." *Southern Historical Society Papers* 25 (1897): 77–90.

Sutherland, George E. "The Negro in the Late War." Wisconsin Commandery, Military Order of the Loyal Legion of the United States. *War Papers,* 1:164–88. Milwaukee: Burdick, Armitage and Allen, 1891.

Thomas, Henry Goddard. "The Colored Troops at Petersburg." In *Battles and Leaders of the Civil War,* ed. Robert U. Johnson and Clarence C. Buel, 4: 563–67. New York: Century, 1887–88.

———. "Twenty-Two Hours Prisoner in Dixie." Maine Commandery, Military Order of the Loyal Legion of the United States. *War Papers,* 1:29–48. Portland: By the commandery, 1898.

Walton, Charles W. "The Battle of the Mine." *National Tribune,* 20 November 1884.

Westwood, Howard C. "Generals David Hunter and Rufus Saxton and Black Soldiers." *South Carolina History Magazine* 86 (1985): 225–37.

Wilkinson, Warren. "Bury Them If They Won't Move." *Civil War Times Illustrated* 29 (March–April 1990): 24ff.

Wilson, Charles. "Exploding a Mine." *National Tribune,* 14 and 23 May 1896.

NEWSPAPERS

Charleston (S.C.) *Daily Courier,* 8 August 1864.

Chicago Daily Tribune, June 1883–November 1865.

Chicago Evening Journal, April–July 1864.

Chicago Times, scattered issues, January 1864–August 1865.

Christian Recorder (Phila.) 20 August, 17 September 1864; 25 March, 1 and 22 April, 29 July, 9 and 23 September, and 4 and 25 November 1865.

Daily Age (Phila.), 3 May 1864.

Daily Courant (Hartford), 1 and 2 August 1864.

Daily Dispatch (Richmond), 1 and 2 August 1864.

Daily Express (Petersburg), 1 August 1864.

Daily Illinois State Journal (Springfield), January 1863–November 1865.

Daily Richmond Enquirer, 1 and 2 August 1864.

Daily Whig and Republican (Quincy), July 1863–November 1865.

Dallas Evening News, 24 March 1904.

Forney's War Press (Phila.), scattered issues, August 1864.

Harper's Weekly, 20 August 1864.

Herald-Whig (Quincy), 15 June 1990.

New York Daily Tribune, 1–6 August 1864.

New York Evening Express, 2 August 1864.

New York Times, August 1864.

Post (Chicago), April–July 1864.

United States Army and Navy Journal and Gazette of the Regular and Volunteer Forces (Washington, D.C.), 2 and 9 July, 6 August 1864.

Worcester Daily Spy, 2 August 1864.

Index

Index

Index

Index

Index

Index